Mick Walker
the ride of my life

REDLINE BOOKS

Mick Walker
the ride of my life

Contents

British Library Cataloguing in Publication Data
A catalogue record for this book is available from the British Library

ISBN: 978-0-9555278-2-1

Designed and published in 2012 by Redline Books
Edited by Andrew Kemp
Printed in Malta

REDLINE BOOKS www.redlinebooks.co.uk

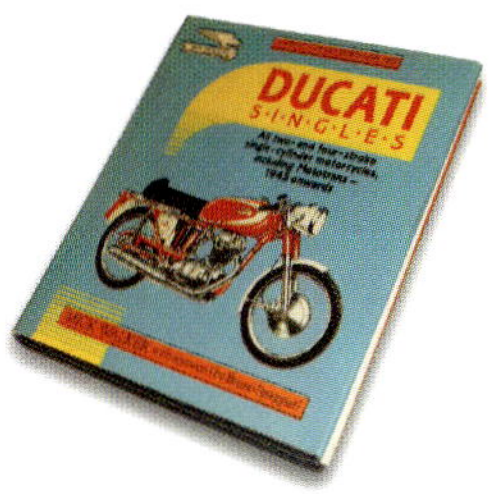

Acknowledgements:

My thanks go to the following for their help, friendship and support over the years:
Bernard Adey, Johnny Angel, Frank Ball, Jan Barszczynski, Vic Bates, Len Bayliss, Peter Bennett, John Blunt, Liz Bridewell, Natasha Brown, Arthur Bullock, Bill and Agnes Cadger, Rob Carrick, Paul Clarkson, Ken Cobbing, Mick Coburn, Eddie Cordle, Brian Crichton, Keith Davies, Alejandro de Tomaso, Ray Elliot, Hoss Elm, Reg Everett, Carl Fogarty, Roy Francis, Alex George, Luigi Giacometti, Peter Greenard, Wolfgang Gruber, Mike Hailwood, John Harris, Pete and Mike Harrison, Mark Heckles, Mick Hemmings, Clew Hughes, Nick Jeffery, Dean Johnson, Walter Kaaden, Andrew Kemp, Roy and John Kirkby, Howard Lindley, Peter Mapes, Bob McKeever, Vicki Michelle, Sammy Miller, Derek and Jenny Minter, Geoff Monty, John and Richard Mushett, Steven Neate, Darren North, George Padget, Tim Parker, Colin and Jill Pascoe, Tony Plumridge, Paddy Reid, Clive Robinson, Stu Rogers, Jim Russell, Brenda Scivyer, John Sear, Barry Sheene, Pat Slinn, Paul Smart, Nigel Stone, Tommy Stoner, John Surtees, Fabio Taglioni, Mick Taylor, James Toseland, Rodney Turner, Ian 'Tiddler' Turner, Chris Vincent, Bill Wait, Lewis Ward, Ian and Rita Welsh and Malc Wheeler.

Publisher's acknowledgement:

Redline Books owes a special debt of gatitude to Mick Walker. With the invaluable help and expertise of Terry Wilson, Mick's Racing Series not only established us as an independent automotive publisher, but also cemented a wonderful working relationship with Mick. We are proud to be counted as Mick's friends and thank him for his unique contribution.

Front cover; The Mark 3-engined Mach 1, Snetterton 1967

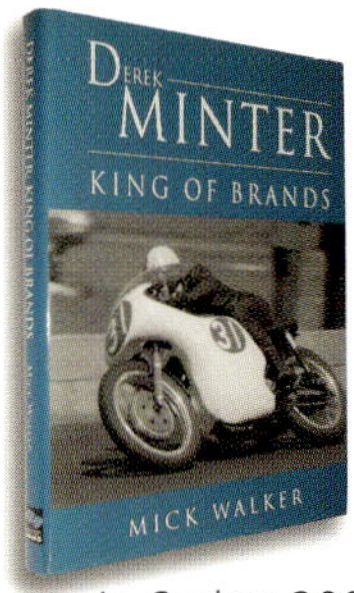

Foreword Derek and Jenny Minter

In Spring 2007, Mick visited us to discuss the *Derek Minter* book. Derek had suffered a brain haemorrhage in October 2000, which resulted in short-term memory loss. We were really impressed with Mick's thorough knowledge. Through his kindness and patience he was able to reawaken some of Derek's memories and tease out all sorts of information that might otherwise have been lost. And all of this hand-written on A4; no laptop for Mick!

When the book came out we were delighted. Every chapter had been sent for our approval long before publication and we felt we could trust Mick completely, putting him apart from most other journalists. There was so much to read and his ability to list every single race of Derek's twelve-year career, including class, machine, circuit, and even retirements, is phenomenal.

Mick has always been involved in the motorcycling world, from competition to importing and dealing, sponsoring and, of course, his prolific writing on the subject. We are certain that Mick's autobiography will be a great read, with something for everyone. We wish him well.

Jenny & Derek

Mike Hailwood's greatest rival

'My choice for the greatest rider of the lot may come as a surprise. He's a man who never became world champion; indeed he never so much as won a 500cc grand prix. But of all the names one could conjure with – Duke, Ago, Bob McIntyre, Alistair King, Jim Redman, Gary Hocking and so on – the man stands out as being the hardest of all to beat was a guy called Derek Minter. I've thought about it a lot and I'm convinced that Derek was, on any circuit and at any time, the toughest competitor I faced.

'Agostini, of course, was the man who in terms of sheer results gave me more trouble than anyone. Ago was superb whenever he raced. Even so, I honestly don't believe I ever felt I could not beat him, given equal machinery, or possibly even something slightly inferior.'

Preface

Having written in excess of 130 books, it could be safely assumed that compiling my autobiography would come easily; nothing could be further from the truth. Many of my close friends and family were forever asking me if I had started, but over eight years after first discussing it with Redline Books, only the onset of a life-threatening illness finally spurred me into action.

My entire life changed in June 2010, when after spending two enjoyable days at the annual Bob McIntyre Memorial meeting at East Fortune, near Edinburgh, I was taken ill on the Sunday evening. My friend Ian Welsh rushed me to the A&E at Edinburgh Royal Infirmary, and 36 hours later Ian's wife Rita ferried me to the acute receiving unit at the Western General Hospital. Since then, I seem to have collected illness after illness, including prostate and bone cancer. The latter has proved the most difficult, as it has robbed me of my energy and mobility – however, I am still here and fighting my problems as best I can.

One positive aspect has been the terrific amount of interest shown by my friends and associates in the motorcycling world; for example, Christmas 2011 saw a vast amount of cards from all over the world – people really do care. Despite this, I haven't found it easy to write about myself, which is why I had spent years putting the project off, preferring to write about other people's achievements.

However, I soon realised (once I felt at ease with the task ahead and finally got started) that my story would be a mixture of detailed factual information, humour, scoops – and the occasional scandal! A major part of what follows is about the personalities I have met along the way; some household names, others less well known, but all significant to my story and, I hope, of interest to you, the reader.

I have never been in the habit of keeping notes, diaries or the like, so I went about the task as if it was a giant jigsaw puzzle. It wasn't written chapter-by-chapter, from start to finish, but one tiny piece of the jigsaw at a time, hoping that it would all fall into place.

Just how well this system worked is for you, the reader, to decide. But I'm happy that finally I have got it down on paper.

The following is a short list of the various medical staff who have cared for me during my continuing illnesses. I am truly grateful for their assistance. God bless you all:

Trinity Surgery, Wisbech; GP Dr Priti Maheshwari and Dr Duraeraj
District Nurses; Kim Strickly, Shirley Clements and Hilary Godfrey
Macmillan Nurse; Jacqueline Havercroft
Staff at the Peterborough Hospital; Dr A Hollingdale,
Anne Nimmo, Sue Pilcher, Evey Bishop, Patience Hamaiabi,
Paul Greenwood, Jackie Clay, Agnus Slinwinska, Laura Doyle
and Celia Alde (Mick Walker, a legend of my teenage years!)
Ambulance crew; Michael Green, Ian Dodsworth and Sophie Wiseman
Occupational Therapist; Pat Parker

Finally, a word about my wife of 42 years, Susan. During the dark days described above she has constantly been at my side. I am a lucky man indeed.

Mick Walker
Wisbech, Cambridgeshire
February 2012

1 Starting Out

the Daytona was the key that transformed my life

It was spring 1961, and I was in full flow, sweeping my new metallic-blue and silver Ducati Daytona through a tight series of hedge-lined bends. The bike felt alive, bursting to be given its head, and every ride was more akin to being on a fire-breathing Manx Norton than a production 250. The Ducati was the best machine in its class, and even at a bank-bursting one-pound-per-cc, the experience was worth every penny.

I had only owned the Daytona a few weeks, and was on the way to my very first motorcycle race meeting, an international at Snetterton, Norfolk. As I parked up, I was already intoxicated by the atmosphere – the noise, the smell of Castrol R and, most of all, the people. My attention was drawn, obviously, to the Ducati riders: Arthur Wheeler and diminutive Gary Dickinson in the 125 event, Brian Clark, Mick Manley and Mike Hailwood in the 250 race (which Mike won on his 250 Desmo twin from Tommy Robb's GMS and Dan Shorey's NSU, with Brian Clark fourth on his 175 Formula 3 Ducati converted to 198cc).

So how come I had plumped for a Ducati, when virtually every other 18 year-old in 1961 would have chosen a far cheaper Royal Enfield Crusader Sports or Ariel Golden Arrow? There is only one explanation; I fell for the magic. Even stationary, the Daytona looked fast, and it had been love at first sight as soon as I saw my future mount pictured in the motorcycling press. Although I had never seen the Ducati in metal until the day that I took delivery, I was certainly not disappointed – and every ride on the Daytona reminded me that this little 250 was a race-bred motorcycle, with its potent overhead-camshaft engine, leech-like roadholding and looks to kill for.

In retrospect, that day 50 years ago was pivotal for me. Buying the Daytona (only the second example imported into the UK) was the key that transformed my life. Not only would I go on to embrace virtually every aspect of motorcycling, but the Ducati marque would play a central role in my journey. I would go on to own many other models from the Bologna factory and become, in time, a Ducati racer, dealer and ultimately the British importer. Of the 130-plus books I was to write in later life, many would involve the Ducati story. Even more amazing was that the riders I witnessed as a spectator all those years ago would become close friends – Arthur Wheeler, Gary Dickinson, Brian Clark, Mick Manley, Tommy Robb and even Mike Hailwood himself. Twenty-five years after I first saw him race, Dan Shorey would kindly write the foreword for one of my earliest books, Osprey's *Spanish Post-war Road & Racing Motorcycles*.

When I became an author, my first publisher at Osprey, Tim Parker, described me as 'a super-enthusiast for all forms of motorcycling', so it is not surprising that my story has my trusty friend the motorcycle at its centre. But I should really start at the beginning, when Michael John Gilbert Walker arrived in this world on 30 November 1942, at Allgoods Farm in Wretton, Norfolk.

Mick and sister Margaret

It was the middle of the Second World War. My father Gilbert and mother Eileen had married a couple of years earlier, and I was soon joined by a sister Margaret, a few days before Christmas 1943, and brother Richard on 20 April 1945. Coincidentally he shared a birthday with Adolf Hitler, while mine was the same day as Winston Churchill's. At least I got that one right!

By the time Richard arrived, I had gone to live with my grandparents Alfred and Maud, who also farmed in Wretton. A fourth member of the 'family' at Willow Farm was Auntie Alice. Alice Bonnett was not a blood relative, but as far as my story is concerned, she was an important person, who I very much looked up to. It was Alice who taught me how to ride on two wheels, albeit only with pedal power.

Wretton is a small village in the west of the county, 14 miles south of Kings Lynn and 7 miles east of Downham Market, and my education began at the village school, only yards from my home. Later, I transferred to school in Stoke Ferry (the next village) and then, when I was 11, to secondary school in Downham Market. Years later, when I was interviewed on the BBC after publishing my 100th book, the interviewer commented that I was obviously very brainy and asked which university I had been to. She was surprised when I replied, 'just a secondary modern.'

I was always one for hobbies. Stamp collecting was an early favourite, but as I grew up, team sports in the shape of soccer and cricket took over. My grandfather took me to see Norwich City, and I have remained a Canary fan ever since. I went on to witness all the games of their heroic FA Cup run in 1958-9, except the semi-final replay, which they lost. Another great interest I developed at an early age was reading, with Biggles books frequently heading the queue in my youth. The reason for this was my equally avid enthusiasm for aircraft.

This led me to join the Air Training Corps group in Downham Market. Besides a weekly get-together, the squadron organised summer camps as far apart as Thorney Island, near Portsmouth, and Towyn in mid-Wales. My first experience of flying came in 1955, thanks to the ATC. We took off from RAF Marham one Sunday afternoon, in a twin-engined Avro Anson that could trace its history to the Second World War, when the type was used by Coastal Command to monitor and attack shipping. Over the next three years or so, my flying took in a varied assortment of planes, including the Avro Shackleton, Blackburn Beverley, Handley Page Hastings, Percival Provost, Vickers Varsity, Valetta, and Viscount.

It was only during the final couple of years at school that I really began to make progress, and I was actually made head boy during my final year. I did not gain any formal qualifications, but this never held me back in life. There was nothing wrong with having stacks of qualifications but in my experience, practical ability and initiative have been just as important, and an enthusiasm for the task at hand is vital.

I had my first motorcycling experience in 1956, thanks to someone in the village who had just purchased a brand-new metallic gunmetal Norton Dominator 88 twin. Although I didn't appreciate it at the time, the machine was one of the very best of its era. Besides a lusty twin-cylinder ohv engine it boasted the Featherbed frame and Roadholder front forks. Its owner was only too pleased to show off his new mount when I answered 'Yes' to his question, 'Would you like a ride?' I was soon straddling the pillion seat and away we went. It was quite an experience, with the wind rushing through my hair and the sensation of speed, which I had never felt during my many car rides. The journey was over all too quickly, and although it had been exciting at the time, it was not to be repeated.

Gilbert Walker with his two-stroke Dunelt in the early 1930s

My brief acquaintance with the motorcycle world would not be renewed until years later. I didn't come from a motorcycling family. To the best of my knowledge my grandparents (and Auntie Alice, for that matter) never owned any form of powered vehicle, although both their sons, my father and uncle Philip, drove. But although my father had owned an ancient Dunelt two-stroke in his younger days, neither of my parents was in the least bit interested in vehicles (except purely as a means of transport) and they were certainly not mechanically minded.

Mum and Dad, Eileen and Gilbert's wedding in Richmond, Surrey.

As far as my own transport went, this was strictly limited to either walking or pedalling. A major disappointment was the new cycle my grandparents had bought for me on my 12th birthday. I had dreamed of a bright-red sports model with drop bars, but what I got instead was a dreary, dark-coloured heavyweight mount. It might have been new, but I truly hated it and the mundane image it portrayed.

I never used my bicycle to ride to school, travelling by bus to Downham Market on a daily basis. But one beautifully sunny summer day in 1957, I cycled over to RAF Watton, a round trip of 60 miles, for a flight in a two-seater de Havilland Chipmunk trainer, during which I was allowed to take the controls for a short time. The need for speed and action was growing. By my 15th birthday that November, I had already decided that I wanted to join the Royal Air Force. My enthusiasm for this career had been fed by my time in the ATC – which is precisely what that organisation was for, and why it had been supported by successive British governments since 1941.

After the Christmas holiday, I prepared myself for a new life that would prove very different from anything I had experienced. 1958 was to be a year of major changes in my life and I would never return to the essentially protected, peaceful environment of my rural childhood.

RICHARD WALKER.

MUM AND DAD WITH NEWLY BORN MICK, 1943

GRANDPARENTS ALFRED AND MAUD AT WILLOW FARM, WRETTON DURING THE 1930s

MRS JAMES WALKER.

MUM AND MICK.

WRETTON RAILWAY STATION.

MICK AGED 6 AT WILLOW FARM CIRCA 1949

MICK AND DONKEY POWER, WILLOW FARM 1947

WRETTON SCHOOL, LATE 1940s

DOWNHAM MARKET SECONDARY SCHOOL 1957

GRANDFATHER ALFRED, GRANDMOTHER MAUD AND AUNTIE ALICE, 1965

AUNTIE ALICE AND GRANDMOTHER MAUD, HUNSTANTON, EARLY 1960'S.

THE FAMILY ALWAYS SAID THAT ONE OF OUR ANCESTORS WAS INVOLVED IN THE DESIGN OF THE FORTH BRIDGE

MICK AND GRANDMOTHER MAUD.

HEAD BOY AT DOWNHAM MARKET SECONDARY SCHOOL, FINAL YEAR BEFORE JOINING R.A.F.

2 Service Life

in retrospect it was the making of me

A 20-year-old SAC Walker, at RAF Steamer Point barracks, Aden

My first stop, after the initial application for entry into the air force via the Boy Entrant scheme, was to visit RAF Cosford, near Wolverhampton, for selection. This lasted a couple of days, then I returned home to wait. Most youngsters of course want to be a pilot, but the vast majority end up as ground staff, which I did, as a trainee 'Supplier'. Funnily enough, this was – although I didn't know it at the time – an excellent choice. Years later, my business was to be built around supplying customers with parts for their motorcycles, but back in January 1958 when I visited Cosford, this couldn't have been further from my mind.

A few weeks later a letter came saying that I had been accepted and that I should report to my first posting, RAF Credenhill on 20 February 1958. This was a training establishment some four miles from Hereford, the base's name stemming from a large hill on the other side of the public highway outside the guardroom and the main gate. RAF Credenhill proved to be a rude awakening. First of all, the only aircraft anywhere in sight was an ancient de Havilland Vampire, which was the establishment's 'Gate Guard' on static display next to the main entrance. The regime could only be described as tough – well tough at least for a wet-behind-the-ears youngster like me who had never been away from home for more than a few days – but in retrospect it was the making of me. The strict regime put a backbone into me and taught me self-discipline, and it also gave me a sense of worth and pride. With the trade training, strict military discipline and daily drill sessions, it could best be described as a second education. I certainly benefited from it, and being a late developer, it was to play a vital role in my progress during future years.

My service number was 1938242, which I had to remember very quickly, for in those days you did not get paid if you could not recite your number, rank and name. I was a member of 37th entry – later to be transferred to the 38th entry. Depending on your trade, young RAF recruits below a certain age were either Boy Entrants or Apprentices. The two were given separate training establishments and did not come into contact with each other. When I joined, young lads had to sign up for 12 years (to date from their 18th birthday) to cover their extensive training, which was 18 months for Boy Entrants and three years for Apprentices. This practice is now illegal and was stopped several years ago.

The first real friend I made in the RAF was Bill Wait from Northern Ireland, whose father was the pro at the Ardglass golf course in Co. Down. We shared the same billet, the living quarters for around a dozen of us raw recruits. At weekends if we were not on duty, Bill and I would walk or take a bus into Hereford. But otherwise our life was centred on or around the base, which even had its own hospital, as I discovered one evening when I suffered a serious ear infection. After several months we were allowed home on leave, and as with other journeys at this time it was by train to Downham Market railway station and then by taxi (a Humber Hawk) to my grandparents' Wretton farm. Another life-long friend I met then was Clive Robinson, from Doncaster, South Yorkshire. Like Bill, Clive was later to become a motorcycle enthusiast – something that bound us together like cement for over half a century.

One of my oldest friends, Bill Wait. We first met at RAF Credenhill during the late 1950s.

I spent nearly two years at Credenhill. Over 50 years later much of it is a blur, but there is absolutely no doubt the experience was crucial for me. Quite simply, the Royal Air Force Boy Entrant scheme toughened me up and provided me with a solid foundation upon which to build. Finally, I took part in the 'Passing Out' ceremony, a couple of weeks before Christmas 1959. The only member of my family to attend was Auntie Alice, who made the long journey from Norfolk by train.

My first posting, the following January, after a well-earned period of leave, was to 214 Squadron RAF Marham, only some 12 miles or so from home. My new rank was SAC (Senior Aircraftsman). The squadron was equipped with the Vickers Valiant V-bombers, which was to be retired early due to metal fatigue problems (unlike the other Vs, the Avro Vulcan and Handley Page Victor). The end of the year saw me on detachment with the squadron to RAF Luqa, Malta, which was the first time I had been out of the United Kingdom.

While still in England, I soon got tired of pedalling back and forth to home, and someone suggested that I should purchase something with an engine. This turned out to be a 1958 Lambretta Li 150 scooter, which I bought from a work colleague for £100. Having my own powered two-wheeler brought an unbelievable independence of a type I had never known before. This really hit me when I had to leave the Lambretta overnight for repair at the local dealers, Lew Sherwood's in Downham Market, a few miles from Marham.

My first scooter, a secondhand 1958 Lambretta Li 150 bought in 1960.

Aboard my new 1960 TV175, still on L plates – as is friend Peter Greenard on one of his many 250 BSAs.

The TV175 near Carlisle after a 14-hour trip from East Anglia.

I soon became an avid scooter fan and later that year purchased a brand new Lambretta TV175 from Sherwood's. While running in, I was invited to visit an RAF friend's home in Glasgow. Leaving Marham at 10 o'clock in the morning in the era before motorways, I reached Carlisle at midnight, sleeping beside my scooter and continuing the journey north at sun-up the following day. One memory of the visit was going to Hampden Park to watch the Scottish national football team in action. I travelled home via Edinburgh, where I experienced my first road accident. Nothing very serious but my previously pristine scooter collected a damaged front mudguard that was repaired at Alexander's, a famous Scottish motorcycle dealership. Years later, I discovered the business had been started by veteran racer Alfie Alexander, who came home third on an Indian in the 1913 Senior TT.

My first-ever experience of piloting a motorcycle came early in 1961, when my friend Peter Greenard, whose father owned a scrapyard in the next village, wanted a ride on the TV175. Peter had owned a succession of BSA 250s that had been rescued from Daddy's scrapyard and rebuilt, and he offered me one to accompany him while he tried the scooter. Up until then, I had always been satisfied with my Lambretta, but riding the BSA (a humble C11G) proved a revelation, and from that moment onwards my attention switched to motorcycles.

It was not long after that that I settled on the Ducati 250 Daytona, after initially targeting a Parilla 175 Sport high cam four-stroke and even a Rumi Junior Gentleman 125 two-stroke twin. But the Ducati it was and so began an entirely new way of life. Scooters had been about commuting, but with the Ducati the word 'sport' came into the frame for the first time. I began to take an interest in the competitive side of motorcycling, attending road race events all over the country and even the occasional scrambles meeting. It was only natural that I began rooting for the Ducati riders – who ranged from top professionals, such as Mike Hailwood, to plucky privateers such as Arthur Wheeler, with whom I was privileged to form a close friendship in years to come.

Triumph Tiger 100SS; a brilliant bike save for one thing, its dreadful brakes.

Besides my Ducati there were scores of motorcycles on the base at Marham. In particular I recall a Puch 250SGS split single two-stroke, various BSA C15 and B40 unit singles, a number of big Triumphs and Nortons and in particular a solitary Bianchi 125 Bernina. Several servicemen owned bubble-cars and I vividly remember one trip in an Isetta with a single cylinder ohv engine based on the BMW R27, increased to 297cc. It certainly did sound like a single-cylinder motorcycle, which in a car was somewhat weird. The other peculiarity about the Isetta was its front opening door; which under current laws is definitely not allowed. Just think what would happen in the event of a head-on crash…

On several occasions during 1960-61, weekend leave was cancelled and we were restricted to base thanks to the Ban-the-Bomb protesters. This probably resulted in five or six lost weekends before tempers finally flared and there was something of a set-to. The violence that followed saw fed-up service personnel physically get the better of the protesters. Despite the hostility, a few bloody noses and some events that should not have taken place, our problem was solved and the protesters went home, never to return.

The purchase of the Ducati had changed my life. After the Italian bike, I flirted with a BSA A7, followed by a Triumph T100SS. Finished in Kingfisher metallic blue and silver, the T100SS was a brilliant bike save for one thing, its dreadful lack of stopping power. Quite honestly the front brake would hardly have been adequate for something like the 250 BSA C15, let alone a model of double the engine size.

I visited many, many race meetings on the Triumph, often with my brother Rick riding pillion, including Mallory Park, Snetterton, Silverstone and Cadwell Park. Solo, I travelled to Oulton Park, Cheshire, one Bank Holiday weekend in 1962 for the meeting in which Bob McIntyre was to sustain fatal injuries in horrifically wet conditions. The subsequent miserable ride back to Marham seemed to take forever, getting back to Norfolk in the early hours of the following morning. Together with Derek Minter, Bob had been my original racing hero. Forty-four years later, my 100th book, *Bob McIntyre – The Flying Scot,* as written in tribute to him.

The poor brakes were the feature of the Tiger 100SS I remember most. There were at least three incidents where the lack of brakes was potentially dangerous, although I never actually suffered an accident. Perhaps the most dramatic was returning from the Thruxton 500-miler. I came round a high-speed bend to be confronted by a set of traffic lights on red, and a queue of stationary traffic. Under full braking I travelled to the front of the queue – simply because I couldn't stop! If Rick had been on the back on that occasion, I don't know what would have happened.

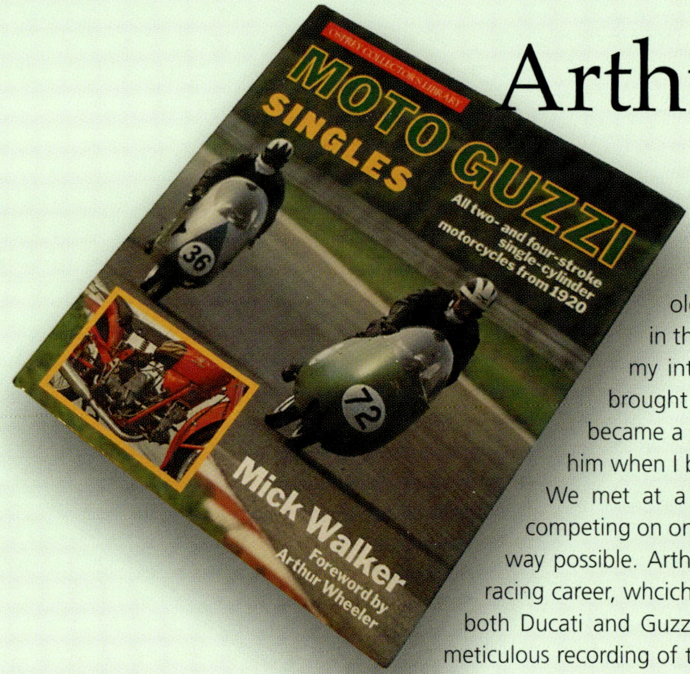

Arthur Wheeler

I was fortunate to be able to witness Arthur Wheeler's performances on a 125 Ducati and 250 Guzzi during his final two years of premier class racing in 1961 and '62. To many older enthusiasts, Arthur Wheeler was 'Mr Guzzi' in the UK as far as racing was concerned, but it was my interest in Ducati, rather than Moto Guzzi, that brought us together in his later years, and Arthur became a very close friend. I originally really got to know him when I began researching my first book *Ducati Singles*. We met at a Snetterton CRMC event, where Arthur was competing on one of his Guzzis, and he was keen to help in any way possible. Arthur produced a diary he had kept of his entire racing career, whcich was a vital tool not only in my early books on both Ducati and Guzzi, but also in future projects, due to Arthur's meticulous recording of the details.

For many years, Arthur was the owner of the motorcycle dealership in Epsom, Surrey that bore his name, and was a real gentleman in every dealing I ever had with him. He had first become a Guzzi convert back in 1951, when, despite finishing fifth in the Lightweight TT and third in the Ulster Grand Prix for Velocette, as Arthur said, 'The Birmingham factory never even said thank you'. At that point, he decided to make the switch to the Italian factory that had won the 250cc championship.

Arthur's first Guzzi was a three-year old Albatros, purchased from Belgian rider Leon Martin. His first victory came in the Irish Leinster 200 in spring 1952, and what followed was a brilliant career aboard Guzzi machinery. He once told me, 'The Isle of Man is the best race in the world,' and it certainly was for him. In a decade of Guzzi TT rides, he finished 4th three times, 6th once, 7th once, 8th and 9th once, together with a couple of lesser places. He was equally impressive in the World Championship series, highlights being 4th in 1954 and 3rd in 1962, his final season – and all this as a privateer!

Arthur Wheeler on a 125 Grand Prix Ducati at Thruxton in 1961.

A feature of Arthur's Guzzi career was the special frames he commissioned to house the Italian power plants. The first of these was made in 1959 – to Arthur's own design – welded from Reynolds 531 tubing by the Birmingham-based firm's Ken Sprayson. From then on, all Arthur's Guzzi singles (both 250 and 350) employed these frames. The essence of the design was a massive top frame rail, which incorporated the steering head and ran backwards to the rear tank and front seat area. Much smaller-diameter twin tubes and large, flat aluminium plates supported the rear of the engine.

I remember being at Brands Hatch in the mid-1980s to witness Arthur falling off his 250 Guzzi. By then, he was in his mid-70s – an age when most people would have been taking things a little more steadily. But he simply picked himself up and was back in the saddle for the next race. Arthur eventually died in the 1990s, of all things from blood poisoning caused by a rusty nail.

During the 1980s, Arthur restored a blue-and-gold wide-case Mark 3 Ducati, and regularly came to me for my advice and spares. At the same time, I was also talking to another Guzzi singles racing legend about his identical restoration project. Maurice Cann hailed from Leicester and had won the 1948 Lightweight TT on his Guzzi. Business interests prevented him from racing on the continent, but during the late 1940s and early 1950s he not only took in the TT, but also the Ulster GP. He really made his mark at the Ulster, winning the 250 race on several occasions. He was also a skilled engine tuner, building a successful dohc cylinder head long before the Guzzi factory did.

Together, Arthur and Maurice epitomised the top British privateer racing scene of the early post-war period – men who could, and did, beat the best in the world on their day.

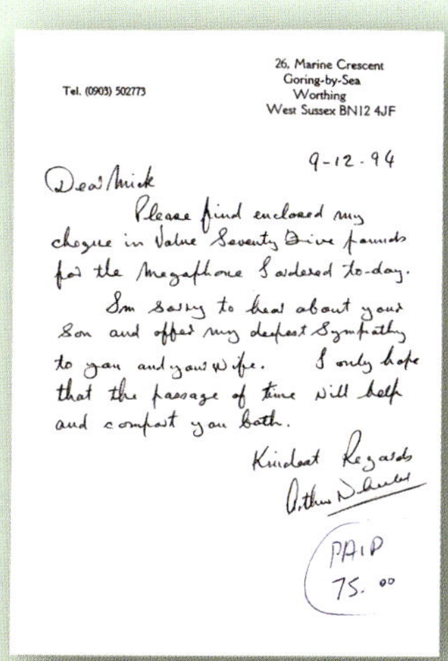
Tel. (0903) 502773

26, Marine Crescent
Goring-by-Sea
Worthing
West Sussex BN12 4JF

9-12-94

Dear Mick

Please find enclosed my cheque in Value Seventy Five pounds for the Megaphone I ordered to-day.

I'm sorry to hear about your Son and offer my deepest Sympathy to you and your wife. I only hope that the passage of time will help and comfort you both.

Kindest Regards
Arthur Wheeler

PAID
75.00

Arthur Wheeler's dustbin-faired Moto Guzzi and impressive array of trophies in 1955.

By this time I had become what would now be called a rocker, complete with the required dress code, making frequent visits to cafes such as The Ace and The Busy Bee. While travelling to a national road race meeting at Mallory Park early one Sunday morning, we were joined by a group of other bikes. We got involved in what is best described as a mad free-for-all dice that included a rider on a Velocette Venom scraping the entire length of a caravan we were all overtaking. How he survived, I simply don't know, but survive he did. Looking back, it is a miracle that I got away with some of my two-wheel escapades at the time.

I did have one accident, although this unfortunate incident was not my fault. While I was staying over at my parents, a few miles from Kings Lynn, my old friend Peter Greenard turned up. This time, it was he who was aboard a scooter, a Vespa. Peter suggested going down to the local cafe, run by John Brundle (father of racing driver and Formula 1 commentator Martin) but we had hardly set off when Peter decided to show off by waggling his backside as were negotiating a series of S-bends. Unfortunately, while he would probably have got away with these antics on a motorcycle, he certainly didn't on the Vespa, which simply threw him off while I, with Rick on the back, was following closely behind. I ended up missing the spinning scooter, but not Peter. Unfortunately, not only did I crash too, but I damaged one of Peter's fingers, which resulted in a trip to the local hospital where it was eventually amputated. The accident didn't cause either Rick or me any lasting injury, in fact the only evidence of the crash on our side was a small dent in the fuel tank of my previously pristine Triumph.

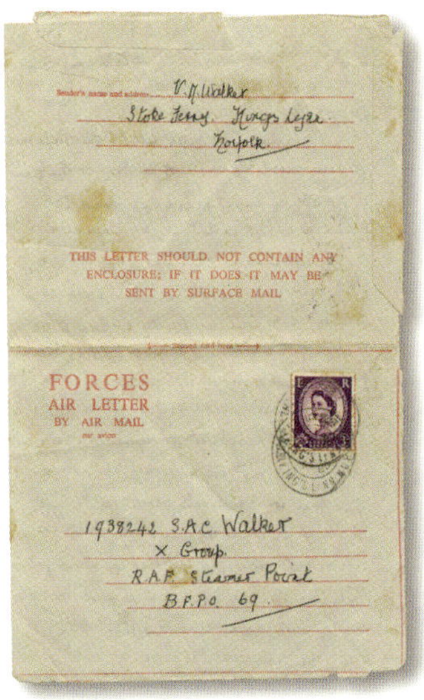

Many years later, when Peter was running a motor garage, I decided to call him. A rather abrupt lady informed me that Mr Greenard was not available and although I said I was an old friend, she wasn't convinced. In the end I mentioned his missing finger and admitted I was responsible. This soon shut her up! Later Peter phoned back and we caught up with the missing years.

In spring 1963, I was informed that I was soon to be posted overseas. This meant that my life was to change drastically, and I would no longer be able to continue my motorcycling activities. What I didn't know at the time was that actually, motorcycling would continue, but in a very different vein. As I would be away for two years, I made the decision to put my trusty Triumph up for sale. It was left at JW Walker & Sons (no relation) of Walpole Cross Keys, two miles from my parents. It was, I heard later, soon sold. Whoever got it had purchased a fine machine, in perfect order, except for the slight dent in the tank and the poor brakes.

RAF X Group in Aden during 1964.

In July I was posted to Aden. My base was at Steamer Point – appropriately named because it was the stopping-off place for passenger liners coming down the Red Sea after negotiating the Suez Canal. Besides being a port, Aden is the commercial centre of trade for Southern Yemen, on a rocky peninsula at the south-west corner of Arabia, commanding the entrance to the Red Sea. A British territory from 1839, it was a colony from 1937 to 1963. After a period of transitional violence between nationalist groups and British forces, it was combined with the former Aden Protectorate to create the Southern Yemen Peoples Republic in 1967, which became the Peoples Democratic Republic of Yemen from 1970-90. When I first arrived, conditions were peaceful, which unfortunately would not be the case for the whole of my tour of duty.

Disembarking on 30 June from the VC10 airliner that had transported us, what hit me immediately was the heat. It felt like stepping into a furnace, but, as with most things in life, I became accustomed to this. Things were different here; minimal clothing, flip-flops instead of shoes, minimum bedding, the constant need for cooling fans in the rooms and ever-present bed bugs. Another thing one had to get used to was a change of working hours, as after 1pm it was simply too hot to do anything. As for riding a motorcycle, no one wore any protective clothing, a helmet or even gloves; the high temperatures simply didn't allow it.

The coastal strip was flat, but close by and in sight was a range of craggy barren hills. My workplace was X Group, essentially a large storage depot for all the military explosives in the area. This was an old Turkish fort, surrounded by hills, with the workforce being transported there on a daily basis in a military Bedford 3-ton truck.

For several months there were no problems, certainly not with the local population, and servicemen like me felt entirely at ease when leaving the military base. We would walk two miles or so into Steamer Point, which because of the vibrant international shipping that regularly called at the port, was awash with shops. We soon learned to drive a hard bargain with the shopkeepers, haggling rather than paying the asking price. This was something the passengers from the cruise liners never seemed to appreciate, usually paying the full (over-inflated) ticket price.

Besides the intense heat, the other thing one had to get used to in Aden was that it virtually never rained; the nearest it got was a few drops in January. This meant that the tarmac roads were shiny, never getting a wash – in fact, had there been any real rain, the surface would have been like a skid-pan.

Because of the weather conditions, motorcycles were a popular means of transport in the colony, and there were many; a lot of British, but also several recently imported Japanese machines. There was also the occasional Italian bike, including a 300cc MV Agusta Raid ohv single; the company's largest production motorcycle at the time. This was owned by one of the more well-off locals (probably one of the shopkeepers) in Steamer Point.

My first motorcycle purchase in Aden was another Triumph, a 650 6T Thunderbird (the bath-tub version). This proved to be something of a disaster, drinking almost as much oil as petrol; and was soon disposed of. My next was another second-hand machine but of much better quality, and my first experience of a Japanese bike. The model in question was the Honda CB92, a brilliant little bike that I described in my book *Honda Production Motorcycles 1946-1980*:

'The CB92 sportster (and its touring brother, the C92) arrived at the beginning of 1959, and in the author's opinion was one of the very finest if not the best of all early Japanese motorcycles.' I continued, 'It was, and still is, a true classic. This enthusiasm comes from ownership of a CB92 back in the 1960s and my 45 years of motorcycle experience, which has included virtually every facet of the sport.'

The CB92 had an air-cooled sohc parallel-twin engine, with a chain-driven camshaft, an alloy head and cast-iron barrel assembly inclined at 40 degrees, Other features of the power unit included unit construction, with a 180-degree crankshaft in horizontally split aluminium crankcases. The frame was of the spine type, built from steel pressings, using the engine as a stressed member, whilst the rear suspension was by swinging arm, with conventional twin shock absorbers. The front suspension was taken care of by a pair of pressed-steel leading-link forks.

Other notable features were a four-speed gearbox, rev counter, 6-volt electrics and a single 22mm Keihin carburettor. The power output was quoted as 15bhp at 10,500rpm; which gave a maximum speed of a genuine 80mph. I remember actually keeping a Norton Dominator 88SS 500 twin in my sights while two-up. Yes the CB92 not only looked good, but it went great as well.

After the CB92, I owned another Japanese mount in Aden. This was completely different in concept; the Suzuki T10, the first of the company's 250 twin-cylinder two-stroke models largely aimed at the world export market. The T10 could trace its origins back to the earlier 1960 TA (Twin Ace). Today, many believe that the T10 was the progenitor of the model that replaced it, the much better known T20 Super Six. Actually, this is totally incorrect, and the similar model designations are almost the only point of commonality, with the T10 representing the end of one design family, whilst the T20/T250 was the beginning of another.

The T10 was characterised by the open pressed-steel frame common to many early Japanese motorcycles, with fully-enclosed telescopic forks up front and swinging arm rear suspension via non-adjustable shocks and a fully shrouded final-drive chaincase integral with the swinging arm. The engine was a 246cc two-stroke with piston-port timing and a 4-speed gearbox built in unit, as was the wet clutch. Lubrication was by petrol at a mixture of 20:1, fed by twin 20mm stub-mounted Mikuni instruments (built under licence from the British Amal concern).

If the Honda CB92 had been my first Japanese machine, the Suzuki T10 was my first two-stroke experience (if one discounts the two Lambretta scooters I had owned back in England). The CB92 and the T10 were completely different, the first being a sports bike, the latter a deluxe touring machine. In a 1964 *Motor Cycle News* road test, Sean Wood began by quoting from Suzuki's own publicity material, 'Designed for pleasure riding' and went on to say, 'It is no idle boast. A more luxurious machine it would be hard to find.

With Johnny Harrison, one of my three room-mates, in 1963.

125cc Honda CB92, my first Japanese bike.

My first two-stroke, Suzuki T10, twin-cylinder 250

Electric starter, direction indicators, leg shields, rear carrier, mirrors and a hydraulic rear brake are all included in the price... There is even provision for an inspection light.' Summing up, Sean pointed out, 'The engine is turbine smooth, even smoother than the average twin two-stroke. Riding the Suzuki is like sitting in a well-ventilated Rolls. If you want it to show a turn of speed, it will do so in no uncertain manner, but it is primarily intended as a touring machine.' Strangely enough, the maximum speed of the T10 was exactly the same as the CB92 whilst the power output was claimed to be higher, developing 21bhp at 8,000rpm.

Which bike did I prefer, the Honda or the Suzuki? Well that's a difficult one, as, they were so different. I think the true answer would depend on what you wanted to do on a certain day. If you fancied a bit of hard riding, it would have to be the CB92, on the other hand the T10 was a more comfortable, relaxed experience. You paid your money and you took your choice; I feel fortunate that I was able to sample both mounts.

In 1964 I was about to rediscover the delights of the Ducati marque. It happened like this. One day I was exploring the back streets of the local Arab town, Ma'alla, when I was amazed to see an absolutely brand-spanking-new Ducati 250 Monza being ridden by a local. He was travelling at little more than walking pace because the narrow street was crowded with people and a fair amount of animals, especially goats.

Running to catch up with the machine and its rider, we arrived virtually together at the rear of some premises, which turned out to be the equally new Ducati agency, that had opened that very day. The rider was actually the firm's mechanic, whilst the owner of the business, whose frontage ran adjacent to the main drag through Ma'alla town, turned out to be a very pleasant Malaysian gentleman. Upon hearing of my interest and past experiences with the Ducati marque I was recruited as a sort of 'Man Friday' in my spare time. I also purchased one of the machines on show, a 200 Elite.

1964 200 Elite, bought from the Aden Ducati agency in Ma'alla.

By now, my old friends Bill Wait and Clive Robinson had been posted to Steamer Point. In fact Bill was billeted in the same room as me with two others, Johnny Harrison (from Manchester) and Tony Vercoe. Bill, Tony and I suffered badly from bedbugs, but never Johnny. It turned out that they lived in his mattress and fed off the other three. Realising this, we stripped Johnny's bed and burned the mattress, which solved the problem.

During his time in Aden, Tony purchased two new Ducatis, the first being a 49cc Piuma moped and the second a 100cc Mountaineer motorcycle. The latter machine was quite interesting, as not only did it feature fan-cooling for the engine, but also came with both small and large rear wheel sprockets; one for conventional road use, the other being for off-road duties. I actually rode this machine in a couple of waste-ground trials organised by the Aden Military Motorcycle Club.

As I explained at the beginning of the preface to my book *BMW Twins The Complete Story*, 'The motorcycle I aspired to own in my youth was an R69S BMW, but I never did.' While in Aden, walking around Ma'alla town one day I saw just such a machine, with the rider, an RAF serviceman, dismounting. This turned out to be Peter Mapes, who lived with his wife and son in a flat nearby. However I did not discover this until a few hours later, when Peter said, 'You should have come to the flat'. Peter and the BMW were a frequent sight on the Aden roads until he returned (with his machine) to the UK.

The Elite featured a curvaceous chrome-plated 'jelly mould' tank. Originally the single pipe branched into twin silencers.

Mick astride his Ducati 200 Elite

Peter Mapes' BMW was a frequent sight on the Aden roads

Off-road riding aboard Tony Vercoe's Ducati Mountaineer, with fan-cooled 100cc two-stroke engine.

When I began racing upon my return home, Peter would often be a spectator at meetings, especially at Snetterton, and even presented me with photographs he had taken of me in action. Then we lost contact, until one day in 1996, when I was working for Three Cross Motorcycles on its Laverda stand at the Birmingham NEC Show. About half way through the 11-day stint and gradually losing the will to live, I was walking from the stand to the toilet block, when a voice said, 'Is that you Mick?'. I turned to see Peter, who I had not seen for almost 30 years. It was then that he gave me more photographs, including the one used here of the R69S in Aden.

The R69S could trace its origins – and a new era for BMW motorcycles – back to the Brussels Show of 1955. The first two models of a new line, the Earles-fork 500cc R50 and 600cc R60, featured long leading-link type front forks (the work of Birmingham engineer Ernie Earles), together with a swinging arm rear suspension closely related to that pioneered by the German factory's racing motorcycles campaigned successfully by Walter Zeller.

By late 1959 a more sporting model, the R69, had entered production. Finally, in August 1960 came the R69S, which produced a claimed 42bhp at 7,000rpm and could reach a speed of 110mph. Later that year, a quartet of British riders broke the world 24-hour record at Montlhéry in France, averaging 109.24mph and covering 2,622 miles in the process. An R69S also emerged victorious in both the Thruxton 500 mile and the Barcelona 24-hours endurance races. Yes, I would have dearly loved to have owned what I still consider to be the Rolls-Royce of the two-wheeled world.

Working in my spare time at the Ducati agency, I first bumped into Ken Watson. He was employed as a civil engineer and before coming to Aden had been a reasonably successful racer with Norton and Aermacchi machines. Both Ken and I took part in some sand races, which were also a feature of the aforementioned military club's sporting activities. The owner of the Ma'alla Ducati agency was keen to import one of the 250 scramblers for Ken and me to compete in the sand races and other events, but Ken told him not to waste his money. Besides racing at circuits such as Brands Hatch, Snetterton and Olivers Mount at Scarborough, Ken had competed in the 1959, 1960, 1961 and 1962 Senior Manx Grand Prix, on each occasion riding a Manx Norton, with his best result so far being 32nd in 1962.

By now I had, via the Aden importer, built up a good working relationship with the Ducati factory in Bologna. So, on behalf of Ken, I was able to order one of the then-new Mach 1/S 250 racers, which had been launched early in 1965. Based on the previous year's 285cc machines (ridden by Bruno Spaggiari and Giuseppe Mandolini) which had been victorious in the gruelling Barcelona 24-hours endurance event, the Mach 1/S was, unfortunately, far too heavy for short circuit racing, or for that matter the Isle of Man. But what it did have was reliability.

Sand racing in Aden on a Triumph Tiger Cub.

Ken returned home to the UK in the spring of 1965, collecting the Mach 1/S from the factory on the way. He also added a CR93 Honda, which he purchased in the UK to give him a 125-class ride. In September that year he finished 9th in the Lightweight Manx GP on the Ducati. The following year, in the same race, Ken caused something of a minor sensation by piloting the machine usually ridden by UK importer Vic Camp's normal runner, Tom Philips, to runner-up spot behind winner Bob Farmer's Aermacchi. After this, Ken only rode in one more Manx, the 1967 Lightweight, where he retired his Suzuki. Then, he returned to his life as a civil engineer. In 1990 he was working in Kuwait when it was invaded by Saddam Hussains's forces during the first Desert Storm. Luckily, he and his wife Olive got back safely to the UK.

Long before Ken had returned home, terrorist problems were beginning to surface in a previously peaceful Aden. One Sunday lunchtime late in 1964, I was travelling with several other servicemen on a local bus from Steamer Point to Khormaksar, via Ma'alla. At that time, locals and service personnel travelled together. At the Steamer Point end of Ma'alla was a roundabout, where the bus stopped and a number of Arabs got on. I was sitting sideways towards the rear of the bus, which by now was crowded. I noticed an Arab put a holdall on the luggage rack above my head. He made his way forward and I didn't see him again. The bus was full and people were hanging out of the doors, so I never thought any more about it until a few days later, when the British newspapers arrived from home. Inside Monday's *Daily Express* was a bold headline in the World News section: 'Bus Britons Escape Terrorist Bomb, Aden Sunday'.

Lining up on the startline for another sand race, with Brian Deller, who would become my race mechanic.

It transpired that the bus reached its final destination at Khormaksar, and when it emptied all of its passengers, that holdall was left behind. When opened, it was found to contain no less than seven sticks of explosive – the timing device had failed to activate its charge! The police interviewed everyone they could trace (including me), but the culprit was never found.

That day changed everything. Eventually a state of emergency was declared, and a series of restrictions imposed. Even so, the Aden Military Motorcycle Club continued to hold events, and they continued after I went home in the early summer of 1965 at the end of my tour. But the problems in the colony were escalating, with a growing terrorist threat which continued to get worse in the months after I left. This resulted in a full withdrawal of British forces two years later in 1967. The danger we had lived under was recognised and I received the Radfan and the Southern Arabian Campaign Medals.

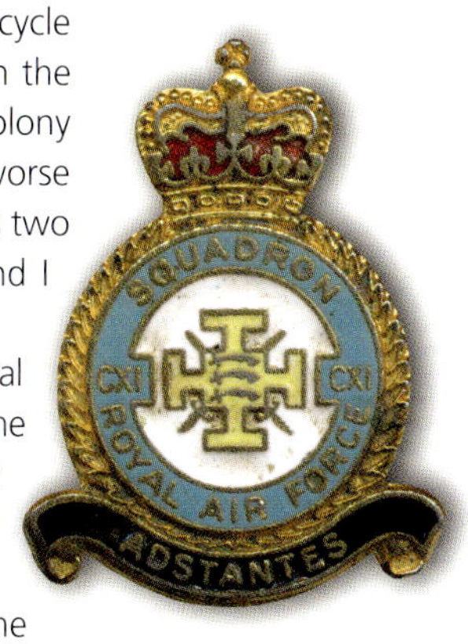

My next posting was Wattisham, with effect from 1 July 1965. In central Suffolk, Wattisham was the home of the legendary 'Treble One' squadron, the Black Arrows, who during the 1950s had been the RAF's premier aerobatic team, flying Hawker Hunters. By the time I joined them they were equipped with the supersonic heavyweight English Electric Lightning interceptor.

During my final few months in Aden I had not only concluded the purchase of a 650 Triton (built by Doug Southwell of Baldock, Hertfordshire), but also my first racing motorcycle, a 175 Formula 3 Ducati. At first, my transport from home to base every weekend was the Southwell Triton. However, I had a crash while travelling to Silverstone, caused by hitting a patch of oil on the road. I reluctantly decided to sell my 'Dream Bike' and in its place purchased a vehicle with which I could transport my racing bike. In retrospect it had been a mistake to commission such an expensive and specialised machine as the Triton and then part with it so quickly. But how was I to know that I would be bitten so strongly by the racing bug?

Something like a Ford Thames van – the racer's transport of the era – would have been ideal. But this was ruled out because I didn't have a car licence. Instead, I decided to part exchange the Triton for a new Reliant Regal van – a three-wheeler which I would be allowed to drive on a motorcycle licence. In truth, it was far more difficult and unsafe, compared with a conventional four-wheeler.

The Reliant deal was done via Monty & Ward Motorcycles in Twickenham, Middlesex. I dealt with Geoff Monty himself, who gave me a fair price for the Triton. Many years later, when I had an established motorcycle business myself, I received a telephone call from a man who was the current owner of my Southwell-built Triton. However, it was far from the dream machine I had sold Monty & Ward. In fact all the exotic components had gone; the Oldani front brake, Manx Norton rear brake, and for that matter the genuine Manx Roadholder forks. Had Monty sold these items off separately? Or had they been robbed at a later date? I shall never know. Later still, after he had moved on from the Twickenham business, Geoff Monty set up another shop in Edenbridge, Kent and was one of my AMF Harley-Davidson dealers in the late 1970s.

At the start of 1966 I was on detachment with 111 Squadron at RAF Akrotiri on Cyprus, a couple of hundred yards down the peri-track from the squadron on which my friend-to-be Rob Carrick worked. I must say that I preferred this experience to my earlier detachment to Malta some years before. Cyprus was much larger and presented many different faces in the years before Partition split the island in two: Turks to the north and Greeks to the south. When I was there, travel between the two areas and peoples was unrestricted. Many of the historic buildings were in the Turkish enclaves – which later became 'out of bounds'. In fact, for many years the only way into the Turkish sector was to fly in from the Turkish mainland. When I was there, Cyprus was unique in that it was possible to go skiing up in the Troodos Mountains then sunbathing and swimming down on the coast, within an hour. It is just a great pity that the Turks and Greeks couldn't live together in harmony.

650 Triton bought from Doug Southwell of Baldock, Hertfordshire.
It was reluctantly sold to finance the purchase of the first race transport – a Reliant Regal van.

After returning from Cyprus just before Easter 1966, it was time for a holiday at home with my family before returning to Wattisham. At around the same time, I part-exchanged my Ducati 175 Formula 3 for a Vic Camp Mach 1 250 racer, and for the 1966 season, I was recruited into the Royal Air Force Motor Sports Association. My initial contact was with Flying Officer WR (Bill) Southcombe, who was also racing (a Greeves in 1965 and a Cotton in 1966). There were several other racing members in the RAFMSA, including CR (Chris) Conn, Brian Moses, John Munn and TG (Terry) Pallister. By far the most successful was Chris Conn, who, I'm sure, would have risen to even greater things had he not been a serviceman. An example of his star quality is that Chris finished on the rostrum in third place behind none other than Mike Hailwood (Honda) and Giacomo Agostini (MV Agusta) in the 1966 Senior TT. He also gained a third in the Junior TT that same year, following Agostini (MV Agusta) and Peter Williams (Arter AJS) home.

There is no doubt that the RAF (probably more so than either the Army or the Navy) was very supportive of its servicemen in motorsport. They not only allowed us time off to compete, but in major events such as the Manx GP and the TT, covered the cost of the entry fees.

For much of the 1967 season, my mechanic was fellow serviceman Brian Deller, who was based at RAF Cranwell in Lincolnshire. Brian owned a Vincent Rapide 1000cc V-twin, a most suitable machine for him, as he was a well-built fellow. While we were working together on my Ducati one day, Brian said that he needed a few bits to complete the job and so he asked me to pop into Sleaford to Peter Davey Motorcycles – on his Vincent – for said parts. The ride there was OK, Brian having kicked the beast into life. However, things were somewhat different when it came for me to make the return journey. I found that my puny efforts to get the big V-twin to fire up didn't come to much. In fact when I stood on the kickstarter, I couldn't move it. Luckily there was a slope outside Peter Davey's, otherwise I'm sure I would still have been there to

At the Manx Grand Prix on a narrowcase 250 Ducati Mark 3, with wife-to-be Susan and mechanic Brian Deller.

this day! Certainly, after that escapade, I wouldn't rate the Vincent amongst my favourite bikes. Brian was a good guy and a good mechanic; he was also a true enthusiast. Sadly, we have long since lost contact with each other.

Another good friend at this time was Frithville dealer and sponsor Sam Coupland. Sam had been involved with many riders over the years, including the ex-Norton and Moto Guzzi works rider Dickie Dale. Austin Monks, winner of no less than four Manx GPs (1933 Junior, 1936 Junior and Senior on Velocettes, plus post-war the 1947 Lightweight on a Moto Guzzi), was also a close associate of Sam.

Besides Sam Coupland himself, both his loyal mechanics Ray and Jim were always on hand to give advice. And whilst Brian Deller was my race mechanic, my racing bikes were often stored on the Coupland premises. Years later, in the late 1990s, I called in to see Jim (Ray having retired), but he wasn't there. Instead a youngster was manning the counter. I decided to wait for Jim to return and after a while said I was going to the toilet. Just as the youngster was about to give directions, a voice shouted, 'He was visiting this establishment long before you was born.' Jim had returned.

On 1 March 1967, I was posted to RAF Cottesmore in Rutland, where I met my old friend Clive Robinson, who was to act as my driver/mechanic for several meetings during the 1967 season, which also included that year's Manx Grand Prix. Brian Deller took Clive over to the Isle of Man on his Vincent.

While I was at Cottesmore, I first considered purchasing my discharge from the service. The opportunity arose whilst I was on detachment to RAF Gaydon in Warwickshire, during the winter of 1967/68. There were four of us in a freezing room, actually snowed in. All four of us had had enough and wanted out, but in the end I was the only one whose reason for leaving was accepted. It cost me £125 to sever my contract, but the other three were not so lucky.

In the period between the acceptance and my actual discharge, 3-4 months, I was given all the dirty jobs. For example, I had to go and collect a prisoner from Gainsborough jail. When I arrived I discovered that he was twice my size, and being handcuffed to him was not a pleasant experience. However, it turned out he was not a serial killer, or even a GBH merchant, and the journey back to Cottesmore passed without incident.

But probably the task I disliked the most was collecting up the human remains after an Avro Vulcan V-bomber (XM 604) crashed a couple of miles after take off from Cottesmore. Amazingly the plane had come down in the garden of a farmhouse, with the farmer's wife standing at the kitchen sink when it happened. The debris from the crash travelled as far as half a mile in the opposite direction and missed the kitchen window completely. How lucky can you get?

The largest body part I found was a finger, and because of this incident I couldn't eat bacon for years afterwards. It was gruesome, and the whole incident was not helped when I discovered a panel from the aircraft with the impression of a human body on it. I subsequently discovered that although the pilot and co-pilot had ejector seats; the remaining four crew members did not. In fact they sat in spring seats that sprung into action in the event of a crash; the theory being that the seat would spin round and assist (push) the occupant towards the open door. In this case it appears the seat spring worked, but the door was still closed.

I was about to make the big switch from military to civilian life, even though I had no experience of a civilian working environment. Was this the right move? Being away from home made me more independent and resourceful, much younger than would have otherwise happened. I had met lots of people, made friends, travelled and learned of other places and cultures. But now I had to build a new life and career for myself and had, of course, forfeited any right to a military pension.

3 Racing Years

who knows what I could have done?

With the 175 F3 and Reliant van in August 1966.

As related in the previous chapter, my competitive motorcycling career began while I was serving in the Royal Air Force in Aden. Among the army and air force personnel in the Protectorate, there was a considerable enthusiasm for motorcycling – particularly the sporting side. This included sand racing, trials and even a touch of scrambling. The machinery was varied to say the least, with almost anything being pressed into service. My mounts included Ducati 100 Mountaineer (for trials), Triumph 200 Cub (sand racing) and a Velocette 500 (scrambling). To be honest, it was all just a bit of fun. Even so, I managed to pick up my most serious competition injury whilst riding the Cub in a sand race and still have the scars today.

I had also purchased my first road-racing bike. The second-hand Ducati 175 Formula 3 came via *Motor Cycle News* for the princely sum of £100, complete with riding gear etc. Back in 1964, while on a month's leave from Aden, Rick and I had attended a meeting at Silverstone run by the British Motor Cycle Racing Club (BMCRC – now known simply as Bemsee) and although we didn't speak to him, we saw the previous owner with the same machine in the paddock. As one of probably only three imported into the UK it would be a very valuable piece of kit today. New in 1959 it cost £521 – compared with just over £400 for a Manx Norton – so it's understandable that few were actually sold, but in today's classic motorcycle scene, such a rarity is in great demand.

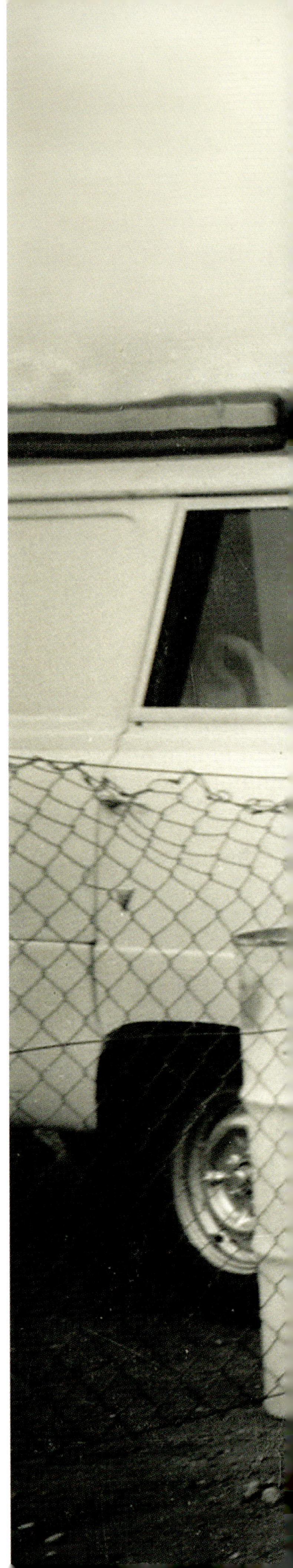

First ever race meeting, Ducati 175 F3,
Snetterton, July 1965

A 1959 175 Formula 3 in standard, unfaired trim

Brother Rick on the F3 in 1965.

That 175 F3 saw me make my début at my local Snetterton circuit in July 1965, where I was accompanied by my brother Rick, and my friend and fellow racer Ken Watson, who had returned from Aden a couple of months earlier. The bike was originally created to take part in the Italian Formula 3 events, hence the inclusion of lighting equipment, centre-stand and the like. But in Britain these 'road-legal' bits were usually thrown straight into the rubbish bin. And so it was with my F3, no lights, stand or even front mudguard by the time I purchased it.

Designed by the inspired engineer, Dipl. Ing. Fabio Taglioni, who joined Ducati in the spring of 1954, my 175 Formula 3 had been developed from a line of smaller models with bevel-driven sohc valve gear. The first, a 98cc known as the GS (Gran Sport) was not only attractive in appearance, but was to prove a particularly reliable mount in the domestic long-distance road races of the day, including the Milano-Taranto and Giro d'Italia (Tour of Italy). Further evidence of its worth came in November 1956, when a fully streamlined 98cc machine set new world records for the one-hour, 100km and the 1000km classes on the banked circuit at the Monza Autodrome. These records were set at over 100mph for the shorter distances and 96mph for the 1000km.

My début race at Snetterton in 1965. It was unfortunate that my bike was outclassed by the 250 two-strokes.

The Ducati was eventually sold to Vic Camp and then on to Scot Alex George, three times TT winner in the 1970s.

Sturdily constructed and easy to maintain, the Gran Sport 100 was – for its engine size – fast and sure-footed. It served to put such famous riders as Francesco Villa, Bruno Spaggiari, Alberto Pagani, Giuseppe Mandolini, Alberto Gandossi and Franco Farné on the road to fame. Together with a subsequent 125 enlargement of the same design, it sold in quite large numbers in Italy, and a 175 version soon followed, while Francesco Villa raced a further 250cc version in the USA with considerable success. The GS and its immediate successors went on to be instrumental in the birth of the series-production bevel-drive overhead cam singles that were to transform Ducati's fortunes from the late 1950s until the mid 1970s, with ever-increasing engine sizes – ultimately peaking at 450cc.

Taglioni's classic sohc design was based on a full-unit construction crankcase and gearbox, carrying a light-alloy cylinder barrel with cast-iron liner, inclined slightly forwards. A bevel shaft on the right of the engine drove the valve gear, which had exposed rockers and hairpin valve springs. On the right were a gear primary drive and multi-plate clutch, transmitting power to a four-speed gearbox. The crankshaft, with full-circle flywheels, carried a small flywheel generator on its drive-side extremity, supplying current for the battery of the coil-ignition system. At the opposite end, outside the timing bevel, a gear with straight-cut teeth provided the drive to the oil pump of the wet-sump lubrication system and the contact breaker system. The contact-breaker points could be adjusted through a spring-retained inspection cap at the front of the outer crankcase cover.

The 98cc version produced an initial power output of 9bhp at 9,000rpm. This was later boosted to 12bhp at 10,500rpm, with maximum speed increasing from 80 to 87mph as a result. The 125 version, achieved by increasing the bore size from 49.4mm to 55.5mm, produced 14bhp at 10,000rpm and could top 90mph. Another enlargement to 175 (62 x 57.8mm) gave 16bhp at 9,000rpm and a top speed of 100mph. The 125 and 175 later gained enclosed rockers and valve gear, and were rebranded as the Formula 3 rather than the Gran Sport. The larger bikes weighed-in at 190lb and 200lb respectively, as against the 180lb of the 98cc original. The arrival of the 125 and 175 models also saw a switch to the use of 18-inch wheels instead of the original 17-inch type, while the 175 was unique in the series by sporting a double-sided front brake similar to the factory's 125 Desmo single-cylinder GP bike.

The latter was Taglioni's masterstroke. For 1956, he had first decided to modify the Gran Sport 125 with a radical new double overhead-cam-cylinder head, boosting power to 16bhp at 11,500rpm. This was followed by an even bolder technical development, which resulted not only in a high point for the Ducati single but also a giant leap forward in motorcycle engine design. Three overhead cams gave the 125 Desmo positive opening and closing of the valves – and this desmodromic system gave the bike enough power to average 100mph over a full race distance.

This was way beyond the potential of the humbler models. It was during my ownership of the F3 that I came across another fellow racer with a 204cc Ducati, Charlie White from Totton, Southampton. It was just unfortunate, that by the mid 1960s, when we were racing these smaller Ducati singles, they were becoming totally outclassed against the new breed of two-stroke 250s, such as the Greeves Silverstone and Cotton Telstar, to say nothing of the latest Yamaha twins. And so I made the decision that the F3 would have to be replaced by something more modern. I first realised this when I competed in a second BMCRC meeting at Snetterton in September 1965. In both meetings I came in about two-thirds down the pack. I can well remember going down the mile-long Norwich straight on the old Snetterton circuit and realising that the 175 was not competitive. The fastest 250s were simply flying past, changing up another gear as they did so.

Desmo explained

The word Desmo has long been associated with Ducati and its design chief, Fabio Taglioni. Many wrongly assume that Taglioni invented it, but while the theoretical advantages have been known since the dawn of the combustion engine itself, what Taglioni did was to make it work, both on the race circuit and later in series production engines which could be ridden on the world's roads.

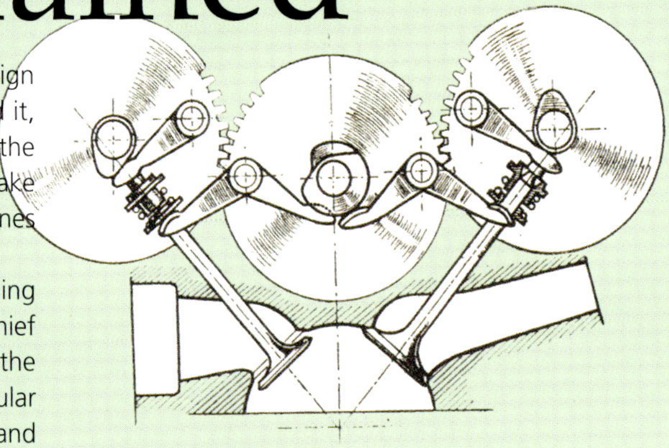

The original desmodromic valves designed by Fabio Taglioni for the 1956 125cc single GP racer. Ducati would later successfully apply the desmo system to its sporting singles and L-twins.

The word desmodromic derives from two Greek words meaning 'linked running'. The idea was to eliminate one of the chief drawbacks of valve operation at high engine revolutions, the phenomenon of valve float, or 'bounce'. This was a particular problem for designers in the days before four-valve technology and the advent of the rev-limiters common on modern power units. Bounce occurs when the valve springs are unable to respond quickly enough to close the valves back onto their seats. The desmodromic principle is to replace the troublesome springs with a mechanical closing system (much like that employed to open them), providing a reliable action. Without springs there will be no bounce, so that the engine becomes capable of higher revs. The desmodromic system either uses a separate camshaft (as on Taglioni's Desmo single-cylinder GP racer of the late 1950s) or the original cam lobes to close the valves through a mechanical linkage.

Much of this technology had been known since the earliest days of the internal combustion engine, but no motorcycle designer had been able to harness it efficiently. Norton and others had tried, but largely unsuccessfully. The automobile industry had done little better, an exception being Mercedes-Benz with its magnificent and highly specialised W196 racing car of 1954. Then the German giants quit racing and shelved the idea. However, Taglioni and Ducati were to buck the trend. Following its exclusive use on the factory GP bikes, the Bologna company later adopted the system for series production with the introduction of the widecase Mark 3D (Desmo) singles of 1968. By 1980, many models were thus equipped, as they are to the present day – Taglioni's legacy.

A 125 Ducati Desmo single with full front and rear streamlining, circa 1956.

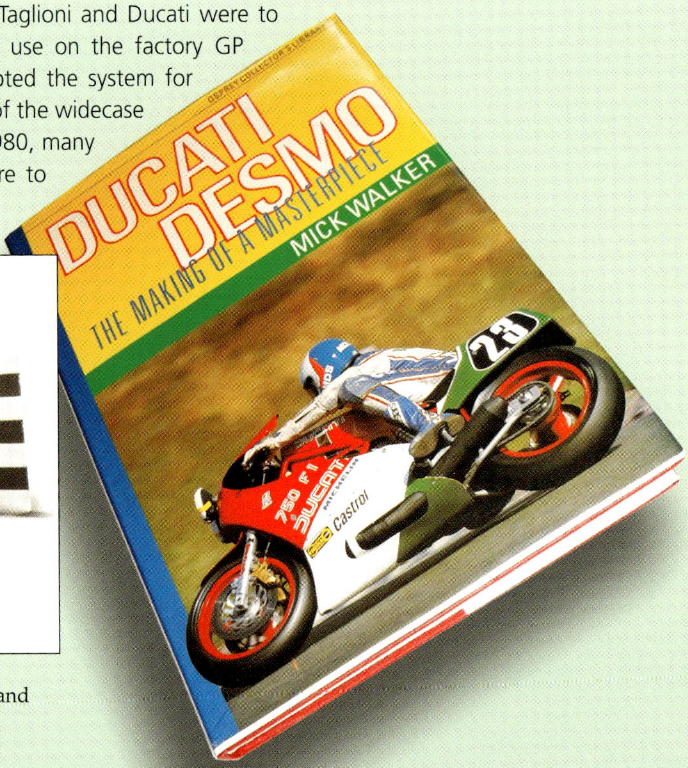

1978 Ducati NCR 900 racer

With the brand new 250 Mach 1, March 1966, Cadwell Park practice

John Kirkby from Lincolnshire also had his first outing on a Mach 1 during a practice day at Cadwell Park. We would go on to become good friends.

The five-speed Mach 1 250 first arrived in the UK during the summer of 1964, replacing the 4-speed Daytona. It was an instant hit, for the fast road rider and the clubman racer alike. In Britain, two of the Mach 1's first racing customers were Brian Jefferies and Mike Rogers, and the early results from this pair prompted Walthamstow Ducati specialist Vic Camp, who had supplied the bikes, to offer a racing conversion. The conversion based on Jefferies' machine was sold during the winter of 1964/1965 (the Rogers mount being run in the 250 production class).

These original early Camp racers were little more than standard production roadsters. Unfortunately, as I was to discover to my cost, so were the later models! In fact they could best be described as fakes. Mechanically they received no special parts or preparation, whilst the bodywork was replaced by fibreglass-ware manufactured for the Camp emporium by the Duguid Brothers, who subsequently produced other more attractive mouldings in the same material, which found their way on to various Camp-produced racers over the next few years. Although impressive for what it was, the Mach 1 in its standard state of tune was not rapid enough to match the performance of pukka race bikes such as the Greeves Silverstone, Cotton Telstar, DMW Hornet, Yamaha TD1 series and Aermacchi Ala d'Oro models of the period.

Following the signing of national star Tom Philips, who had won the 250 British championship on a Greeves Silverstone in 1963, Vic Camp found the demand for his race-kitted Mach 1 increasing. Customers included GR Bunting, Ken Finney, John Kirkby and me. In 1965 the price had been £299 (£30 more than a stock Mach 1 roadster), but for 1966 this price had risen to £319-10s. To justify this new figure, the following changes were listed as improvements: a twin-plug cylinder head (a second smaller 10mm plug being fitted at the rear of the bevel drive tube), a modified clutch (drilled lobes on the clutch basket), air-scoop slots drilled for improved brake cooling on the front stopper, Girling rear suspension units, a 30mm Dell'Orto carburettor (in place of the standard 29mm SSI unit), Dunlop triangular racing tyres, a modified rear seat frame rail and new fibreglass bodywork, which comprised the tank, seat, oil flap, front mudguard and fairing. Colour choice for the fibreglass components included blue, white, yellow and the most popular option, red.

In reality, the Camp modifications did not achieve much in the way of additional performance. In fact, I soon switched back to the single 14mm plug set-up and slung the Dell'Orto in favour of a British Amal Monobloc ($1^3/_{16}$ inch), which was much easier to set up. It also meant that the bike fired up instantly when it was pushed into action – a vital requirement at that time, as riders had to bump-start their mounts at the beginning of the race. With the Dell'Orto it was frequently a hit-or-miss affair, and all too often the rear wheel would simply lock up, which resulted in getting away at the rear of the field.

I first met the brothers John and Roy Kirkby at a Sunday practice day at Cadwell Park in mid March 1966, only a few weeks after collecting my Mach 1 from Camp's East London showrooms. The Kirkbys were local Lincolnshire lads, with John the rider and Roy the mechanic. We were to become good friends over the coming years. That practice was the first outing for both John's and my newly purchased machines.

The first race meeting with my new Camp Mach 1 was a BMCRC event at Silverstone on Saturday 1 April 1966. And a wintry start it was too, with snow greeting the competitors early that morning. By race time, conditions had cleared, but it was still bitterly cold. In my race, the bike was slow to fire up, so I had no chance of making up any real ground, resulting in a lowly finishing position.

Campaigning the Mach 1 at Snetterton in 1966.

The first crash came while challenging for the lead on an atrociously wet Snetterton track during the 1966 Baragwanath Trophy Meeting.

A few more meetings included the Baragwanath Trophy race at Snetterton (an event named after the famous pre-war Brooklands rider Ted 'Barry' Baragwanath). In terribly wet conditions I fought my way through the field to challenge for the lead before crashing out at the infamous Russell's Bend, which had just been added to the Norfolk circuit that year. In truth it was more akin to a skidpan in the wet – as many star riders, including Mike Hailwood, were to find out shortly afterwards.

Within days I had my second crash, I was making my début at Oulton Park in the ACU Clubmans meeting. During practice, a rider on a DMW seized directly in front of me on the approach to the super-elevated Esso Bend. In avoiding the rider and his machine, I hit the tarmac and slid up to the top of the banking. Luckily neither the machine or I had sustained any damage of consequence and that afternoon saw me on the starting grid. However, I felt somewhat detuned and failed to qualify for the 250 final.

Then some time in June or July 1966 I joined Ed Layn, who was helping two young Kings Lynn-based riders. This meant not only that I was able to share travelling costs, but also enjoyed the occasional ride on one of his Layn-prepared Formula Bantam machines. It was on one of these two-strokes that I had my first top-three finish, at a Bantam Club Snetterton meeting. It was also with the Layn team that I had my first experience of Cadwell Park. Cadwell was much more of a rider's circuit, where Snetterton was all about speed.

And so to the Manx Grand Prix, which was my first ever visit to the Isle of Man. I travelled there with Roy Kirkby and RAF comrade John Chillingworth, with Roy acting as my mechanic/pit-man. On our way to Douglas, aboard a Manx Steam Packet ferry, we got to know ML (Michael) Bennett, an experienced MGP competitor between 1963 and 1976 who lived next to the Silverstone circuit in Northamptonshire. Sadly he was killed in a racing accident, but I shall always remember his generous nature and enthusiasm for the sport. My group stayed at 34 Murray's Road, Douglas. That year the TT had been delayed due to a seamen's strike, and when we arrived our rooms were still occupied by TT teams, so we had to wait until we could move in. Already in residence were Peter Williams, Robin Miller (*MCN*) and the South African Ray Flack, with his controversial Norton Kneeler machine.

My first top-three finishes were scored with Ed Layn's racing Bantam, on which I enjoyed an occasional outing.

Relaxing between events with the Mach 1 at a sunny Cadwell in June 1966.

In retrospect I was absolutely unprepared to race on such a difficult and demanding course as the 37.73 mile Mountain circuit. My only experience of the course prior to the first practice session was half a lap on John Chillingworth's Greeves Scottish trials bike before it broke down. Geoff Duke spent weeks walking around the course before his début there, by comparison with which my preparation was virtually non-existent.

The first practice session began at around 5am on Tuesday morning, riding the machine up to the start line on the Glencrutchery Road, at the very top of Douglas, ready to get under way at 6am. Riding around such a complex circuit with which I was completely unfamiliar was certainly an experience. However, I thought I was getting on with the job well enough. That was until I reached the middle of Sulby Straight on the second lap. Then my fortunes took on a massive change for the worse. The engine locked up when I was flat out in top gear at well over 100mph. I failed to disengage the clutch in time, which resulted in the machine and me parting company. I still vividly remember sliding at high speed down the road. As I began to slow, I was overtaken by a fellow competitor, who was still on his motorcycle. Eventually I came to a stop and, finding myself uninjured (except for a cut hand), I picked up my machine, only to find the remains of the con-rod hanging out of the shattered crankcases. At the end of practice the machine and I were collected, and I was deposited at Nobles Hospital. With my hand duly bandaged, I was back at the hotel in time for breakfast.

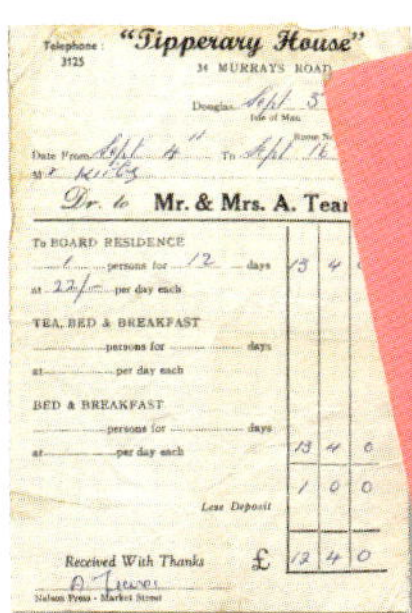

The Mark 3 engined Mach 1, Snetterton 1967.
In the background is brother-in-law to be Tony Plumridge's Ford Consul, RAF J2 van and Bob Frith's AJS 7R

The 1966 Manx Grand Prix with tape repair to my helmet and a replacement Mach 1 engine after a practice seizure at over 100mph wrecked the original and threw me off.

Amazingly, my two friends soon found another engine taken from a spectator's Mach 1. In truth, it must have been the slowest power unit in the event, much slower than my Camp unit. However, I did manage to complete the requisite number of practice laps in order to qualify and I actually finished the race. I wasn't last either, this honour going to an Aermacchi rider who was staying in the same hotel. He was so disgusted with his performance that he did not even bother to attend the prize-giving ceremony. An interesting footnote to my 1966 Manx GP was that, unlike today, no official inspected me, my riding gear, or machine. As a race photograph shows, I took part with tape around my damaged helmet.

After the Manx, I had intended travelling to Northern Ireland to race in the Carrowdore 100, but only having the remains of my original motor, my racing plans for the rest of the season suddenly became out of the question. As far as the engine we had borrowed was concerned, ominous clouds of smoke were being emitted from the breather pipe at the end of the race, and it was definitely past its best.

Fast-forward over 40 years to a club meeting at Snetterton at the beginning of the 21st century. I was standing at Coram Curve, awaiting the start of a 600 Supersport race, when a van pulled up, and I was joined by, as it turned out, the father of one of the riders. We got talking and when he realised I knew what I was on about, he asked for my name and telephone number. It turned out that neither of us had pen or paper. So he suggested we go to the van where one of his friends could take my details. Well, the friend almost fell out of the van. It turned out that he had been the owner of the Ducati from which we borrowed the engine back in 1966 – he had loaned the bike to a friend to go to the Island and received it back with a somewhat second-hand power unit!

Over the winter of 1966-67 my main task was to find a replacement engine, as my unit was a write-off – only the cylinder head was left in a serviceable condition. Not only had the rod destroyed the crankcase halves, but also the cylinder barrel and piston, together with several cogs from the gearbox cluster. It was beyond economical repair, but luckily, I eventually discovered a new 250 Mark 3 motor for sale in Bedford, where it had gone after being purchased from Vic Camp with the intention of fitting it into a Formula 3 racing car.

It was around this time my wife-to-be entered my life. Susan was the sister of fellow racer Tony Plumridge, Soon, she, Tony and me were travelling to meetings together, which meant that I now took in circuits further afield. During what would be my last couple of years in the RAF, I was stationed in Suffolk and then Rutland, and since my entry to the 1966 MGP, I was racing with support from the RAFMSA. For the 1967 season Tony and I purchased a trailer, which was towed by his Ford Consul. Everything went well until early one Sunday morning, travelling from Wisbech to Snetterton with my Ducati and Tony's Greeves, the trailer suffered a puncture at Downham Market river bridge.

Rick on the first incarnation of his BB32 Gold Star as a 350cc racer.

We did not have a spare wheel, so we left the trailer (and bikes) and carried on to Snetterton hoping we could borrow another trailer. The only one available was a pig trailer, but the owner assured us that it towed fine. Today, of course, there would be little likelihood of either our trailer or machines still being where we left them, but luckily in the 1960s things were different. We returned to Downham Market and loaded the bikes into the new trailer, but rather than just lay the bikes side-by-side we thought it would be a good idea if I got into the trailer and sat on one of the bikes and held the other. Everything was fine going through the town, but when we reached the open road Tony increased the speed. The trailer developed a horrendous speed wobble, which all but pulled Tony's car off the road. Eventually Tony got the rig under control. When we stopped I said there was no way I would be getting back into the trailer, so we laid the bikes over and I completed the journey in the car.

We made it in time for our race (a fully-fledged national status event). As I pushed off, I made a lightning start, but as I weaved side-saddle through the field, the front two riders suddenly closed the gap between them and I had nowhere to go! The only choice was to brake hard or collide with them, and the next thing I knew I was down. Several riders ploughed into me and my machine – including, I was later to learn, Tony on his Greeves. Somehow in the mêlée a Bultaco expansion chamber got caught in the webbing of my pudding-basin helmet, and I couldn't hear a thing for days afterwards. The race had to be red-flagged, as the debris could not be cleared by the time the leaders came round to complete their lap. Tony and I were ruled out of the restart due to the damage sustained to our bikes. All in all not a very successful day.

Another national meeting, this time at Mallory Park (my first time at the Leicestershire circuit) saw me in a 350 heat, having entered my Ducati as a 252cc due to the 250 class being over-subscribed. This saw me lead a race for the first time, a position I retained for a complete lap. But then I got really frustrated, because every lap, coming out of the Hairpin section, I had trouble selecting gears. Later, upon inspection, the selector box proved to be the problem. It was after this incident that my brother Rick came up with a modification that cured the weakness of the original Ducati design.

In 1967, Rick had a 350 BB32 Gold Star on the road (the first of the swinging arm models), and to gain a second ride he converted this into a racer for me to campaign. Except for a megaphone exhaust and a weight-saving exercise it was pretty much standard. Even so, it acquitted itself with distinction, often getting the better of Manx Nortons and AJS 7Rs. This encouraged Rick to go a stage further and seek out a 500 DBD34 motor to fit into the rolling chassis. He ended up buying an engine from County Durham-based Johnny Weston. As with my friendship with the Kirkby brothers, Johnny and Rick became good pals.

The 350 Clubman's Goldie in road trim.

With Susan's Mum, Susan and Rick, Snetterton 1967

1967 Manx Grand Prix, 250 narrowcase Mark 3, the first of many home-tuned Mick Walker machines

Unfortunately, fitting the larger engine was to cause plenty of problems. The small-fin BB32 engine had proved to be outstandingly robust, while the chassis performed well. However, the DBD34 power unit proved unreliable, failures including broken con-rods and sheared flywheel shafts, while the frame proved to be incapable of handling the additional horsepower. Eventually, we improved the handling by fitting a Taylor-Dow fork conversion. Later Rick replaced the Gold Star with a Manx Norton/pre-unit Tiger 100 Triton. However, I never even rode this machine, never mind race it.

During a Cadwell Park national meeting in May 1967, my Mark 3-engined Ducati had been overtaken by none other than Vic Camp's official rider, Tom Philips, on the approach to the Mountain section. Although I was able to stay close to Tom through the hairpin and Barn corner, as soon as we came off these sections onto the start and finish straight, his Ducati simply flew away. Afterwards I tracked down Vic in the paddock, and he was eventually forced to admit that 'his' bike was considerably different from the customer's models. The result was a promise that I would be able to buy the go-faster goodies. These consisted of a double-webbed titanium con-rod, a higher compression slipper piston (11:1) and a high-lift 'works' camshaft.

With these changes the machine was transformed, with the maximum rpm going up from 9,000 to 11,000 with a corresponding increase in top speed of some 10 per cent. This extra power in turn showed up the inadequacy of the standard 180mm single-sided twin leading-shoe front stopper, and also the stock 31.5mm Mach 1 front forks. The ideal solution, if cost and availability had not been a problem, would have been a new front end comprising a twin-leading-shoe, single-sided Oldani front brake, and a pair of Ceriani GP forks (the combination found on the Aermacchi Ala d'Oro).

I came very close to owning one of these pure-bred Italian racers. Travelling over to the 1967 Manx Grand Prix I had met Syd Lawton, the Aermacchi importer, and having known him for several years, we had discussed the possibility of me purchasing a new 350 Ala d'Oro for the following season. However, once again the Isle of Man did me no favours. This time it was a full-blown fire that actually occurred after finishing the race. Because of high winds and torrential rain, the start had been delayed for a couple of hours. When we finally got under way, the distance had been reduced from four to three laps. For practice and race periods I was sharing a garage with two other riders, Bob Grimson and Roger Corbett. We were queuing up at a Douglas newsagent for our copy of the post-race TT Special when news of a fire in our garage reached us. Together with another rider I lost everything; bike, spare engine, tools and spares, you name it – it all went up in smoke.

One of several Finisher's Medals from the Manx Grand Prix

It turned out that the landlord who rented us the garage had not bothered to obtain any insurance, which meant that our losses were not covered. This painful episode also signalled the end of my dream to own an Aermacchi. For some reason the Isle of Man fairies always had it in for me. Needless to say, my one and only appearance in the Southern 100 races (In July 1967) had also been jinxed. My Ducati, which had run the previous weekend at Cadwell without a hitch, decided to play up as soon as I reached the Island once again. With my bike out of action, I was recruited as a sidecar passenger when another competitor had been taken ill and the driver invited me to be his ballast. I must say this was the most hair-raising ride that I have ever experienced throughout my entire motorcycle racing career. Having your nose inches from the kerb or a brick wall at mind-bending speeds is not my way of having fun, but I will admit that it certainly was an experience. And years later in 2010 it came in handy when I was compiling my book *Sidecar Champions since 1923*.

Unlike the previous year, my Manx GP problems were not to rule me out for the rest of the year. During the latter part of 1967, while still in the RAF and stationed at Cottesmore, I raced at national meetings on an AJS 7R loaned to me by Flying Officer Bob Frith. Collecting the bike from the officer's mess on the base turned out to be a very embarrassing experience. Bob was away on flying duties and I, a mere corporal, had been given permission by Bob to collect the 7R from his room, and get it ready for Snetterton the following weekend. I went to Bob's room and collected the bike and proceeded to push it down an extremely long plush-carpeted corridor. Just before I reached the other end after what seemed a long journey, I was halted in my tracks by a loud command from the other end. As I turned to face a very irate Wing Commander, I noticed a trail of oil that had leaked from the 7R's chain oiler device all the way down the corridor. How I escaped without being thrown into the guardroom I will never know, and I never found out what happened to the oil slick I had created. I can only imagine that Bob Frith sweet-talked his way out of this potentially costly mistake.

As for me, I was soon charging around Snetterton on the 7R in the company of stars such as Derek Minter, Dave Croxford and John Cooper. On one occasion I remember being caught and lapped on the final circuit at Coram Curve by John Hartle, riding his race-winning Aermacchi Metisse.

I was an official RAFMSA entry, together with Chris Conn and other RAF riders at the time, and as such was able to use service transport to race meetings. In this case it was one of the infamous Austin J2 vans, which was driven by friend and fellow serviceman Clive Robinson. The J2, it has to be said, was always considered to be the biggest heap on wheels and someone in high authority must have taken a large back-hander to allow such an awful vehicle into RAF service; the palm-greasing coming from BMC (British Motor Corporation) the forerunner of British Leyland, which in turn became the ill-fated Rover Group.

At the end of that season, the 7R – of mid 1950s vintage, complete with Burman gearbox – was advertised by Bob in *MCN* for the princely sum of £95. In hindsight I should have somehow found this amount and salted the bike away for the future. But at that time I lived weekend-to-weekend, racing on a shoestring; much more pressing was the finding of entry fees and other race-related running costs. At around the same time in 1967, another service friend and I visited his ancient aunt in rural Suffolk one summer evening. At the bottom of her garden was a wooden shed, and inside lurked a truly

Clive Robinson, friend for over 50 years, with his customised Honda CB72 in 1966

With Rick at Snetterton in 1967 on an AJS 7R on loan from Flying Officer Bob Frith.

immaculate Douglas 90 Plus, which I could have purchased for a mere £10. The classic movement had not been thought of in 1967 and such bikes were then classed as old junk. Today the 7R would be worth in excess of £25,000 and the Douglas around £15,000. With the pair being available for a shade over £100, it doesn't bear thinking about.

At the end of 1967 I purchased another 250 Ducati, and rebuilt the engine using the valuable Camp extras rescued from my fire-damaged Mark 3. I had also managed to acquire, at last, an Oldani front brake, and was able to approach the 1968 season with an air of confidence. However, this was soon shattered, thanks to the arrival of the latest Yamaha TD1C, which was some 20 mph faster than my Ducati and far more reliable than the twin-cylinder Japanese two-strokes that preceded it. The time had come to part company with the Ducati. But it is worth relating an incident at Cadwell Park, at the first meeting of the season. Susan and I were asleep in our van at the Lincolnshire circuit, when I was woken up by a brightness in the sky. Assuming it was morning I was ready to get up, but checking my watch it only showed 3am. I then realised the brightness was in fact snow, which resulted in the meeting being abandoned at mid-day. Not a very good start to the 1968 season.

As my budget had been destroyed by the Isle of Man fire I was forced to re-examine my racing career. Although I managed to sell my rebuilt Ducati (via the *MCN* classifieds) this hadn't done much to restore my finances. Luckily, salvation was at hand in the form of an immaculately prepared – and competitive in its class – Formula Cub. Essentially it was a carefully assembled Sports Cub, the model with the distributor at the rear of the cylinder barrel. I bought it from Ray Noble of Sandhurst, Kent, and it can only be described as a brilliant little bike. Running on Duckhams oil it never missed a beat, or broke down during my ownership, and in truth its handling was marvellous. If I had purchased the Cub earlier than midway through the year, I am pretty certain that I could have won the championship title, but I still managed victories at the first two circuits I competed at, Snetterton and Lydden Hill, and there was better yet to come.

MOTOR CYCLE NEWS, Wednesday, October 16, 1968

RUNAWAY MICK WALKER'S TREBLE AT LAST CADWELL

MICK WALKER had runaway wins in his three rides at the British Formula Racing Club's last meeting of the season at Cadwell Park on Saturday.

Over 100 competitors took part in brilliant sunshine, the day marred only by strong winds.

The 250 cc class once again produced some exciting racing. Austin Hockley led the field for a while but the experience of club champion Tony Spencer paid off at the flag.

Surprise of the day was the brilliant riding of Paddy Reid (250 cc Cotton) when taking second place to Gerald Carter's Bonneville in the first production machine event. After two creditable wins Carter's hat-trick was prevented by the dedicated riding of Mike Pusey third time out.

Gearbox troubles plagued both Don Grant and Cyril Crosy in the allcomers events and two wins apiece was a very fair outcome. Mixing with them was Steve Billingham on his Triton to provide some of the most thrilling racing seen here this season

PROVISIONAL RESULTS

First allcomers 1000 cc: 1 D Grant (499 Norton) 8m 31.8s—63.61 mph. 2 M Spencer (650 Triton), 3 G Thomas (489 Triton), 4 S Billingham (650 Triton), 5 K Littlechild (350 AJS), 6 J Marshall (498 Norton). **Fastest lap:** Grant, 1m 21.2s—66.5 mph.

Second allcomers 1000 cc: 1 C Crosby (650 Triton) 8m 9.4s—66.24 mph. 2 D Grant, 3 S Billingham, 4 G Thomas, 5 D Stephenson (650 Triton), 6 R Garner. **Fastest lap:** Grant, 1m 17.8s—69.41 mph.

Third allcomers 1000 cc: 1 C Crosby 8m 5s—66.8 mph. 2 S Billingham, 3 D Grant, 4 J Marshall 5 G Thomas 6 G Brown (750 Norton). **Fastest lap:** Crosby, 1m 17.4s—69.77 mph.

Fourth allcomers 1000 cc: 1 D Grant 8m 1.6s—67.36 mph 2 C Crosby, 3 G Thomas, 4 G Naylor (614 Norton), 5 W Roberts (500 Norton), 6 S Billingham. **Fastest lap:** Grant, 1m 17.2s—69.95 mph.

First 250 cc: 1 J Kernan (Bultaco) 8m 40.8s—62.21 mph, 2 P Thompson (Yamaha), 3 J Ford (Greeves) 4 C Hewson (Ducati), 5 L Parson (Parilla), 6 C Curtis (Ducati). **Fastest lap:** Thompson, 1m 24.6s—63.83 mph.

Second 250 cc: 1 P Martindale (Yamaha) 8m 33.2s—63.13 mph, 2 J Kernan, 3 D Chapman (Cotton), 4 A Clatworthy (Greeves), 5 W Hill (Ducati), 6 C Hewson. **Fastest lap:** Kernan, 1m 24s—64.29 mph.

Third 250 cc: 1 P Martindale 8m 44.6s—61.76 mph. 2 W Byard (Aermacchi), 3 L Parson, 4 C Curtis, 5 S Hall (Bultaco), 6 A Glazebrook (Suzuki). **Fastest lap:** Byard, 1m 23.3s—64.44 mph.

Fourth 250 cc: 1 A Spencer (Yamaha) 8m 15s—64.45 mph. 2 A Hockley (Yamaha) 3 W Byard, 4 P Reid (Cotton), 5 W Hill 6 J Ford. **Fastest lap:** Spencer, 1m 20.4s—67.16 mph.

First 1000 production: 1 G Carter (650 Triumph) 8m 42.2s—61.97 mph. 2 P Reid (250 Cotton), 3 J Vincent (650 Triumph), 4 J Bassindale (750 Norton), 5 P Haslam (650 Triumph), 6 A Glazebrook (247 Suzuki). **Fastest lap:** Carter, 1m 22.8s—65.22 mph.

Second 1000 production: 1 G Carter, 8m 18.6s—64.98 mph, 2 M Pusey (650 Triumph), 3 J Vincent, 4 M McClelland (750 Norton), 5 P Haslam **Fastest lap:** Carter, 1m 19.6s—67.84 mph.

Third 1000 cc production: 1 M Pusey, 8m 17.6s—65.11 mph, 2 J Vincent, 3 G Carter, 4 J Bassindale, 5 T Oddin (650 Norton), 6 G Millward (654 BSA). **Fastest lap:** Vincent, Bassindale, Carter, 1m 21.2s—66.5 mph

First Bantam Cub: 1 M Walker (Cub) 9m 17.8s—58.09 mph, 2 J Adkin (Cub), 3 D Ward (Cub), 4 J Ford (Bantam), 5 P Hanmore (Cub), 6 M McGrath (Cub). **Fastest lap:** Walker, 1m 31s—59.34 mph.

Second Bantam Cub: 1 M Walker 9m 14.6s—58.42 mph 2 J Adkin 3 B Hanmore, 4 C Miller (Cub), 5 J Taylor (Cub), 6 M McGrath. **Fastest lap:** Walker, 1m 30.6s—59.6 mph.

Formula Cub: 1 M Walker, 9m 9.3s—58.93 mph, 2 J Adkin (MP Hanmore), 3 C Miller, 4 J Taylor, 5 M McGrath. **Fastest lap:** Walker, 1m 29s—60.67 mph.

Formula Bantam: 1 J Ford 9m 39.6s—55.9 mph, 2 L Notman, 3 R Lane, 4 F Robinson, 5 P Barnes, 6 S Smith. **Fastest lap:** Ford, 1m 34s—57.45 mph

Even though I left the Air Force on 23 July 1968, I still had a large number of friends in the service, and many of them continued to support my racing by following me round the circuits. Several were there to witness the final meeting of the 1968 Formula Cub season which was held at Cadwell Park in October. It was here that I gained the one-and-only headline I would have in *Motor Cycle News* during the whole of my competitive career: 'Runaway Mick Walker's treble at last Cadwell'. This was to be my last meeting with the Cub, but it was certainly a superb way to bow out – three wins in three rides and the fastest lap in each.

Over the winter months Susan and I had decided to get married, which we did on 24 May 1969 at Leverington, North Cambridgeshire, her parent's home, where she and her brother Tony had grown up. Getting married obviously changed my view of life. Prior to the wedding I had sold the Cub to Derek Ward, a fellow Cub racer from Great Yarmouth. Over the winter I had totally rebuilt the bike and in the process changed the colour scheme from light blue to a Ford metallic light green. Derek raced the bike under the 'Walker Cub' banner – my first involvement in what could be described as sponsorship.

I returned to racing after purchasing a new Ducati 250 Mark 3 from Elite Motors of Tooting in South London during the summer of 1969, as related in Chapter 5. I had initially bought it as a means of transport, rather than for competitive riding. But by the spring of 1970 I was missing the sport, and on the spur of the moment I took out an international racing licence and entered the Thruxton 500 endurance race, nominating Tony Plumridge (my new brother-in-law) as my co-rider. As a shake-down prior to Thruxton I took part in a Sunbac (Sutton Coldfield and North Birmingham) club meeting at Silverstone, over the club circuit. Not only this, but I also rode the Ducati there and home again after the event.

Tony Plumridge – brother-in-law and co-rider for the Thruxton 500 endurance race.

Brilliant Sports Cub bought from Ray Noble of Sandhurst, Kent. It brought me the only *Motor Cycle News* headline of my entire racing career.

During my racing career, I had ridden both the full Silverstone GP circuit and the shorter club one, so was pretty familiar with the Northamptonshire venue's layout. The Sunbac meeting was a combination of high-speed trials and scratch races. I took part in one of each of these, and the class I entered catered for bikes up to 500cc. In both events I found myself wheel-to-wheel with a 499cc Egli Vincent ridden by Roger Slater. In the 1970s, Roger was the British (and later American) Laverda importer and also the instigator of the legendary Jota model. I well remember my battles with Roger, as the performance of the Egli Vincent was slightly superior to my Ducati – well, it was double the cubic capacity – while the Italian 250 was more agile around the bends.

Agony for Alan Barnett . . .
The picture that sums up the Thruxton 500-miler on Sunday. In torrential rain, race leader Alan Barnett crashed Reg Curley's Norton Commando in front of the pits. He appeals to his pit for help.

Besides the Silverstone track time I also tested my Ducati Mark 3 out on the roads near Wisbech. Today, with the vast increase in traffic, this would be suicidal. Tony (who had never ridden the Ducati prior to race day) and I were entered for the International 500-mile Grand Prix at the Thruxton circuit on Sunday 10 May 1970 by our local Wisbech & District Motor Cycle Club. Prior to race day, the weather had been dry, warm and sunny for several weeks, but all this changed within an hour of the 10am Le Mans-style start. I had undertaken to ride the first session and, considering the international status and star riders, our club-entered, standard and unfaired production 250 was lying third in its class – amazing! Then came the rain, or should I say monsoon, which lasted for the remainder of the day. The following week's *MCN* had a front-page picture of Alan Barnett covered from head to toe in mud after crashing out on his Norton Commando.

At least we kept circulating, but with only one Barbour jacket between the two of us, we were soon wet and cold and putting on a soaking jacket slowed us even more. The professional teams and riders had waterproof suits

Taking part in the 1970 Sunbac meeting at Silverstone on the Hannah Ducati 250 Mark 3 bought new as transport in 1969 and ridden to the event.

and fairings, but we were less well prepared. However, we managed to bring the little Ducati home 7th in class, and 27th overall. Years later at a special 50th anniversary dinner for the Wisbech Club, Tony and I were guests of honour, with our heroics still fondly remembered. A programme from the event was on display and the list of riders read like a Who's Who of motorcycle racing: Barry Sheene, Dave Croxford, Percy Tait, Malcolm Uphill, Peter Williams, Ray Pickrell, Alan Barnett, Stuart Graham, Ralph Bryans, Chas Mortimer, John Blanchard, Barry Ditchburn and Paul Smart – just about every star of the era, plus Tony and me. Today it would be like putting a couple of club riders on a Moto GP grid.

By now, I had been selling Ducati spares for almost a year. The business was expanding, and so I decided to make a return to the Manx Grand Prix that September – my third race meeting of the year, but not on my road-going Mark 3. Instead I had located a racerised 200 Elite (actually 210cc). Transport was arranged by two of my customers, who had become friends and offered to take me to the Island in their van. But unlike 1966 and 1967 we had decided to camp in the paddock at the rear of the grandstand – mainly on the grounds of cost – the same reason I had brought the Elite, rather than something more competitive.

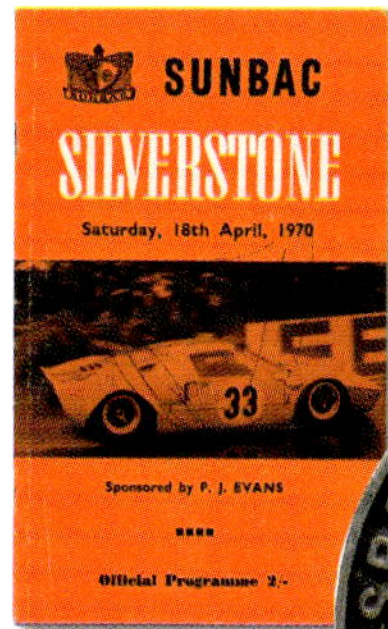

By the middle of practice week I had a major problem. A piston circlip had come out, ruining not only the piston but also the liner of the cylinder barrel. By visiting every motorcycle dealer on the Island, I eventually unearthed the required items from a machine being broken up for spares, but a far bigger problem was waiting just around the corner. One afternoon I decided to take a walk down into Douglas, and came back to a very nasty shock. My two friends had gone home, leaving my suitcase, tools and motorcycle alone and forlorn in the paddock. In retrospect this was probably the best thing that could have happened as the rest of the paddock quickly came to my aid. Everyone wanted to help and I was soon taken in by fellow-racer Denis Rapley, his mechanic and their respective girlfriends. Another competitor, Brian 'Snowy' Cammock from Lincoln – a regular MGP rider from 1962 to 1976 – promised to transport the bike and me back home to Wisbech after the race was over. If all this kind-heartedness was not enough, Denis decided that I should ride his spare bike – a Camp 250 Mark 3. This I used for the remainder of the practice sessions and in the race itself. I brought the Rapley machine home in 32nd position, my best place in the event so far, even though the field was now dominated by the Yamaha twins.

The demands of my fledgling but expanding business allowed me only to take in one race the following year. This was the 1971 Manx Grand Prix, which was destined to be my last visit as a rider to this famous event. Once again I rode Denis Rapley's bike. Although my 30th only improved a couple of places on the previous year, my lap times were much better, and a 5 minute stop to rectify a misfire lost me many places. Who knows what I could have done? Even so, I now had a record of finishing all four Manx GPs that I had entered, something to be proud of considering the problems I had encountered along the way.

My racing career finally ended in 1972. 'About time!' I hear you say. In May I had my one and only race in the 50cc Enduro. The last in the series, this was held over the Lydden Hill circuit in Kent, as opposed to Snetterton where it had been staged since its inception in 1960. Over the years, many famous riders had taken part in this unique event, including world champions Bill Ivy and Dave Simmonds. My 50cc ride had come about due to helping Pete Harrison when he experienced problems with his Spanish-built Ducati purchased from Vic Camp, as explained in Chapter 5. Pete's son Mike had originally been scheduled to ride the Harrison machine with co-rider Terry Stimpson, but Mike had Isle of Man TT commitments.

The machine was interesting, in that it comprised a Honda CR110 rolling chassis into which had been grafted a much-modified series production pushrod Honda engine with a horizontal cylinder. This engine was in fact the work of Honda's Alfie Briggs (himself a racer) and its performance and reliability were to prove superb. Terry and I finished 5th overall, only beaten by a quartet of Grand Prix Kreidler two-strokes.

My final outing, a few weeks later, was at my local track at Snetterton, where I had begun my racing career seven years earlier. My machine on that occasion was the Ducati 24 Hours my dealership had prepared for our sponsored rider Mick Taylor for the Production races that year.

I had enjoyed my racing years greatly, and the numerous minor setbacks recalled in this chapter were no different from those suffered by many other riders who made up the majority of the grid during what is today regarded as the classic period of motorcycle racing. I was also lucky to have experienced numerous high points during my racing career, not only chalking up top-three places at most circuits, but also a fair spattering of victories at Snetterton, Cadwell Park and Silverstone, among others. I also had the great honour of competing at a higher level against the likes of Hailwood, Minter, Hartle, Croxford, Sheene and many other household names, at national and international level.

From then on I transferred my racing efforts into supporting other riders. During the 1970s, besides Mick Taylor, these included Dave Arnold, Paddy Reid, Dave Cartwright and Ian Gittens. The lessons I learned from my own racing experience were to benefit others, so all was not lost. I was able to continue to support riders from that time until fairly recently.

As far as the Manx was concerned, 1972, 1973 and 1974 were spent sponsoring other riders in the event. These included Andy Vaughan-Jones 250 Ducati (20th in 1972), Stuart Morrell 350 Saxon-framed Ducati (retired when well placed in 1973) and Norman Tricoglus 500 Yamaha (2nd in 1974). Actually Norman was just 3 seconds away from a sensational victory.

I had the honour of competing against some of the most talented riders of all time – including Mike Hailwood, shown campaigning a Benelli single in my favourite picture, painted by Peter Haynes.

Norman Tricoglus (centre) on a Mick Walker-sponsored Yamaha in the 1974 Senior Manx Grand Prix, in which he came second.

I also became really involved with speedway during the late 1970s, via various sponsorship deals with my local team, the Kings Lynn Stars, whose home track was just outside the town on Saddlebow Road. My first year with the squad was during the 1976 season, when amongst other things I bank-rolled Lynn's number three rider Ian 'Tiddler' Turner. As the nickname implies, Ian was small in stature, but just like Bill Ivy in road racing, he had the heart of a lion, with a never-say-die attitude. Besides my rider, that team included captain Terry Betts and an up-and-coming Michael Lee, who became World Champion in 1980.

At this time Kings Lynn was one of the country's leading teams, challenging hard for both league and cup competition honours. Beside my help to Ian Turner, which lasted until the end of the 1978 season, my company also gave other financial assistance, including even sponsoring one-off meetings, and in 1979, I helped a younger, less experienced member of the Kings Lynn squad, Billy Spiers.

The sport of speedway is essentially a team effort; not individual, as in other forms of two-wheel competition. Even so, there is an individual world champion each year. I found the average speedway fan very much like a soccer fan, supportive, enthusiastic and loyal to his team above all else. Yes, there were fans of individual riders, but ultimately the team performance was what mattered.

Speedway racing can trace its origins back to the American dirt tracks of the early 1900s. But it was really the Australians who refined the sport. Speedway arrived in England in early 1928, with the first meeting being staged in Epping Forest on the outskirts of north London. This was followed by tracks appearing in several major cities, including London (Crystal Palace), Edinburgh and Wolverhampton.

With future world speedway champion Michael Lee and Mick Walker Motorcycles salesman Chris Handley.

The early British speedway scene included several major competitions, the best-known being the renowned Golden Helmet. There was also the novelty of women riders, who, although banned in 1929, created quite a sensation during the short period they competed. The next step was the creation of a league system in much the same vein as soccer clubs, with track teams riding against each other. In fact, after the Second World War, speedway became Britain's second-largest spectator sport, with the early 1950s witnessing truly vast crowds. Even today, speedway remains popular in many countries around the world; notably in Scandinavia and former Soviet-bloc countries. I can fully appreciate why this is so, having experienced its unique blend of noise, excitement and spectacular floodlit viewing of short but marvellously intensive racing.

With my involvement at Kings Lynn I got to know not only the sport, but the personalities. One particular friend was Kings Lynn's manager, Martin Rogers. Unlike the soccer manager, Martin was both team boss and promoter, and under his guidance the team emerged as a major force in British speedway – and his enthusiasm rubbed off on me, hence my support for his team. My friendship with Martin meant that I even got to test-ride a speedway bike. Having tried virtually every other branch of the sport, this was a real eye-opener. What hit me straight away was that there were no brakes. Essentially a speedway bike has a 500cc single-cylinder engine, a single-speed gearbox, rigid rear suspension and very little else. On a speedway bike the throttle is the all-important control, power on to accelerate, power off to slow down, whilst the key is in the art of broadsliding, pouring on the power via the rear wheel enabling the bike to slide through the bends in one controlled drift. Well that is the theory, but my efforts were not quite so fluid, certainly not so during the first few hectic laps in which my progress was very kangaroo like. But eventually I got the hang of it, which really made me appreciate the skill and throttle control exercised by the top riders.

Sadly, I was forced to end my speedway connections in 1980 due to a combination of increased workload and the onset of the economic recession. However, I still look out for the Kings Lynn team's results and was pleased to see them re-join the top division in 2011. I also keep in touch with Ian Turner, who still lives only a few miles from Wisbech.

Ian 'Tiddler' Turner
sponsored by Mick Walker Motorcycles 1977-78

With ‘Tiddler’ Turner, John Blunt and his girlfriend Angela Sims, Susan and Chris Handley

4 A New Direction

I preferred looking after customers to selling bikes

After leaving the Royal Air Force in 1968, I had found a job as an export manager at a firm in Kings Lynn, where I worked alongside my father and brother Rick. But when Susan and I were married in May 1969, we moved to Wisbech, and I was soon looking for work nearer home. I found a position at a local canning factory where I was in charge of 70 women, but my boss decided that I was not being harsh enough with my staff. Actually, with three production floors to look after, the heavy-handed tactics he demanded wouldn't have worked, even if I had agreed with him, so I handed in my notice.

By this time, my Ducati connection had already led to me servicing and supplying parts to Ducati owners in my spare time, so I decided to turn my enthusiasm into a fully-fledged business venture. What that really meant was that I began operating in the smallest way possible for a new enterprise. As I still had lots of things related to riding and racing Ducatis, I had already built a sturdy wooden shed at the rear of our house, 20 The Grove, Magazine Lane, and this became my original business premises when I finally took the plunge. My transport in those days (besides my new 250 Ducati Mark 3) was a tradesman's cycle, given to me by my father-in-law, Bill Plumridge.

Soon a second wooden shed was built and I pressed ahead, taking a small weekly classified advertisement in *Motor Cycle News*. Mick Walker Motorcycles was in business. Right from the start, I used my own name for two very good reasons: the first was so that the customer would know exactly who he was dealing with (to my mind, using your own name should tell the customer that you are answerable to him and that he will always get good service); secondly, having raced Ducatis and being known as an enthusiast for the marque, it was a name that other Ducati buffs would be familiar with. Trading as Mick Walker Motorcycles and later as Rick & Mick Walker the business would last for several decades.

During 1970, my cottage industry rapidly expanded to such a point that I had outgrown both my sheds and I soon found better premises at 10 Hill Street, a brick-built shop in Wisbech town centre that was my base for the next three years or so. Being new to business, the main problem was how on earth I would manage to finance the new project. The shop purchase price was, I believe, in the region of £1200. As I didn't have that sort of money, the owner, a Mr Chater who owned travel agencies in both Kings Lynn and Wisbech, allowed me to pay the balance in stages, which I did in less than 12 months.

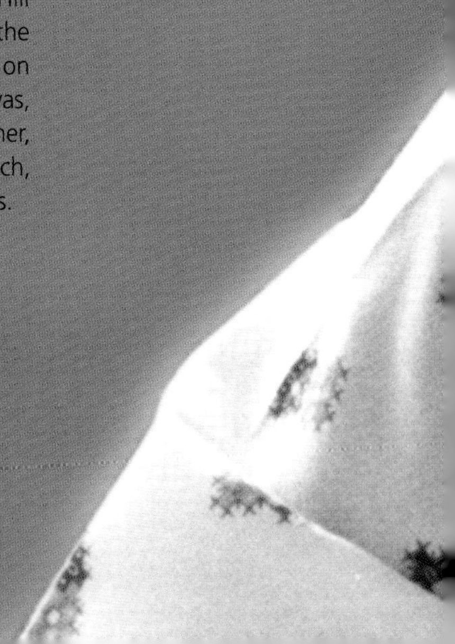

The EMC Puch racer that proved surprisingly desirable.

With larger premises, several things changed. I sold my original home (a caravan), together with the wooden sheds, and Susan and I moved into rooms over the shop. At this stage I took on my first employee, my brother Rick as mechanic, soon followed by my father and John Blunt. John had owned a Suzuki Super Six, was a keen motorcyclist and a big racing fan. Thanks to my staff I was able to enter the Manx Grand Prix that year. As a one-man operation this would not have been possible.

By the end of 1970, we had begun to sell a few motorcycles – mainly second-hand. But as 1970 became 1971, one bike simply would not move, a 125 EMC Puch racer of early 1950s vintage. It sat in the showroom for many, many months. What could be done? Steve Hackett, my contact at *MCN*, suggested that I put an advert in the racing section of the classified ads of his journal. I did so, not really expecting this would achieve much. Over time I have forgotten the exact asking price, but it was low. Anyway, when we opened on Wednesday morning, someone immediately telephoned to say that he was coming to buy the Puch. I said that I'd keep it for him. No sooner had I put the phone down, it rang again, another person wanting the Puch – 'Sorry it's sold,' I said. This continued not just that day but for a whole week. Anyway, the first caller eventually arrived – and so did another potential buyer. The second one simply would not accept that I had already promised the machine, and offered ever-increasing amounts of cash for the bike. I refused his offers and eventually he ended up telling me that I was a fool for not allowing the original customer to be gazumped and stormed out of the shop. But a promise is a promise!

Once I had moved into the shop at Hill Street, suppliers' representatives started to call, including ones from Ken Cobbing, WE Wassell and MCE (Motor Cycle Equipment Birmingham). It was not long before John Blunt and I visited the Ken Cobbing warehouse in Waltham Cross, just north of London, where I met Ken for the first time. During the 1960s and 1970s he was a major player in the aftermarket spares and accessories business. This had begun in the scooter sector, but by this time, scooters were rapidly going out of fashion. Ken looked to other areas in order to replace his shrinking customer base, so, rather unexpectedly for his old customers, he chose motorcycles. He and his wife were avid collectors of those older bikes that are now referred to as classics. Ken had a wide range of contacts within the Italian accessory industry, including the likes of Meteor (pistons and rings), Aprilia (electrical equipment), Borrani and San Remo (wheel rims). He could even source smaller items such as fuel taps. As we shared a mutual interest in all things Italian Ken and I instantly hit it off. Because he had been in the business much longer than I had, I always regarded him as the senior partner in our discussions.

At the Hill Street premises with Rick and John Blunt, on the 350 Saxon-framed Ducati racer

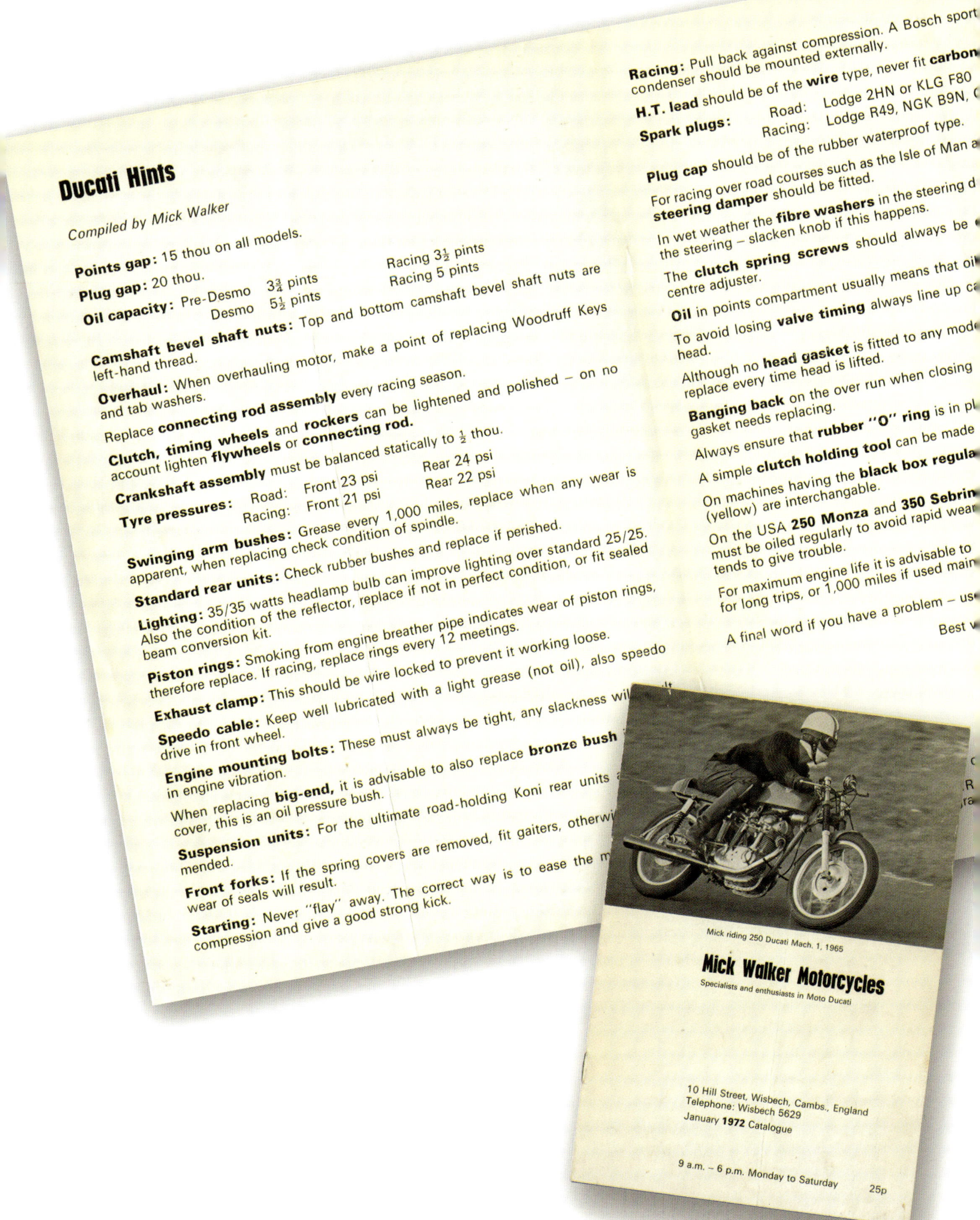

Ducati Hints

Compiled by Mick Walker

Points gap: 15 thou on all models.

Plug gap: 20 thou.

Oil capacity: Pre-Desmo $3\frac{3}{4}$ pints Racing $3\frac{1}{2}$ pints
Desmo $5\frac{1}{2}$ pints Racing 5 pints

Camshaft bevel shaft nuts: Top and bottom camshaft bevel shaft nuts are left-hand thread.

Overhaul: When overhauling motor, make a point of replacing Woodruff Keys and tab washers.

Replace **connecting rod assembly** every racing season.

Clutch, timing wheels and **rockers** can be lightened and polished – on no account lighten **flywheels** or **connecting rod.**

Crankshaft assembly must be balanced statically to $\frac{1}{2}$ thou.

Tyre pressures: Road: Front 23 psi Rear 24 psi
Racing: Front 21 psi Rear 22 psi

Swinging arm bushes: Grease every 1,000 miles, replace when any wear is apparent, when replacing check condition of spindle.

Standard rear units: Check rubber bushes and replace if perished.

Lighting: 35/35 watts headlamp bulb can improve lighting over standard 25/25. Also the condition of the reflector, replace if not in perfect condition, or fit sealed beam conversion kit.

Piston rings: Smoking from engine breather pipe indicates wear of piston rings, therefore replace. If racing, replace rings every 12 meetings.

Exhaust clamp: This should be wire locked to prevent it working loose.

Speedo cable: Keep well lubricated with a light grease (not oil), also speedo drive in front wheel.

Engine mounting bolts: These must always be tight, any slackness wil…
in engine vibration.

When replacing **big-end,** it is advisable to also replace **bronze bush** …
cover, this is an oil pressure bush.

Suspension units: For the ultimate road-holding Koni rear units …
mended.

Front forks: If the spring covers are removed, fit gaiters, otherwi…
wear of seals will result.

Starting: Never "flay" away. The correct way is to ease the m…
compression and give a good strong kick.

Racing: Pull back against compression. A Bosch sport…
condenser should be mounted externally.

H.T. lead should be of the **wire** type, never fit **carbon**…

Spark plugs: Road: Lodge 2HN or KLG F80 …
Racing: Lodge R49, NGK B9N, …

Plug cap should be of the rubber waterproof type.

For racing over road courses such as the Isle of Man a…
steering damper should be fitted.

In wet weather the **fibre washers** in the steering d…
the steering – slacken knob if this happens.

The **clutch spring screws** should always be …
centre adjuster.

Oil in points compartment usually means that oi…

To avoid losing **valve timing** always line up ca…
head.

Although no **head gasket** is fitted to any mod…
replace every time head is lifted.

Banging back on the over run when closing …
gasket needs replacing.

Always ensure that **rubber "O" ring** is in pl…

A simple **clutch holding tool** can be made …

On machines having the **black box regula**…
(yellow) are interchangable.

On the USA **250 Monza** and **350 Sebrin**…
must be oiled regularly to avoid rapid wear…
tends to give trouble.

For maximum engine life it is advisable to …
for long trips, or 1,000 miles if used main…

A final word if you have a problem – us…

Best v…

Mick riding 250 Ducati Mach. 1, 1965

Mick Walker Motorcycles

Specialists and enthusiasts in Moto Ducati

10 Hill Street, Wisbech, Cambs., England
Telephone: Wisbech 5629
January **1972** Catalogue

9 a.m. – 6 p.m. Monday to Saturday

25p

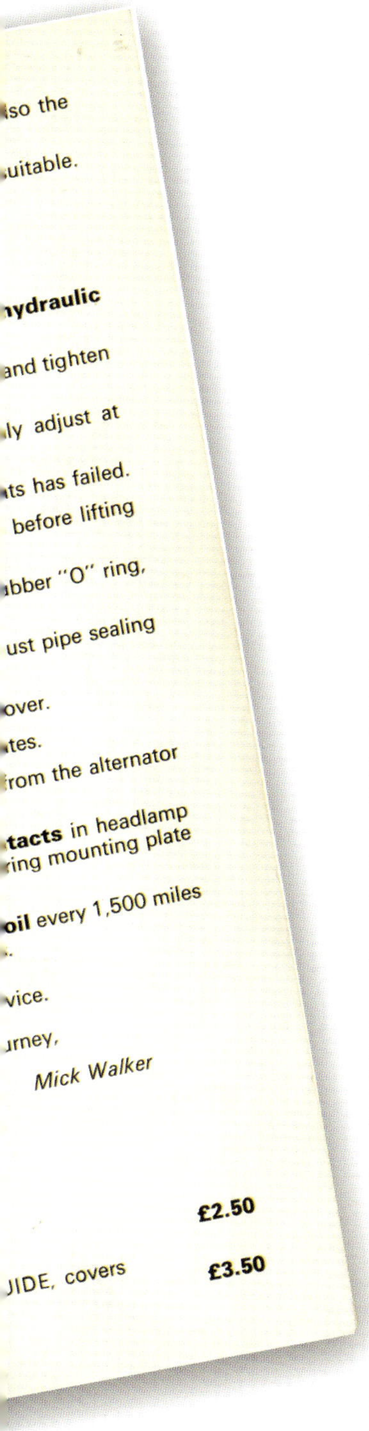

By 1972 our business relationship had grown to such an extent that I was doing a considerable amount of business with the Cobbing empire. Later Ken even broached the subject of a joint venture to import the new Moto Morini 3½ V-twin machine, but eventually we decided to stick to the spares game and so the Morini project never happened. But it was still a significant milestone for me, as it was my first brush with the concept of importing motorcycles. This all happened several months before Wilf Harrison and Peter Glover, who traded as Harglo, took on the job. Sadly, as with many other motorcycle enterprises during the early 1980s, Ken Cobbing, like myself, was affected by the major recession that hit the industry. His company went into liquidation and just as he was about to drive away on the very last day Ken suffered a fatal heart attack. I had lost a true friend and someone I very much respected.

Like everyone else in business Ken made the occasional error of judgement. The biggest one in his case concerned the unsaleable vast stock of surplus Dutch-made Anker 50cc two-stroke engines that he purchased from the ailing BSA empire in 1972. These engines, thousands of them, had come via the Ariel 3 trike, which had proved to be a massive sales flop for the BSA group. Only a few hundred were sold to dealers – and even fewer on to customers. The tooling costs were never recouped, whilst the BSA computer continued to buy-in components, including the Anker engine units in vast numbers. The whole exercise is estimated to have cost BSA a minimum of £2 million and was certainly a major factor in the group's ultimate demise.

To illustrate why the Ariel 3 did not sell, I need only to relate my own experiences with one of these machines that came into my Hill Street shop in 1972. Owned by a local lady customer, it was suffering from an almost total lack of performance. This was found to be caused by a blocked exhaust system. On replacing this with a new component, the engine started and ran sweetly. However not one of my staff could be persuaded to test-ride the machine; all saying something like, 'You must be joking, I wouldn't be seen dead on that!'

So it was down to me to give the Ariel its required test before handing it back to the customer. Not only did it provide an insight into what it was like to ride – not too bad actually – but it also provided a unique experience. Never before – or since – have I been subjected to quite so many questions, usually, 'What is it?' True, the Ariel 3 didn't look like anything else on the street, regardless of how many wheels other vehicles might have. I don't know why BSA took on such a risky project – and more importantly, where was the market research?

I must say that I always considered customer service the most vital part of running a motorcycle dealership. In fact I preferred looking after customers to selling bikes, which is probably why I was always happiest supplying spare parts. From 1970 to 1972, while Susan and I lived over the shop, on many occasions we played host to customers who, for whatever reason, were unable to travel home. An example of this was recalled by a former customer at a recent Stafford Classic Motor Cycle Show. I was there selling my books, when this guy walked up to me and asked, 'Remember me?' Well, usually after a while a name would come, or at least where we had previously met. In this case I drew a blank, but he certainly knew me. Back in 1972, on his way to holiday in Great Yarmouth aboard his 450 Ducati, he had broken down several miles from Wisbech, and telephoned the shop asking for assistance. As it was late in the day I drove out and collected him, bringing him and the bike back to Hill Street. We fixed the bike and put him up for the night, giving him breakfast and sending him on his way to start his holiday. That was the only time we had ever met, but he remembered and appreciated it enough to find me and thank me nearly forty years later.

Mick Walker Motorcycles continued to expand and we built up a solid customer base, thanks to our ability to supply both new and used Ducati parts. At this time the second-hand business outstripped the supply of new components. When I had first started trading, my parts mainly came from the items I had collected over the years of Ducati ownership. But soon these stocks began to dwindle. So I restocked by dashing all over the country to buy up Ducatis for breaking. You could, at that time, find a plentiful supply of bikes at what can only be described as giveaway prices. But then came the big break that would transform the business from lower division to Premier League status. I will call it the Bill Hannah saga.

Born in Cumbria in 1928, Bill Hannah was a speedway rider during his younger days, before eventually moving to Liverpool, where he became a motorcycle dealer and later began selling cars in a big way, too. Bill was a flamboyant character who first sprang to national attention when he sponsored sidecar star Chris Vincent – also a solo racer of considerable ability – on a Honda CR93 during 1964. The following season the Hannah Honda was ridden by future world champion Bill Ivy. Like Chris, Bill racked up many wins on this machine.

Giuseppe Pattoni with the Hannah Paton 500cc racing twin. Paton sponsor Bill Hannah would play a key role in the Ducati story.

A little later, Bill Hannah bankrolled the Italian Paton Grand Prix team, with riders including Angelo Bergamonti, Fred Stevens and Billy Nelson. The 500 Paton dohc vertical twins were the work of Giuseppe Pattoni, the former chief mechanic of the FB Mondial GP squad. The machines were generally faster than the best of the British singles and proved themselves reliable over several seasons' use. In two-valve guise the engine produced 65bhp, but the final version with four-valve heads was good for 70bhp. Usually the Paton had to take second best to Giacomo Agostini's MV Agusta, but when this suffered one of its infrequent retirements, the Paton was able to record a victory. The best year was 1969 when Nelson finished the season fourth in the championship table, whilst 1967 had seen Bergamonti defeat Agostini for the 500cc Italian Senior title. In 1970 Hannah withdrew his support, keeping the bikes, whilst Pattoni continued with new machines but on a reduced scale.

My own part in the Hannah saga had its roots back in mid-1966 when the American Ducati importers, the Berliner Corporation of New Jersey, refused a shipment of 3,500 bikes ordered from the Italian factory. At that time the Berliner brothers Joe and Mike wielded great power as a major stateside supplier of imported motorcycles. Not only did they import Ducati, but also held the agency for AMC (Associated Motor Cycles) of Woolwich, London, manufacturers of AJS, Matchless and Norton. When they refused to take delivery of the Ducatis, the Berliners sent a letter to WA (Bill) Smith, then chairman of AMC, telling him in no uncertain terms to find another home for a certain shipment of Ducati motorcycles. The contents of the letter (the original of which later came into my possession) made it crystal clear that until this happened there would be no more AMC products required. As AMC itself was facing financial disaster, the problems the letter presented to Smith need hardly be emphasised. How much Berliner's demands played a role in AMC's final collapse later that year is not known, but it is certain that can not have helped matters.

The shipment that caused all the trouble consisted of 500 350cc Sebrings, 400 250cc Mark 3s, 300 250cc Monzas, 1,800 160cc Monza Juniors, 300 100cc Cadets, and 100 Brio scooters. Actually, the problem took many months to resolve, and it was not until late 1967 that a financial agreement was finally thrashed out. The intermediary was a merchant bank in London, and the consignee was none other than Liverpool businessman Bill Hannah. The exact financial sum involved is not known, but it was reported to be in the region of three-quarters of a million pounds, a serious amount in 1967.

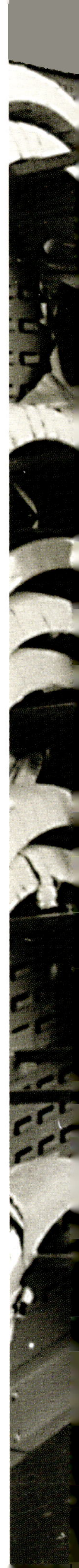

A fraction of our Ducati spares stock in 1976

At the time Bill Hannah was probably at his business peak, having built up a sizable financial empire that included what was claimed to be the largest car showroom in Europe. Bill was definitely an extrovert, and enjoyed showing photographs of his luxurious mansion and his ex-Mike Hailwood Iso Grifo supercar (essentially an Italian body on an American V8 engine), which he made a point of parking in a prominent position. Besides the Ducati deal and the car business, Bill imported reconditioned Honda Super Cubs from Japan and, amongst other ventures, marketed a fire-escape ladder.

The number of machines Bill Hannah imported dwarfed the figure achieved by Vic Camp over his many years as the official UK importer. This was something of an insult in Vic's view, and was to cause a major problem for British Ducati owners over the next few years. To begin with, Ducati's 'exclusive' tag was quickly tarnished, and spares supplies for new Ducati owners were erratic, partly because Vic Camp was none too keen on supplying spares for Hannah bikes – a very short-sighted position in my opinion. In fact, this was the very reason I was able to make such a success during the early years of my own business venture.

Having owned and raced Ducatis for many years, I found myself getting more and more requests for parts and help. Many owners just wanted someone who was interested in them, since large numbers of Hannah Ducati customers found a total lack of anyone who remotely understood them or their bikes. Having purchased one of the Hannah machines myself – a 250 Mark 3 registration number XML 962G – from Elite Motors in spring 1969, I had something of a personal interest in the Hannah/Camp argument. Nor was this to be my only connection with the Hannah bikes, since during early 1972 my Ducati spares stock was now beginning to run short of particular items, and something needed to be done to replenish the dwindling pile. Imagining that the Bill Hannah organization had perhaps half a dozen bikes and hopefully a few spares left, I telephoned the office in Liverpool. Although it was a 'cold' call and my first direct contact with the man or his company. I received a positive response. I drove up to Liverpool in my 1950 side-valve, split-screen Morris Minor. When I stopped for fuel and directions, the pump attendant warned me against Bill Hannah, but having travelled all this way, I ignored his advice.

At the Hannah car showrooms there was no sign of anything Ducati. Eventually I was escorted into the manager's office, where I was introduced to Bill himself and saw a couple of framed photographs of the Team Hannah Paton GP bikes in action. Bill took me next door to a large warehouse with no windows. Opening the door, I was absolutely amazed to see that my original estimate of 'half a dozen' bikes was wildly inaccurate and could be multiplied many times over, as there were in fact around four hundred! Almost every bike had been robbed of bits, and although some were pristine many were going rusty. This situation was not helped by the water covering parts of the warehouse floor.

The next surprise met me in a building at the rear of the car showroom. I was staggered to find a storeroom full of Ducati parts, many in unopened bags. I was later to discover that the staff had found it easier to take a component from a new machine, than to go to the trouble of finding it in the stores. No wonder there had been so many unhappy customers. The remaining 'new' machines could not be sold, as they were missing vital parts and were in a poor state of repair after being stored in the waterlogged warehouse. The other problem was that nobody in the stores seemed to know what was there, let alone where it was.

Road racer and journalist Alan Cathcart campaigning the Hannah Paton dohc 500 twin.

1966 Hannah Ducati 350 Sebring – an American-spec model named in honour of Franco Farné's class win at the Sebring Raceway, Florida.

Feeling stunned, I was led back to the office. Bill Hannah said he was taking me out to lunch, and we left the building in the ex-Hailwood Iso sports car. I had a major problem. My finances were limited, to say the least, although I realised that Bill Hannah was pretty desperate to rid himself of what he himself described as the 'curse of Ducati'. He had parted with all the saleable stock and was getting a load of hassle from an irate dealer network over the issue of spares, which Vic Camp did not want to supply. So what was Bill to do? Here was someone keen to take over his remaining stock of bikes and spares – but I had to admit that I simply did not have the money. I had never operated an overdraft so we settled on a number of post-dated cheques. My next problem was how to get the machines to Wisbech. 'Easy!' said Bill, and he simply hired a fleet of Hertz rent-a-trucks!

Where was I to store this vast amount of bikes in my tiny Hill Street shop? This problem was solved by my friend and employee John Blunt, whose father had a huge barn on the outskirts of the town. And so I departed from Liverpool as the owner of everything that remained of the Hannah Ducati empire. With this at my disposal, I was able to solve all of the problems for owners and dealers alike. It really was an amazing coup and the Hannah deal was to prove the turning point for the Mick Walker business.

I must say that all my dealings with Bill Hannah were a good experience. As the pump attendant's warning suggested, others seemed to have had a bad deal with Bill, but he treated me very fairly, and there were no hidden charges or complications, none whatsoever. Several months later Bill phoned me. Was I interested in purchasing the Hannah Paton race bikes? Now, this was in the years before the concept of the classic bike, and motorcycles had not yet been considered as a form of investment, so I turned down the offer. Not long after this it transpired that Bill Hannah was in big, big trouble. Eventually he wound up in prison on a charge of tax evasion. Bill was certainly a larger-than-life character who liked to do things in a big way; but I liked the man, even though we probably didn't share a single thing in common.

Someone who became a great friend over many years was Arthur Bullock. Arthur was the service and warranty manager for the Nottingham-based Agrati Sales organisation, which was based at St Marks Street in the city. He had joined back in 1964, remaining there for 19 years until 1983, shortly before the firm, an offshoot of the parent Italian Agrati company, closed. My first contact with Agrati Sales came in the early 1970s when I augmented my Ducati business by becoming a Garelli dealer. Ducati did not sell anything below 250cc at that time, and it was the beginning of the Sports moped boom, with the main contenders being the Yamaha FS1E 'Fizzy', the Suzuki AP50 and the Garelli duo of Rekord and Tiger Cross. Garelli's range consisted almost exclusively of 50cc mopeds in virtually every guise: sports, trail, small wheel, single-speed, multi-speed and automatic – you name it and Garelli supplied it.

The used bike department at Norwich Road

Certainly, the Garellis were the quickest, although they were not famous for their reliability. One of my very first experiences of their mechanical woes came when a customer on an outlying farm phoned to say that a part of his engine had dropped off. I always believed in personal service (probably why I never made much money) and went to investigate this problem myself. Arriving at the address, I was taken to a barn to find the Garelli, a Rekord, with one of its outer engine covers removed. This was the cover that protected the machine's flywheel magneto, and yes the customer was correct – the flywheel had actually fallen off. Later I determined just why this had occurred (and why it was to happen many more times thereafter). In their wisdom, Garelli had decided to make a switch from CEV to Bosch flywheel magnetos. Unfortunately, this switch had not been thought through. The Bosch flywheel was made of steel where the CEV was aluminium, so the German component weighed at least three times more than the Italian product. In service in the hands of an inexperienced novice who was only interested in wringing the last ounce of performance from the tiny engine, when the throttle was snapped shut from peak revs, the inertia of the much heavier flywheel would simply snap the rotor clean off the crankshaft taper. As a result Agrati was to suffer a flood of claims, and it was Arthur Bullock who had to deal with them.

My Agrati representative (who visited the Wisbech dealership on a regular basis) was Roy Edge. Later Roy became one of my employees, working on the Harley-Davidson and then the Cagiva import side of the business. Roy and Arthur eventually sorted out the many and varied Garelli warranty problems I experienced. Because of this we remained close friends, and when Arthur left Agrati, I kept in touch with him and was able to help him with the restoration of his disc-valve 50cc Garelli racer which had won the British championship title in 1969, ridden by George Ashton. One of my very last contacts with Arthur before he died in the late 1990s was supplying him with a pair of Marzocchi rear suspension units for the racer. And later, after Arthur died, I was reunited with the machine at Stafford, together with its new owner. Somehow my input into the machine felt like a link with a true gentleman.

By the beginning of 1973, the Hill Street premises was bursting at the seams, and so began a search for bigger property. This was found at 72/74 Norwich Road on the other side of Wisbech. It was some four or five times larger and also gave us the opportunity to move home. Our son Steven had been born on 4 July 1971 and now Susan was expecting another baby, Gary, who arrived on 19 September 1973. The Hill Street shop had served us well, but it was time to move on. We bought a bungalow (with a granny loft) in Popes Lane, Leverington. For Susan, there was quite a difference in living conditions. The old Hill Street kitchen had been more akin to a workshop – with the cooker doubling up as a means of removing bearings from crankcases. At Popes Lane, we had something that we could now look on as a home, rather than an extended part of the business premises.

Barry Sheene and his father Frank at Brands Hatch in October 1969 with Francisco Bulto, boss of the Bultaco factory.

The future double 500cc World Champion Barry Sheene cut the ribbon to open my new Norwich road premises at a ceremony in July 1973. It was through John Blunt that I had become a friend of Barry, who during the period 1970-72 spent the winter months with John at his West Walton home. Eventually in the mid-70s, Barry made his base in a large farmhouse just outside Wisbech, where he lived with his father Frank and mother Iris. Later that decade, Barry moved back south, but he told me that he had enjoyed living in the area.

Barry was a very genuine person and I never found that fame changed him. Yes, he was what today would be termed as 'media friendly', but to his friends Barry Sheene remained the likeable fun-loving individual he had always been. While Barry lived near us, Susan and I, together with John and his girlfriend Angela, went out socially with Barry and Stephanie on several occasions. An example of Barry's personality occurred at Donington Park on the weekend of the 1988 British Grand Prix meeting. I was walking across the paddock with a photographer and next thing I knew Barry was flinging his arms round me as he exclaimed 'Mick, great to see you, how are you doing?' The photographer was surprised to realise that Barry and I were close friends, but of course he didn't know our history. When Barry spent time in Wisbech during the closed season of 1970-72, he used my dealership as a base for picking up girlfriends; Barry would arrive around 2pm each afternoon, and spend time chatting to John and me. Then at 3.30 on the dot he would dash out just in time to intercept the girls coming out of the local high school, and it was almost a different one each day. However, he slipped up one afternoon – quite literally. As he dashed out, he tripped and landed headlong in the roadway, grazing his chin, but undaunted, he still walked off with a newly recruited female companion.

Barry Sheene opening the first Norwich Road premises in summer 1973

Paul Smart, former race rival, who I got to know in 1972.

Through my friendship with Barry I got to know Paul Smart, who I had campaigned against early in my racing career, when he began racing with a 250 Cotton Telstar at the beginning of 1966. Paul was Barry's brother-in-law, having married Barry's sister Maggie. In April 1972 Paul had, famously, won the prestigious Imola 200 on a Ducati 750 V-twin, beating team-mate Bruno Spaggiari. Subsequently, the Ducati management presented Paul with his winning bike and, after returning to the UK, Paul took in a couple of international events on the British short circuits, before laying the bike up.

For several months, it was on display in my Norwich Road showroom, but eventually I phoned Paul to ask when he wanted the Imola machine returned. His reply stunned me, for he admitted he had actually forgotten that I had the bike. Even though this was in the pre-classic days when racing bikes were only metal, rather than gold, I was still surprised. Paul did collect the bike in the end, and today it must be one of the most valuable racing machines of its era.

After moving into the Norwich Road showrooms, I was able to expand my parts and servicing operation, but I could also increase the sale of motorcycles. Besides new and used street machines, from the summer of 1973, I had begun to stock up on an increasing numbers of racers. Just about everything came through my showroom doors during the next few months and it was a period that I really enjoyed. None of the machines were new, for I specialised in good quality second-hand bikes. Looking back, my stock then would have been worth millions at today's prices – and in light of the classic boom, which began a few years later, many enthusiasts got a real bargain from me.

Paul Smart on the 500 Ducati V-twin in practice for the Italian Grand Prix in May 1972. The legendary works rider and development engineer Franco Farné is on the right.

'The Motorcyclist's Friend'

Brian Crichton with his Suzuki GT380 two-stroke triple.

I first met Mick Walker in late 1970 or early 1971 when working on the *Wisbech Advertiser* – now known as the *Fenland Citizen*. A nearby lane led to the rear of Mick's shop, which was how I discovered the dealership on first moving to the town. I would often walk round after work to the front of the shop to look in the window. For a while Mick had a Thruxton Bonneville on a plinth that I ogled for several nights. I can still see it.

I had decided to ride the 1959 BSA A7SS I owned at the time to the south of France and tentatively asked Mick if he would check it over and strengthen the tall sissy bar so that I could strap a tent to it. The bike was mildly chopper customised – all the rage then, thanks to the film *Easy Rider*.

This was the first time I met Mick. With a smile he agreed to do the work. Now that I look back and think about it, that smile was probably one of indulgence from a man with a more refined taste for pure sporting and racing motorcycles than a Jack the Lad with a peanut-tank Beeza. And the more I think about this first encounter the more I realise now that I had just met a genuinely friendly character. He could have told me to clear off, taking the thoroughbred-motorcycle moral high ground. He could have lectured me about having a non-standard bike. He could have shaken his head in resignation while reluctantly agreeing to take on the work. I have come across all these attitudes over the years.

But no, Mick Walker took on the work without prejudice. He didn't give me a hard time over a new fashion in bikes that the established motorcycle world then regarded with much disdain. I guess he could sense youthful enthusiasm and it was in his character to befriend rather than to belittle. Though that was the first time I had met Mick, I knew of him and his Ducati associations through bike magazines and *MCN*. Little did I realise our paths would cross many times in the future.

The key to this was the fact that in September 1971 I moved from Cambridgeshire to Northamptonshire to join *Motor Cycle News*. Now I would occasionally see Mick at a race meeting and always felt comfortable asking him questions because he was always helpful and always had a welcoming smile.

When he became the Cagiva importer, I was involved in organising some testing, including some comparative tests against rival Japanese manufacturers. What I especially liked about Mick was that he didn't get upset if the Cagiva didn't come out as well as some of the rivals. He always kept his composure. I think this aspect of his nature has been the key to dealing with some of the rougher hands life has dealt him.

Mick would go on to become a prolific motorcycle book writer, and it's thanks to him and Roy Bacon that would-be purchasers of classic bikes of all types had someone to turn to when needing information and background on their next potential purchase, both being 'friendly uncles in print' in effect.

Mick has been a constant in the motorcycle world. And he has served his following well. He is almost altruistic in this sense. Outwardly his enthusiasm never seems to have wavered. We all owe him a debt of gratitude for this contribution.

I cannot believe that 40 years have passed since I first met Mick. I have yet to see him minus a smile and a friendly greeting. I admire him for all the things he has done, and the way he has coped with life's setbacks, and I look forward to our next meeting.

Brian Crichton, Editor *British Dealer News*
ex-Editor *Classic Bike* and *The Classic Motor Cycle*

In my AJS 7R book, I recalled one incident as, 'How would you like a 7R for £180?' That's what Dumfries man Colin Dunbar paid back in 1973. While on a visit to nearby Koni importers JWE Banks of Crowland, Lincolnshire, Colin decided to book into a hotel in Wisbech and visited my dealership. Actually, it was bang on closing time, but I stayed behind to show Colin the 7R, which essentially was a complete rolling chassis of 1953 vintage, together with a 1954 Burman gearbox and partly stripped, but complete, engine assembly of the same age. Colin carried out a full restoration over the following years to create an immaculate 7R that is now worth £25,000-plus. Before heading back north Colin spent a pleasurable evening with me in the hotel bar. This meant that I was late home, and Susan was asleep. The next morning she was still asleep – so I tiptoed out of the bedroom and went to work. Later that morning John Blunt received a phone call from a worried Susan, asking if he had seen me as she thought I had not been home the night before. For many years thereafter, Susan didn't believe that I had actually made it home that night. But finally one day in July 1985, at Donington Park I bumped into Colin – and the rebuilt 7R – and finally Susan believed my story!

With John Blunt outside the first Norwich Road premises in 1973.

At the Wisbech dealership I looked after many local racers, helping them with advice and parts for their home-brewed specials. One such special was built by Wisbech farmer and neighbour Frank Ball, who had acquired an ex-factory Greeves experimental single-cylinder engine. The twin-port 498cc engine (91 x 76mm) was of unit construction, with a geared primary drive, and fitted into a special frame equipped with Ducati front forks and rear wheel, together with a Spondon front brake and Krober electronic ignition, all of which was supplied by my dealership. Unfortunately Frank was killed in a flying accident and the special was eventually sold off in 2010.

Another local competitor was Bantam Bob, who raced with the Formula Bantam Club. Bob was never that quick, but he told many stories of his exploits on the racetrack. His great claim to fame was a near-death experience when he was almost run over by Emerson Fittipaldi's Formula One car in the Bomb Hole at the Snetterton circuit. This was during the days of mixed practice at the Norfolk venue, with Emerson lapping three times quicker than the Bantam, and Bob just got in the way. The escapade in this case resulted in a near miss, but thankfully it put an end to the dangerous practice of running cars and bikes on the same track

I first came into contact with Ducati concessionaires Coburn & Hughes in September 1973, the week after my riders Dave Arnold and Paddy Reid had competed in the Thruxton endurance race for series production machines. Riding a Ducati 250 Mach 1, they had led the 250 class only to be let down by a flat battery towards the end of the event. On the Monday morning Ray Elliott from C&H phoned to say how pleased he'd been at seeing a Ducati leading its class. As this was just after C&H had been appointed as the Ducati factory importers, replacing Vic Camp, this was a nice surprise. But then Ray went on to say that as C&H did not have expertise or finance to handle the spares operation, could Mick Walker Motorcycles look after this side of the new business? It was soon agreed that I would.

Mike Coburn and Clew Hughes had begun during the late 1960s with a showroom in Haringey, north London, which they still had in 1973, and there was also a third member of the team, Ray Elliott. The company had expanded rapidly, helped by selling large numbers of mainly British bikes to foreigners (Americans) who were visiting Europe. Essentially Mike Coburn was the moneyman, Clew Hughes the salesman and Ray Elliott the worker. Ray lived in Luton, where C&H had opened a second showroom, and he was the frontman for the new Ducati operation that was to be run from there.

As can be seen in my chapters on Ducati and Moto Guzzi, the mid and late 1970s was a period of healthy co-operation between C&H and Mick Walker Motorcycles, with a degree of friendship and respect. We experienced an exciting explosion of sales, both of machines and component parts and it was often great fun. My first requirement as the UK official Ducati spares importer was to assemble an order of parts for the new models that C&H would be buying in – 250/350/450 Mark 3s (in blue and gold), 750GT and 750 Sport V-twins. This also provided the chance to replenish my dwindling stocks of parts for the older singles. As the November launch day approached, the phone lines between Wisbech and Luton began to hum, a situation that was to continue for several years.

C&H owned their own aircraft, a twin-engined four-seater Beechcraft Baron, based at Luton Airport. It was frequently used for travel to Italy and I travelled in it on several occasions with Clew Hughes and Ray Elliott, but from memory only once with Mike Coburn. However, my first trip to Italy in my new role with C&H was by road. In February 1974, Ray, journalist John Nutting and I travelled in the Luton branch C&H truck. I went mainly to resolve outstanding parts issues, John to test the latest machinery (which included a prototype of the forthcoming 860GT), and Ray with fresh orders for motorcycles. This was the very first time that I actually saw the yellow Desmo singles, and as soon as I saw them in the metal, I was convinced that this was 'the' Ducati and asked why C&H were not interested in these machines. Ray said that there would be no market for them in Great Britain – but there was at least one buyer, because together with the spares I had gone to collect I also loaded up a 350 Desmo (disc brake) for me.

My subsequent enthusiasm convinced Ray that he should be importing the Desmos and that they would sell. Coburn & Hughes remained unconvinced, but when the bikes arrived in the showrooms, they simply couldn't get enough to satisfy the hunger of the bike-buying public. In the summer of 1974, the UK retail prices for the Desmo singles were £599 for the 250 and £669 for the 450. Apart from my own 350, only six others were officially brought in. The blue-and-gold Mark 3 valve-spring versions were considerably cheaper, at £519 for the 250 and £549 for the 350, and it was, no doubt, this price differential that convinced C&H that the sportier versions would not sell.

Happily there is always a market for something special. Looking back at all the Ducati singles I have owned and ridden through the years, that 350 was the nicest of all, with perhaps the exception of my first Ducati racer, the 175 Formula 3. It was one of the rare breed of motorcycles capable of feeding a message back to the rider all the time it was being ridden, and making man and machine one. The only things that I would have preferred on my Desmo were the forks and front brake of the drum brake version – in my opinion the 35mm Ceriani forks of the disc version just did not suit the bike as well as the Marzocchis. In all other respects I could honestly not fault the bike. It did what it was built to do, pure enjoyable sporting riding, although customers who purchased one as a ride-to-work plodder might have been disappointed, except for the frugal fuel economy!

As it is, the yellow Desmo signifies to me and countless other enthusiasts all around the world, just what Ducatis are all about: style, speed and stamina. Those yellow masterpieces had these virtues in abundance, and even when I first saw one standing in the factory yard it looked hungry for the open road.

Ducati 350 Desmo, which Coburn & Hughes were initially reluctant to import.

1976, outside the second Norwich Road premises

Motor Cycle News

Motor Cycle News was founded in 1955 by Cyril Quantrill, a former *Motor Cycling* journalist. In 1956 he sold the title to East Midlands Allied Press (EMAP) of Peterborough remaining as editor and in EMAP's ownership it quickly prospered, virtually killing off two of the biggest names in British motoring journalism, *Motor Cycling* and *Motor Cycle*. They eventually combined to form a rival newspaper, but *Motor Cycle Weekly* came a poor second to *MCN* and, after reverting to magazine format, died in 1983.

From the mid 1970s, *MCN* became more interested in its advertising revenue than providing serious reading. Its original journalists were knowledgeable, enthusiastic motorcyclists, such as Roger Maughfling, Mick Woollett, Ralph Venables, Charlie Rous and Peter Howdle, but most had moved on, to be replaced by a new breed of less well-informed writers. In 1972, *MCN* ran a full-page story of my emergence as 'Ducati guru', which caused a lot of hassle. The reporter would not allow me to see what he had written, and when it appeared in print, my business rival Vic Camp was none too pleased. Neither was I; *MCN* had twisted what I had said and added things that I definitely had not said. Eventually, relations between Vic and I returned to normal, but the episode left me feeling disappointed that a journalist could write a story and not have it checked.

I had a more serious run-in with *MCN* in the late 1970s, when I was importer for the lightweight (Italian) Harley-Davidsons. The paper ran a test of our SX250 headlined, 'Trailing Behind the Rest'. The report was so awful, I decided to inspect the motorcycle myself, finding it had been 'down the road' on both sides and the test mileage was exactly the one-way distance between Wisbech and *MCN*'s offices. The mechanic who took the bike back into our premises told me that it was returned on a trailer. Not happy, I phoned *MCN* to speak to the tester, only to be told that he was no longer there. Friends at the paper revealed that he had been fired when it was found that he did not even have a driving licence!

Much later, in 1995, *MCN* held its annual event with stars from the various disciplines of motorcycle sport. As Mick Walker Racing's rider Dean Johnson had just won the British Superteen Championship, we were invited to loan *MCN* the bike. However, as the Cagiva Mito Evo SP belonged to the importers Three Cross, I was not prepared to do this until *MCN* provided a certified letter agreeing to pay for any damage caused to the bike. When road racer Chris Walker (no relation) fell off the machine during the session, causing some £4,000 worth of damage, I thanked goodness for my caution – until I asked *MCN* to honour the agreement. After several fruitless months, I demanded the telephone number of the insurance company, whose rep was amused by my request. He explained that *MCN*'s insurance excess was around £20,000, basically meaning that its staff could legally take to the road, rather than that his company would cover any damage. I immediately wrote to *MCN*, and a cheque was received almost by return of post.

A Harley-Davidson SX250 caused a falling out with *MCN*.

Unfortunately, production of all the singles, and for that matter the round-case 750 V-twin models, was soon to come to an end. But before the 750 V-twins were axed, there was an embarrassing event for the C&H team. In 1974 the three C&H directors and I had flown to Italy for a high-level meeting arranged by the Ducati bosses. I was somewhat taken aback at the meeting when the C&H men produced one of their adverts, picturing a scantily dressed young lady draped over a 750 Sport. The unfortunate thing was that somehow the headline,'La Dolce Vita' (the sweet life) was misspelled and read 'La Dolce Vite' (the sweet screw). I knew immediately what was wrong, but Clew, Ray and Mike certainly didn't. There were a lot of red faces that day.

This was to be followed by another trip and another clanger – but this time not of C&H's making. As usual, we were to fly from Luton in the Beechcraft. Besides Clew (the pilot) Ray and me, was a journalist, who ought to remain nameless. This individual was not only late, but he had forgotten his passport, Clew's answer to the problem was, 'Well, son, you will just have to blag your way through at the other end.' We took off but about halfway there, the journalist said that he needed to go to the toilet. This was a four-seater with no such facilities and Clew's reply was short and to the point, 'Well son, you are going to have to do it in your crash helmet.' And that is exactly what the poor guy had to do, arriving in Italy with no passport and a very wet helmet. We left him to explain the situation to the Italian immigration officials and some time later he was allowed to rejoin us.

Long before the arrival of the World Wide Web, promotion and advertising was vital if one wished to establish a national or international business. My initial advertising campaign, if one could call it that, was via *Motor Cycle News*. *MCN* did not get top marks from me for its journalistic activities. However, in my dealings with the newspaper's advertising staff, things were much more positive. During the late 1960s and throughout the 1970s several good people not only helped my business to grow, but became good friends at the same time. The first was Steve Hackett, followed by Mick Hemmings and finally Colin Hill.

Sadly, I have lost contact with Steve, but Mick Hemmings went on to found his own motorcycle dealership in Northampton, whilst Colin ran a motorcycle accessory firm in Kettering, where the *MCN* editorial offices were based in the 1970s, and in 2005 republished the Greeves history that I had penned with Rob Carrick. Mick Hemmings recalls what happened, 'I first met Mick Walker while I was working at *MCN* in the period 1970-76. I left *MCN* in 1976 and set up my first shop in Northampton. I had a nice workshop, stores and also a very large but empty showroom! I mentioned this to Mick, and he declared straight away – come and get some bikes! So off to Wisbech I went in my old Transit van and came back with it full of Derbi mopeds! About a week later Mick rang and asked if I would like to borrow a Guzzi Le Mans. You bet! Off I went to Wisbech again. I have always been grateful to Mick for helping me to start up, and over the years we have remained very good friends.'

Mick Hemmings, former *MCN* staffer, in his own motorcycle shop, far left.

Besides the various Italian marques for which I was a British representative, there was also the Spanish Derbi company, with which I had a close and successful relationship during the mid-1970s. The name Derbi is an acronym of DERivados de BIcicletas (derivatives of bicycles). In 1922, Simeón Rabasa Singla had opened a small workshop for the repair and hire of pedal cycles. The location was in the village of Mollet, 12 miles from Barcelona, and from these humble beginnings emerged what has since become Spain's strongest and most successful motorcycle manufacturer.

It was during early 1975 that my first contact with Derbi was established, when the newly set up London-based Derbi Concessionaires, in the shape of Norman Bronstein and Max Findon approached me to handle the spares side of the business. Later I would become the East Anglian distributor for the machines themselves (which were all 50cc at this time). My first visit to Spain and the Derbi works came that summer, accompanied by Norman and Max. Then in November the same year came another more interesting visit, when I was introduced to Derbi race supremo Francisco Tombas, the man behind the factory's world championship success both before and since. Knowing by now of my interest in racing and the fact that I had only recently retired from active competition in the sport, Tombas and Derbi had organised something special for me. They closed off all the roads near the factory (just how they managed that I never discovered) then Tombas produced riding equipment and one of the new 125cc twin cylinder racers, offering me a ride. How could I refuse? Well, the end result was that I was speed-trapped at 133 mph! Where else could an event of this nature have taken place I asked myself? Certainly not in Great Britain!

Derbi's tuning wizard Francisco Tombas had joined the company in 1953, having previously designed and raced several home-built 100cc prototypes and in the process not only proved just about unbeatable in his class around the twists and turns of Montjuïc Park, Barcelona, but established his worth as a skilled designer and tuner. In my opinion, Francisco was the Spanish equivalent of Germany's Walter Kaaden; a truly brilliant engineer and two-stroke engine genius. Tombas was largely responsible for the myriad of championship titles that Derbi amassed over the years, and the 13-time World Champion Angel Nieto gained the majority of his titles aboard Derbi machinery prepared by Tombas.

Following my test session I came very close to establishing a British Derbi race team. The most likely rider would have been 125 specialist Clive Horton, with whom I had talks, amongst other leading British lightweight jockeys. Sadly the idea never got off the ground. This was mainly due to changes in the British laws regarding novice riders – which effectively killed off the highly popular 'Sixteener' moped class and with it 50cc sales. Unfortunately, this virtually wiped out Derbi's UK presence almost overnight.

During early 1976 I had purchased a 50cc Angel Nieto replica racer brand new from the Spanish factory via Derbi Concessionaires. This was one of 50 manufactured, and although a truly superb looking bike, it proved to be a major disappointment. Unlike the works racers of the era, the replica was air-cooled and not a patch on Nieto's actual machine. Although mainly used by my company as a showpiece, it was ridden once at Snetterton by Mick Grant for a proposed racer test by *MCN*. The test never appeared, for, quite simply, the bike's performance was not in the class that the 'Angel Nieto' tag suggested. Eventually, the bike was sold off during the late 1970s, still unraced.

Following the test session of the new 125cc Derbi twin racer in 1975, on closed roads near the factory. Also in the picture are Derbi management plus (centre) Norman Bronstein and (right) Max Findon from the British Derbi Concessionaires.

The Angel Nieto replica, unfortunately not a patch on the real thing

However, even with this blip, my overall memories of Derbi and its factory are superb. I found them friendly, helpful and very different from the majority of the other manufacturers I dealt with over the years. It was at that time a real family concern, and the Rabasa family were excellent people.

I visited the Barcelona works yet again later in April 1976, this time with several of the by-now established dealer network. The trip was over several days and not only was our British party given access to the manufacturing processes of the Derbi factory, but also Andreu Rabasa (the founder's son), said during his welcome speech, 'We do not want your visit to Spain to be work only, but it should also be an occasion to become acquainted with a small part of our country. Therefore we have prepared some trips to show you the most typical places, which we hope you will like.' He was good as his word. The next few days turned out to be a visit that members of the party still remember to this day. As Jim Lee (of Jim Lee Motorcycles) said recently, 'It was the trip of a lifetime.' At a celebration dinner everyone was presented with a medal commemorating the 50th anniversary of the Derbi foundation, in 1922, inscribed with their company's details. I still have mine, together with its presentation box.

During 1975, Moto Guzzi (see Chapter 6), was added to our model portfolio, with the same set-up of C&H looking after the bikes and Mick Walker Motorcycles looking after the spares. Compared to the Ducati Bologna works, the Moto Guzzi factory was totally different. The Guzzi headquarters was in a large village – rural rather than urban – and the works was much, much older than the relatively modern Ducati plant. The workforce was entirely different too, with Guzzi staff in the main having been there for many, many years. The Ducati export manager, Franco Valentini, and the Guzzi incumbent, Joe Ermilini, were as different as chalk and cheese. In fact Signor Ermilini could well have been mistaken for an Italian count. On one of the C&H trips I met the American importers of both Ducati and Guzzi, the Berliner brothers, Joe and Mike, who in truth seemed more Al Capone than straightforward businessmen, contrasting sharply with the dignified quiet approach of Joe Ermilini.

A little-known fact is that on one of our visits during spring 1976 C&H held secret talks with MV Agusta, at the company's Gallarate factory, after the original British importers Gus Kuhn quit in 1975. But these discussions ultimately came to nothing, and later that year another company, essentially a Saab car dealership in Slough, Buckinghamshire, took over, trading under the title Agusta Concessionaires (GB) Ltd. Peter Bate, boss of Agusta Concessionaires did succeed in appointing several dealers, including me. But when the 750 America became available in December 1976, it cost a whopping £3,187, the most expensive production street-going motorcycle on the UK market at that time. This figure did not include the optional cast-alloy wheels with triple 280mm discs or the factory-made fibre-glass full fairing. These made the MV look like a replica Agostini racer, but when fired up there was a shock in store. It sounded mechanically noisy, more like a gravel-crusher in fact! And the stock matt-black silencers were ugly in the extreme, so most customers opted for the much prettier chrome system, also at additional cost.

In the 17 July 1976 edition of *Motor Cycle* I was described as 'the man behind the Ducati and Moto Guzzi spares organisation.' The headline to a two-page article was 'Mick Walker – 100% Enthusiast.'

As *Motor Cycle* said: 'By all the rules it should be impossible to divide the concession for spares and machines in two, run them by two separate companies miles apart and expect success. To split the concession like this, between two companies is absolutely unique in the motorcycle trade – but it does work if you have real enthusiasts operating it. Mick Walker Motorcycles employs twenty staff, and while it operates under one company, internally it is broken down into three. The spares side is the most complex and has some £1/2 million-worth of parts in stock at the moment. Up to 300 orders a week are processed and sent out to countries all over the world, even Japan."

The first hint of problems on the Coburn & Hughes front came in 1977 when, out of the blue, and with no prior consultation, they appointed four additional spares distributors. This was a real kick in the teeth for me. The newcomers were Sports Motorcycles, Apple Motorcycles, John Blanchard and the London Motorcycle Centre. At a stroke all the goodwill and trust had vanished. Probably, C&H thought they could repeat the success they had with Mick Walker Motorcycles, but in truth, none of these companies had the enthusiasm or commitment to the parts business and certainly nowhere near the expertise gained over the years of trading to make the grade.

So, eventually, besides undermining my enthusiasm, C&H lost much more. The others and I quit the scene, to be replaced by Coburn & Hughes themselves. At great cost, millions in fact, C&H purchased a massive warehouse at Wolverton, Milton Keynes and made the fatal mistake of appointing an ex-Volvo Cars storeman to run the new operation. His lack of knowledge cost C&H a fortune, as he simply ordered 50 of everything. This meant that after a relatively short time they ran out of quick turnover items such as oil filters, gaskets and the like, but still had 50 swinging arms and 50 rear wheels!

The problems with C&H resulted in me talking to other marques. At the end of 1977, we signed an agreement with AMF Harley-Davidson to become the UK importers for its range of Italian-made motorcycles (as related in full in Chapter 7). Later still, in 1979 we added the Testi range of 50cc motorcycles and mopeds to our range of imports. The Testi, with a Minarelli engine, was displayed for the first time alongside the Harleys, which from September 1978 had been marketed under the Cagiva brand name.

The ultimate 50cc machine, 1980 Testi Champion, cast alloy wheels, front disc brake, monoshock rear suspension, one-piece bodywork and six speed Minarelli engine.

Most of the 649cc Ural flat twins sold by Mick Walker Motorcycles in 1974/75 came with sidecar attached, unlike this solo example.

Although a large slice of our business was now trade, rather than retail, the private customer was still important. During the course of the 1970s, at various times, Mick Walker Motorcycles retailed several marques besides Ducati, Moto Guzzi, Harley-Davidson (Cagiva) and Testi. These were: Garelli 1972-1980, Benelli 1973-1980, Russian models (Ural, Voskhod and Jupiter) 1974-1975, Jawa/CZ 1975-1978, MV Agusta 1976-1978 and Suzuki 1976-1981.

Suzuki was the only Japanese marque for which I was to hold a franchise throughout my business career. The Suzuki link was down to my friendship with Barry Sheene, then a works rider for the Japanese factory.

Each of these makes brings back memories. The Garelli ones are mentioned earlier in this chapter, while my association with Benelli predated by a few months my involvement with Coburn & Hughes. In fact, I attended the launch of the Benelli range by importers Agrati Sales in Nottingham in September 1973. I must admit that the main model I was interested in was the Tornado, a 650 vertical twin four-stroke. However, Agrati never brought examples over for sale to its dealer network.

The remainder of the range comprised the 750 Sei, 500 Quattro, 250 2C, 125 2C and the 125 Enduro. It was the two 125s and the 250 that sold in quantity, but after a few months I dropped them, because they were no match for the Japanese opposition. Yes, performance, handling and braking were good, but they were let down by weak 6 volt electrics and petroil mixture. However, the real killer was the poor finish (except for the highly polished aluminium castings). We continued with the four-stroke Benellis but very few were sold. This was probably due to the popularity of the Ducati and Moto Guzzi bikes, and latterly the MV, and so the Benelli had to take something of a back seat – at least in our Wisbech showrooms.

The Suzuki link was down to my friendship with Barry Sheene, then a works rider for the Japanese factory

The Jawa/CZ importers – Motokov (the Czech Vehicle Export Agency) – was just up the road at Kings Lynn, so perhaps it was natural that we would stock these models. The CZ range comprised a 175 road, 175 trail, 250 twin and 175/250 enduro models. To me, the 175s were akin to the recently defunct BSA Bantam – cheap and cheerful, reliable runabouts. The 250 twin somehow didn't fit in too well, its only real assets being low price and reasonable reliability. The enduro machines were altogether different, virtually factory motocross models with lighting equipment. The sole Jawa model was the 634 350cc twin, almost a bigger engined, de luxe version of the CZ 250 twin.

Even compared to the Jawa/CZs the Russian bikes could only be described as agricultural. By far the best of the bunch was the Ural flat twin, based on the pre-war BMW, and the majority of these were sold with a sidecar attached. As for the two-strokes, the 350 Jupiter was endowed with the worst brakes I've ever found on any motorcycle – so bad that I am sure that a standard brand new bike would have failed its MOT. All the ones we sold had the brakes relined with better-quality Ferodo material. That leaves the 175 Voskhod, one of which nearly severed my fingers when I attempted to lift the machine by its rear carrier. The underside of this was badly finished and as sharp as a razor blade, so I ended up with severely lacerated digits! But on the plus side, of the 50 or so examples we sold, we never had a single warranty claim. Some of this, I think, was down to doing a proper PDI (Pre Delivery Inspection).

We sold quantities of almost every Suzuki model, which during our time ranged from the AP50 sports moped to the GS1000 superbike. We also sponsored a local rider on an X7 250 twin in production racing during the late 1970s. Probably the only Suzuki of the era that we never sold was the RE5 Rotary – even though one of my mechanics attended a workshop course on the machine at the Heron Suzuki importers headquarters in Surrey. Besides the AP50, the best sellers were the GT380 triple and the TS185 trail bike. My time with Suzuki bridged the gap between a two-stroke-only range and the arrival of the new four-stroke models, which included the SP370, GS400 twin, GS750 and GS1000. And I suppose even without the Barry Sheene connection I had something of a soft spot for Suzuki ever since I had owed a T10 250 twin back in Aden

My involvement with Coburn & Hughes and other activities had seen Mick Walker Motorcycles expand to such a degree that it was now amongst the leading names in the British motorcycle world of the 1970s. So once again the problem of space, or lack of it, began to rear its ugly head. Firstly, the workshop was moved over the road, directly opposite the Norwich Road showrooms. For a while, this tactic freed up space, but not for long. As I owned a plot of land at the rear of the showroom, I asked for planning permission to extend the building. This was flatly refused by the authorities. The next shock came when the very same officials decreed that I could no longer use the building we now occupied across the road as the workshops. The time was ripe to find a new home for my expanding enterprise and its workforce, which had also grown.

Eventually, a site was located further down Norwich Road, a massive site, with the buildings alone measuring a huge 220,000 square feet – if anything, too big. However at least it would allow for further expansion, if needed. And so in February 1976 we officially opened the new enterprise. But behind the scenes there had been problems. The first was that, unlike 72/74 Norwich Road, I no longer owned the site; instead I was paying rent to BP. Secondly, moving the well-over-a-million different part numbers that now comprised our spares stock and relocating them was a major task – something I would never want to do again.

We sponsored a local rider on an X7, which Suzuki promoted as the first 100mph production 250.

Dave Croxford and Terry Betts opening the new 'superstore' in Norwich Road

The official opening ceremony of what was to be referred to by the press and public alike as a superstore was performed by celebrities from the world of motorcycling, including road racer Dave Croxford and speedway ace Terry Betts. By the end of the 1970s, the company – now under the umbrella of the Mick Walker Group, of which the 'Motorcycles' applied to the retail side – the company had grown to post a yearly turnover in excess of £3 million. Employing over 50 staff and having taken on the duties of UK importer for Cagiva and Testi, I had come to feel that the whole operation was a millstone around my neck, rather than a source of pride and pleasure in my working life.

The whole enterprise had always taken up much of my time, but without realising it, that time was now being spent on administration and negotiating with officials such as bankers, government officials and high-powered businessmen, none of which I much cared for. Also the expansion had brought in many newcomers, some of whom didn't have the same drive, enthusiasm or expertise of me and my core team. Expansion showed up weaknesses in the management structure and there were disagreements and tensions.

There were diversions. Early 1981 saw a request from a film company for the supply of seven Cagiva SX250 trail bikes for a forthcoming production entitled *Riding High*. The film wasn't a major box office production, but did feature Irene Handl, Bill Mitchell, Murray Salem and Marella Oppenheim. In one scene Eddie Kidd jumps over the Blackwater River in Maldon, Essex. The only other scene in which a bike appears is when Eddie performs a doughnut on a table during a banquet sequence and the end of filming all seven bikes were in a very poor condition after being wrecked by the film crew. Another Eddie Kidd adventure that same summer was when his contract with Yamaha ran out. Remembering the Cagiva he rode in the film sequences, he acquired another example to complete his busy summertime display schedule that year, this time a MXR250 moto-cross model. One display was put on during the August Bank Holiday Monday of 1981 in the central recreational area of Kings Lynn, known as the Walks, and was transformed into a huge media event to entertain the population of this Norfolk town. The highlight of the display was when Eddie jumped his bike over the 17 surviving heart transplant patients, who had been assembled by the Papworth Heart Hospital. It can only be assumed that this was a test to ascertain that the new hearts were still in good working condition! Of course today this just wouldn't happen; too risky, too much chance of litigation!

The late 1970s had seen the introduction of the first British consumer laws, and also the beginning of the litigation culture. This brought about the need to have a legal buffer on hand to advise Mick Walker Motorcycles. My solicitor was John Aitken, who became a good friend. Sadly, many of the cases he dealt with were what are best described as 'try-ons'. Some people viewed consumer laws as an opportunity to claim some easy money, or, if they couldn't afford the repayments of a motorcycle on hire purchase, a possible legal way to provide some way of wriggling out of their responsibilities.

All too soon, the 1980s brought the final straw, the economic recession that was to cripple good and bad dealers alike. As explained elsewhere, the import side suffered from the fact that my competitors began to offer more and more extended credit (Mitsui the Yamaha importers increased this to an amazing 18 months in 1981), while my Italian suppliers wouldn't budge from 60 days credit. Meanwhile, the big four Japanese companies allowed a discount war to break out, which might have helped their sales graphs back in Japan, but virtually bankrupted the smaller British dealer network overnight. And so over the winter of 1981/82, one of the coldest and bleakest on record, the Mick Walker Group was dismantled. By the spring of 1982, nothing remained except the original Ducati spares operation, which traded as Rick and Mick Walker for almost the next quarter of a century. The main reason this division survived was the huge number of letters I received from Ducati owners all around the world pleading for me to continue.

After the Mick Walker Group ceased to trade, my need for a solicitor ceased too. But a couple of years later I needed advice regarding my home. Afterwards I asked John Aitken for an invoice, and he replied, 'You owe me nothing, as you have more than enough paid your dues when the business was in operation.' John has never since wanted any payment for his services, and Susan and I now refer to him as the 'No-fee Solicitor.'

Strangely, after closing down my own business I received numerous enquiries from hard-pressed dealers asking me to sort their problems out for them. I was usually successful in this role, although as the task was highly confidential, I cannot reveal any names. But one story, which concerned a 5-star Honda dealer, is noteworthy. His problem was excessive, slow-moving parts stock. Going there once a week, I soon discovered the problem, or at least how it had come about. Over a period of many years, this dealer had employed a storeman who owned several different Honda models. What this employee had done over time was to order one of every part for his respective motorcycles. As I explained to the dealer he might just as well have given the storeman a series of signed blank cheques; it would have probably worked out cheaper in the end.

On my final visit to this dealer at the end of my contract, I arrived on my Ducati 350 Mark 3, and one of the staff invited me back to his home for a spot of lunch. It turned out that he was a Ducati enthusiast and before leaving the house to return to the dealership, he took me down to the bottom of his garden where he had garaged his collection of motorcycles. There he set about showing me various pieces of literature concerning Ducati. He picked up one of the leaflets I'd had printed a few years earlier. He turned a page and was confronted with a mug shot of me. He turned to me, awestruck, 'It's you' he gasped. Now my cover had been blown, but luckily this was my last day on that particular job.

In retrospect if the Mick Walker Group had not ceased to exist at the beginning of 1982, nothing of what followed would have happened – no work with *Motorcycle Enthusiast*, no books and no involvement with young British racing talent, and I would probably have died from the stress of the business. As things turned out, it was all for the best. I was on the verge of an entirely new life and career.

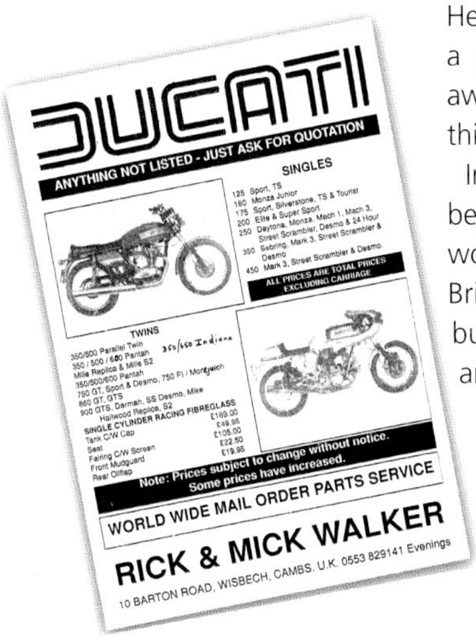

Mick Walker Motorcycles' staff before the recession of the 1980s.

Angela Sims Chris English MW Richard Alan Roper Linda Sims
John Rollison John Blunt Paul Parry Dave Tavener Grahame Smith

5 Mr Ducati

I could never have imagined that my passion would take over my life

My first loves were all Italian. After my two Lambretta scooters, I seriously considered two smaller motorcycles, the Parilla 175 Sport and the Rumi 125 Junior Gentleman, before I finally decided on the freshly launched 250cc Ducati Daytona (Diana in other markets). In early 1961, all three machines cost around the £250 mark. By way of comparison, an Ariel (Golden) Arrow Super Sports was £187 11s 5d, a BSA C15 Super Sports £180 0s 8d and the Matchless G2CS was £215. The three British bikes were all considerably cheaper, but to me, a teenager at the time, they just didn't have the style or performance of the Italian irons.

Before I saw the Ducati, my original choice had been the Parilla, but at the beginning of May 1961 the British Ducati Concessionaires (essentially the Manchester branch of Kings of Oxford, headed by Mike Hailwood's father, Stan) introduced three new models, led by the Daytona. As *Motor Cycle* of the day reported, 'Ducati's first two-fifty roadster, the Daytona has a substantially oversquare engine (74 x 57mm) claimed to produce 20bhp at 7,500rpm. A compartment beneath the twin-seat houses the battery, tools and air filter (actually there were two elongated side panels); fitted with snap (lever-operated) filler, the bulbous fuel tank is surprisingly narrow at the back. Tyre sizes are 3.00 x 18in rear and 2.75 x 18in front. Finish is blue and silver (both metallic).'

After deciding on the costly Ducati, how was I going to get one? At the time, I was in the Royal Air Force, working alongside a civilian, Gavin Trippe, who was, at the time, much more experienced in the two-wheeled world than me. (Gavin would go on to perform several motocross tests for *Motor Cycle News*, before crossing the Atlantic to launch a stateside version of *MCN* with Bruce Cox.) Besides scrambling a 500cc BSA Gold Star, he was a close friend of Andy Lee and Ken Covell, who ran a dealership in Ely, Cambridgeshire. Not only could they obtain one of the new Ducatis, they would also take my Lambretta TV175 scooter in part exchange.

The Ducati duly arrived and I travelled the 30 miles or so from Marham to Ely to collect the machine – only the second one to be imported I was told. My only previous motorcycle riding experience aboard my friend Peter Greenard's ancient BSA C11G machine had done little to prepare me for the race-bred Ducati. My ride home was a revelation. For its day, the Daytona was just about the fastest and best handling road-going two-fifty money could buy. I was smitten. Even so, I could never have dreamed that this little machine would lead to a passion for the marque that was to last for decades.

Armed with the two-fifty Ducati I discovered a whole new world; one of excitement, speed, new friends, new places and probably the greatest of all, the glamorous road racing scene. Although as a factory, Ducati had quit the Grand Prix scene by 1961, there was still a major Ducati presence by many leading riders, notably in the 125cc class. So at Silverstone, Mallory Park, Cadwell Park and my local track at Snetterton, I revelled in the aura of many a

My first Ducati, the 1961 Daytona after I had fitted a Butler fairing.

Summer 1972, on a Ducati special built from bits

Ducati victory that year. The riders campaigning Ducatis on British short circuits included Arthur Wheeler, Tommy Robb, Ivor Walton, Brian Clark, Mick Manley and Terry Grotefeld, but in the larger capacity classes there was also a host of legendary names, including Mike Hailwood, Bob McIntyre and Derek Minter.

Personally I tended to look out for the last two, Bob Mac because of his never-give-up attitude and Derek Minter because of his fantastic ability to recover from his trademark poor start. This was in the era of bump-starting, not the clutch starts of today's scene. The following is how *Motor Cycle News* journalist Charlie Rous described Minter's situation to readers, 'Derek Minter's trouble just lately has been starting. Not once this season has the Mint been first away at the drop of the flag; more generally he's been way down the field and has had to carve his way through to head the field.' Sadly, Bob was to lose his life at Oulton Park in August 1962, but later on I raced against both Derek and Mike. Later still, I became friends with both, something that seemed a million miles away when merely an enthusiastic spectator.

Looking back now, owning one of the very first Ducati 250s in the country made me many new friends. One of the very first was Rodney Turner whom I met shortly after purchasing the Daytona. My grandparents' house in Wretton was not far from Stoke Ferry, which had a hump-back bridge very similar to Ballaugh Bridge on the Isle of Man. This became something of a challenge, as it would to any spirited rider of that period. Late one evening I flew over the Stoke Ferry bridge on the Ducati, leaving the tarmac by a considerable distance. On the return run (at a slower speed) someone flagged me down. He was impressed with the motorcycle and my lurid riding style. This was to be the beginning of a friendship with Rodney that has survived to the present day.

There is no doubt that my Ducati was instrumental in teaching me many things and, in truth, I served my motorcycling apprenticeship aboard that bike. I owned the machine for 15 months from spring 1961 until late summer 1962, during which I honed my riding skills, learned basic mechanics, and much more. I had my first breakdown on it, and when a much more experienced motorcyclist stopped to help me rectify an electrical problem, I discovered the brotherhood of motorcyclists. Other recollections include several dices on the public highway with much larger and more powerful bikes, including one with a group of lads when I was returning from a race meeting at Cadwell Park. I (wrongly) thought that the leader was on a Royal Enfield 250 Crusader Sports, when actually he was riding a 700cc Constellation. Even more bizarrely, I once attempted to keep up with a Manx Norton, which years later I discovered had been owned by Hugh Brown from Wisbech, who often rode to Cadwell Park on his machine which, except for its number plates, bulb horn and very basic silencer, was straight off the race track. Of course it was no contest between the 250 Ducati with its novice rider and the 500 Manx with its highly experienced pilot.

The BSA A7 500cc twin was a good pillion carrier through the winter, but after six months its ponderous handling signalled that it was time to move it on.

The matching pair of Hannah Ducati Mark 3s. XML 962G was mine and 963 was Rick's.

Finally in late August 1962 I decided to trade in the little Ducati for a BSA 500. By this time my brother Rick was a frequent passenger, and carrying a pillion instantly restricted the Ducati's sporting personality, whereas with a bigger touring bike, it wouldn't really make much difference. Also winter was coming and I needed a bike that would be better suited to survive the cold, wet and sometimes icy conditions. It should be remembered that for many people in those days a motorcycle was a main form of everyday transport, not the rich man's fair-weather toy that many are today. So the Ducati had to go, replaced by a 1958 BSA 500cc A7 twin, HJE 2. By the time I finally parted with the Ducati (I can't remember its registration number) it was fitted with a Butler Mouldings dolphin fairing, but otherwise was stock.

Quite frankly the British bike was the exact opposite to the Italian one. For starters it was very heavy (420lb against 250) and totally different in character. The Ducati was virtually a racer, whereas the BSA was a comfortable tourer, but the bigger twin proved to be an important stepping-stone in my motorcycling education. Where the little Ducati responded instantly to my wishes when cornering, the BSA had to be set up before the bend. If you attempted to ride the A7 like a Ducati you would soon be in trouble. After the winter, the A7 in turn was traded-in during February 1963 for a Triumph Tiger 100 SS of 1962 vintage. Finished in Kingfisher metallic blue and with the registration number 4 FAT, I covered my experiences with this machine in some detail in Chapter 2.

My next Ducati came along in 1964, the new 200 Elite that was purchased during my time serving with the RAF Middle East Command in the Aden Protectorate. It was then that I first made contact with the Italian factory, and became closely linked with the Aden's Ducati importer.

After I had raced several Ducatis in the mid-60s, my brother Rick and I purchased a pair of Hannah (ex-Berliner) Ducati 250 Mark 3s new from Elite Motors of Tooting in the late spring of 1969. These were XML 962G (mine) and XML963G (Rick's). Besides being used as daily transport, the Mark 3 was pressed into use when I resumed my racing career in 1970. Strangely, while I never had any form of mechanical trouble with my Mark 3, Rick's machine suffered a big-end failure – even though it had never been raced.

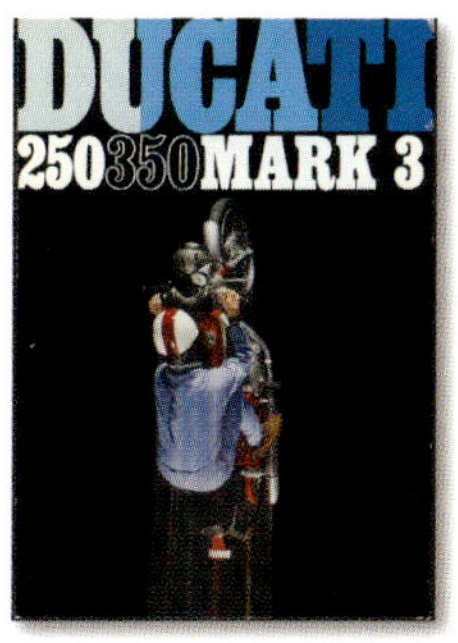

Ingegnere Fabio Taglioni with a cylinder head from a 125 Desmo single-cylinder GP racer, circa 1958.

I could never have imagined that my passion for Ducati motorcycles would take over my life in the way that it did when a combination of no job satisfaction and a demand for my services from enthusiastic owners led me to establish Mick Walker Motorcycles – the smallest of small businesses – in late 1969, but that is exactly what happened. As I said at the start of this book, there is a touch of magic in the Ducati marque – and that is largely the creation of one man, Fabio Taglioni.

For almost four decades Taglioni was the inspirational force behind the extraordinary success of the Ducati marque, both on the street and the race circuit. His vision as an engineer, and his talent for exploiting radical ideas, produced a series of innovative motorcycles that established Ducati as the most charismatic of Italian sporting machines. As described in my book *Ducati Taglioni And His World-Beating Motorcycles*, 'The impact Taglioni had during his years at Ducati cannot be overstated, When he joined them, Ducati was a manufacturer mass-produced small capacity pushrod-engined commuter bikes that were no different from countless others. When he left, the marque had a worldwide following and a reputation as makers of sporting and racing motorcycles with their own unique identity and mystique.

I first met the great man when I paid a visit to the Bologna works with my road-going Ducati 250 Mark 3 as I was just about to start my own motorcycle business specialising in Ducati spare parts. Luckily, I already had contacts at the Italian factory from the work I had done in Aden during my spare time while serving in the Royal Air Force. Upon my arrival, I was amazed to be taken straight to Taglioni's office. He greeted me warmly and I was instantly impressed by his unbridled enthusiasm. What other chief designer would have pulled out blueprints of a V4 engine (which he had conceived as a student of Bologna University back in 1947) to show to a foreigner who he had never met before? From that day onward, I was fortunate enough to rank Fabio as a friend – and I dedicated my 70th book to the great man, who had celebrated his 80th birthday weeks before the Taglioni book was published.

Taglioni's precocious gift as a designer was apparent in that 1947 V4 engine (which had a displacement of just 250cc). After university, Taglioni cut his design teeth at factory level with Ceccato, followed by FB Mondial, and joined Ducati Meccanica on 1 April 1954 as their design chief. The rapid success of the early models he created at Ducati was to established him as one of the great innovators of his day. His machines scored victories in the great long distance Italian road races, which included the Giro d'Italia and the Milano-Taranto events. But the début victory of the Ducati Desmo single (ridden by Gianni Degli Antoni) in the 1956 Swedish Grand Prix, firmly placed Ducati as one of the leading factories at the very top level of international motorcycle racing. The death of Antoni a few weeks later whilst testing at Monza set back Taglioni's GP racing programme, but the momentum soon returned, culminating in the arrival of the British teenager Mike Hailwood. Mike was to score his very first Grand Prix victory (the 1959 125cc Ulster), on a Ducati machine.

During the 1960s and 1970s, Taglioni created a succession of overhead-camshaft engined street bikes that took advantage of the technical knowledge derived from racing at the highest level. These included the Mach 1 (launched in 1964), the first 100mph 250cc street bike (whatever claims might later be made), and the ground-breaking desmodromic roadsters, in particular the 3D (Desmo) single of 1968. Then, in 1970, came the most charismatic Ducati, the 90-degree V-twin. The arrival of the twin brought a series of dramatic successes for the Taglioni Ducatis, including the now legendary Imola victory, in April 1972, over world champions Giacomo Agostini and MV Agusta, together with Mike Hailwood's famous 1978 Isle of Man TT return.

Fabio Taglioni

Despite being a gifted engineer, Fabio Taglioni was also a cultured man with several interests. He was a great family man, an accomplished artist who enjoyed painting the ancient architecture of the Middle East, and a keen gardener. The great designer was fascinated by how plants grow from tiny seedlings – the 'miracle of nature' as he once described it. When Taglioni was under pressure at work, his escape was his garden and its tropical greenhouse, where his special forté was orchids. In fact, he became a world authority on this exotic cultivated species. His plants were a major source of enjoyment and relaxation. Away from the bustle and noise at Ducati's Bologna works, Fabio Taglioni relished opportunities to retreat to this world of peace and wonderment, far removed from the challenges of a busy factory.

Fabio Taglioni with development engineer Franco Farné on 30 May 1989, the great designer's last day at the Bologna plant.

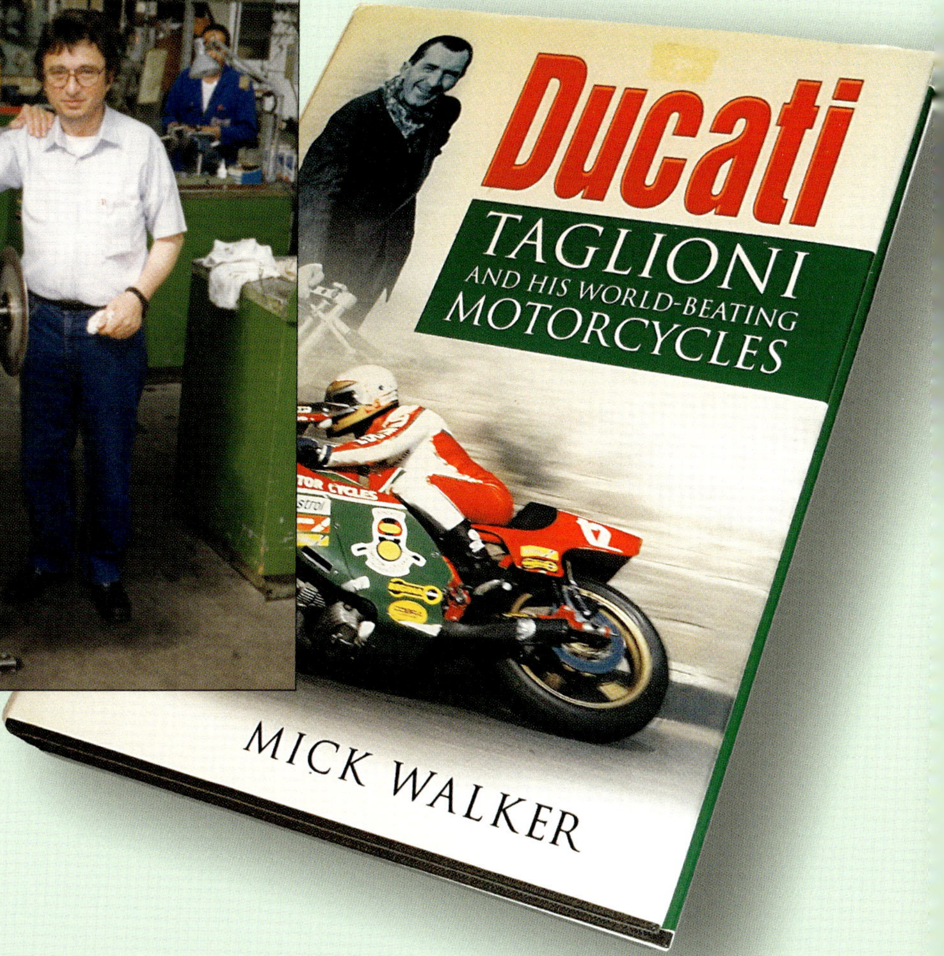

Ing. Taglioni and Franco Farné – the two men behind Ducati's success on both road and track.

The 1980s was a difficult period for the world's motorcycle industry. However, Taglioni and Ducati still managed to innovate. They produced a new series of V-twins with belt-drive valve gear (the first being the Pantah) and won no less than four world championship titles in Formula 2, with Englishman Tony Rutter as rider. Fabio Taglioni's final design, the 750F1, was launched a few weeks before Cagiva took over Ducati on 1 May 1985. During his final years at the factory in the late 1980s, Taglioni became more of a consultant than design chief, this role having been taken over by his protégé, Massimo Bordi.

During his years at the Bologna factory, Fabio Taglioni designed over 1,000 different engines, either in outline or detail. The machines he created ranged from humble mopeds and scooters right through to massive V-twins and V4 superbikes. He was also the first motorcycle engineer to perfect the desmodromic system of positive valve operation for both racing and series production use. Quite simply, in my opinion Fabio Taglioni was one of the greatest motorcycle designers of the 20th century.

To quote from my introduction to *Ducati Taglioni and His World-Beating Motorcycles*: 'This has given me probably the greatest satisfaction since my first book, *Ducati Singles*, even though almost 70 other publications have come between the two. More than anyone else, Fabio Taglioni has shaped my own motorcycling life since I purchased my first Ducati back in 1961. This book would not have been possible without the many years I spent with his designs and machines, each one of which has a certain something that gives it its own character – one would call it motorcycling DNA.'

Not that all Ducatis were true inheritors of the bloodline. Back in the spring of 1972, Derbyshire enthusiast Pete Harrison purchased a new-to-Britain 24 Horas (24 Hours) Ducati 250 from Vic Camp, the UK importer. What followed demonstrated what a dissatisfied customer felt he had to do before consumer laws and the onset of litigation culture. Very soon afterwards, an advertisement appeared in *Motor Cycle News* classifieds: 'Ducati "24 Horrors" for sale'. The ad explained that this virtually brand-new yet undesirable motorcycle was being auctioned for scrap outside Camp's showrooms in Walthamstow, London the following Saturday morning.

This event was to go down in Ducati folklore, to haunt the 24 Horas ever since. The model was made under licence by the Spanish Mototrans factory, and its '24 Hours' name tag commemorated Ducati's success at the local Barcelona race. Although the machine went unsold on the day of the auction, the advertisement brought the public's attention to the fact that the material specification used on the cams and rockers of the Spanish-made engine was vastly inferior to that found on the traditional Italian Ducatis. Vic Camp's lack of sympathy for his customers had triggered the *MCN* advert and its aftermath. Instead of resolving the problem, which after all was a warranty matter (or should have been on a machine only a few weeks old), the importer's failure to deal with it caused the whole incident to become nationally known.

Ducati's Borgo Panigale, Bologna factory

1972 24 Horas from the main batch imported, featuring a racing seat and twin-leading-shoe front brake.

The truth was that the hardening on the cam and rockers was very poor and their durability suffered. My own experience of stripping a brand new 24 Horas down for spares showed that the material employed was way below the standard on the Italian models. However, there was a simple cure; fit Italian components, consisting of Italian locknut rockers together with an early 175/200 camshaft. Another weakness was the habit of the Spanish-made Motoplat alternator rotor to shake its taper-flange rivets loose.

However, in defence of the model I would say that the balance of the engine was generally robust and reliable in service. Many of the cycle parts of the machine were superior to some of the earlier Italian Ducatis, particularly the front forks and brakes. My last competitive race, a production event at Snetterton in late spring 1972, was on a 24 Horas. From that experience I found the Spanish bike to be superior to the highly rated Mach 1 in both roadholding and braking. As for maximum speed, it was only down by 5mph on the Mach 1 – and for everyday convenience, the kickstart and footrest layout was far superior to the Italian machine.

During a season's racing in 1972, besides my own solitary outing, the same 24 Horas was used by my sponsored rider, Mick Taylor of York, who competed at the Isle of Man Production TT and the Production race at the Silverstone British Grand Prix. Except for fitting an Italian cam and rockers before we began, the machine was completely standard and in all that time and hard use I cannot recall any problems whatsoever, not even with the dreaded rotor. The Walker-prepared 24 Horas was also tested at Silverstone that year by *Motorcycle Sport* journalist Marcus (Marc) Ramsay Wigan (MRW), who not only raced a Mach 1 at this time, but also later purchased a 750SS Desmo V-twin which was raced under the Mick Walker banner during the 1974 season.

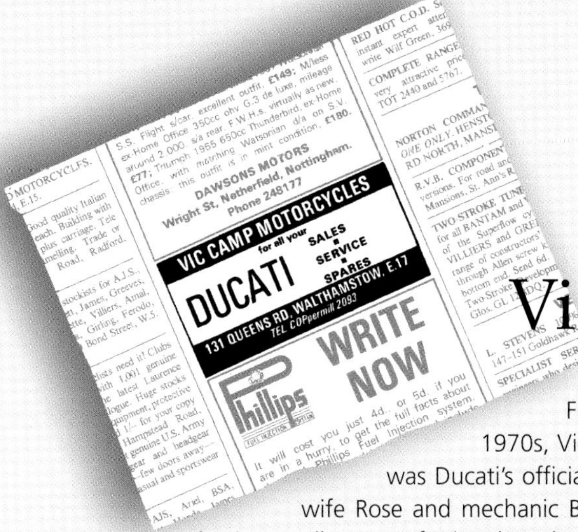

Vic Camp Motorcycles

From the mid 1960s to the early 1970s, Vic Camp Motorcycles of Walthamstow was Ducati's official British importer. Vic, along with his wife Rose and mechanic Bert Furness, would became not only business colleagues of mine, but also friends.

During the late 1950s, Vic was a Francis Barnett dealer and specialist in 'trials and scrambles' models, and later become a main agent for BSA, Ariel and Norton. The first mention of Ducati came in the 4 April 1961 issue of *Motor Cycle News*, in which the Italian marque was added to the weekly advertisement. At this time, the official importer was Ducati Concessionaires (Kings) of Stretford, Manchester, and Ted Broad, another dealer/entrant, promoted the Ducati name in the London area. Ted claimed to be 'Southern England's Ducati Centre', but it was Vic who took a stand at the Earls Court Show in November 1964, just in time to show off the new Mach 1.

Vic had quickly realised the newcomer's potential not only for clubman's racing, but also for making money. He stripped off all the road equipment and fitted a Smiths rev-counter kit, alloy rims and a full set of his own glass-fibre products, including a dolphin fairing. The bikes used by Vic's own riders were specially tuned, unlike the over-the-counter customers models, as I found to my cost after purchasing a new Camp Mach 1 racer in 1966. Vic was an all-round motorcycle sport enthusiast and during the early 1970s, he built a number of grass track machines in conjunction with grass specialist Alf Hagon, using Ducati single-cylinder engines. I was also involved in this, not only selling a few examples but also sponsoring Brian Havelock (father of future speedway World Champion Gary).

Vic was never keen on the Ducati V-twin so only imported a couple of the new 750GTs. It was this that ultimately opened the door for a joint venture between me (as spares specialist) and Coburn & Hughes (selling the machines) to take over the import rights for the Italian factory. In September 1973, this brought Vic's time as Ducati's official UK agent to an end. By then Vic's relationship with Ducati had become somewhat strained. This began in 1968 when Bill Hannah picked up the unwanted American-market Ducatis and brought them in as parallel imports. Vic was so annoyed that he later refused to supply spares for these machines, thus opening the door to my own spares operation. Although, ultimately, we became business competitors, Vic and I remained friends, which illustrates the difference between the motorcycle business then and now. Of course, we didn't always agree, but at least it was friendly rivalry.

Vic continued to sell Ducatis under the Coburn & Hughes/Mick Walker operation, and also became a Suzuki dealer until he and Rose decided to retire in late 1977. They closed the Walthamstow business and moved to Malta. Sadly, ten days later, Vic suffered a fatal massive heart attack. Rose returned to the UK, where she married the managing director of motorcycle insurance specialist, Devitt DA. Bert Furness transferred to Alf Hagon's Leytonstone dealership, where he continued building the Suzuki 250 single-cylinder racers that he and Vic had begun in Walthamstow premises. While writing my first book, *Ducati Singles* in the early 1980s, I tracked down Bert, who was able to give me details of the 160 Ducati trials bike he had constructed during the late 1960s.

Vic Camp and Bert Furness (left).

1970 prototype of the round-case 750 twin as tested at Modena for Daytona by Spaggiari and Farné.

I had my own very small part to play in the 750SS story. As with the now well-known 'narrow-case' and 'wide-case' terms to indicate the difference between the two basic layouts of the ohc singles, I was also responsible for the description of 'round-case' and 'square-case' to differentiate the two generations of Ducati's bevel-drive V-twins. To many enthusiasts, the 750SS and 900SS V-twins were *the* definitive factory-built café racers of the 1970s. They were as near to being pukka racing motorcycles as any street-legal machine could be, and as I said in my 1985 book *Ducati Twins*, they performed 'on the world's race tracks with great credit, in addition to providing their owners with a sporting roadster par excellence.' The first of the breed, the 'round-case' 750SS, was directly spawned by racing. Indeed, without the legendary Imola race victory of 1972, it is extremely unlikely that either the 750 or 900 would have ever seen the light of day in SS (Super Sports) form. In fact, the original 750SS was simply referred to as the 'Imola Replica' when it débuted in pre-production guise during March 1973.

Paul Smart's historic win at Imola created a state of euphoria at the Bologna factory, with the result that their other racing projects were quickly axed. Amongst these was the 500cc V-twin that had been ridden in the GPs by the likes of Phil Read and Bruno Spaggiari, and even later, after the Imola success, by Paul Smart himself. Another project underway at this time was a liquid-cooled three-cylinder 350 with seven speeds and fuel injection. This engine, I understand, never reached the stage of being fitted into a frame.

The cancellation of both these racing projects was announced in the winter of 1972, at the same time as General Manager Fredmano Spairani was given the boot. Ducati's Competitions Department was left with considerable spare capacity, so they decided to fill the gap by taking advantage of the Imola victory and built a small batch (25) of 'replicas'. These bikes were road-legal production-racing versions of the Imola machine, and at the outset, the project was intended to be a one-off exercise. But as soon as the machines appeared, the demand proved to be far in excess of even the factory's most optimistic expectations, which dictated the need for further batches to be produced.

In my opinion the 750SS (in round-case form) was the most beautiful of all the factory's bevel-drive V-twins. In the engine department, the 750SS was identical in bore and stroke (80 x 74.4mm) and displacement to that of the 750GT and Sport. However, there were several differences. Firstly, there were Desmo cylinder heads (as the valve-spring type were still used for the lesser models). Then the compression ratio was increased to 9.65:1, and the standard 22mm gudgeon pins and small-end bushes were replaced by 20mm components. Other differences included forged slipper pistons, connecting rods with double webbing at the bottom for added strength, together with huge 40mm Dell'Orto pumper carburettors in place of the 30mm (GT) and 32mm (Sport) instruments. The offside crankcases even featured a flat to enable the piping for an oil cooler to be mounted.

In SS guise, the engine would rev to 8,800 and drove through the stock five-speed gearbox. For riders who wanted even greater performance than that offered by the 'standard' SS, there was a race kit on offer to transform the machine into a full Formula 750 racer. This kit included a set of racing camshafts and a special exhaust system consisting of new high-level header pipes and open megaphones. An oil cooler and attachment kit was also supplied, as were racing sparkplugs, Bosch condensers and a Renold racing final drive chain. There was also a selection of replacement main jets, and eight alternative rear wheel sprockets (34 to 42 teeth). Finally, the purchaser received a full racing fairing, which included the screen and mounting kit.

The colour scheme of the 750SS was identical to the works racers – metallic duck-egg green frame and swinging arm, with silver fibreglass ware. Fibreglass was used extensively for components such as the fuel tank (which featured a clear panel like those found on the Imola racer, enabling the fuel level to be determined at a glance), the mudguards, side panels and seat base.

A 1971 750GT; this is the very first production example manufactured.

JAN 75
DUCATI
750

Rick's 750GT and Mick's 350 Desmo, Spring 1974

A 1974 750SS at Brands in July 1997.

The first batch of 25 models of the 750SS differed in several details from later versions. Unique to them were the front mudguard (retained by hose clips, rather than studs and nuts), leading-axle (instead of central-axle) front forks, Lockheed brake equipment (for the triple disc set-up), a different half fairing and black outer engine covers.

As a race sponsor, Ducati dealer, and UK parts importer, I took delivery of the very first 750SS to be used in anger in this country, in April 1974. The specification was much changed (as noted above) from the small batch constructed in 1973 – none of which had been exported officially. On delivery, no instructions whatsoever came with the motorcycle – not even a data sheet. What we didn't know at the time was that the standard low-level exhaust system was entirely unsuitable for serious track use. My brother Rick departed to our local circuit at Snetterton for the brand-new 750SS's initial testing. Later that day, he returned with a rather second-hand motorcycle. The exhaust had grounded, throwing rider Mick James off and leaving the bike sliding along the track surface. At that time, Rick and I both owned 750GTs and had never suffered any grounding problems. However, our bikes were used on the public roads, and both had 19in front wheels. The SS sported an 18in wheel, which effectively reduced the ground clearance. The factory never gave us any sort of guidance on this problem, other than a 'here it is, get on with it' attitude.

Motorcycle Sport journalist Marc Ramsey Wigan on the 750SS raced under the Mick Walker banner in 1974.

The prototype and production version of the 1973/74 750 Sport.

The outcome of this rather expensive lesson was an extensive, and expensive, repair session in the MWM workshop, which included fitting our own set of high-level pipes. But Mick James more than made up for the early disaster by winning the inaugural 500-kilometre race at Cadwell Park in July that year. Amazingly, his co-rider Johnny Hascott had never raced before. Mick James rode the 750SS exclusively during the time it remained in my stable, with the exception of the 500 kilometre event and an occasional outing by myself on the public highway. He secured several victories at club and national level before the machine was sold to motorcycle-racing journalist Marcus Ramsay Wigan. Its only mechanical glitch had been due to the left-hand conrod shim wearing, allowing the rod to rub on the side of the crank flywheels. Before it was sold, a completely new crank assembly was fitted.

In those days, the technicalities of the Ducati V-twin were virtually unknown in the UK as imports only began with the GT and Sport at the end of 1973. No information at all came with the first batch of 24 750SS machines – no handbook or list of technical data, not even a specifications sheet and certainly no workshop manual. For the owners it was a case of learning by experience – hands-on lessons, which once learnt were shared with other enthusiasts.

Rick's 1974 750 GT after he painted it green.

Mick James winning the 500km race at Cadwell Park, July 1974 on the Mick Walker 750SS

Gulf
WALKER M/CS

The 750 GT and 750 Sport

It was during this period that I first met Steve Wynne, a fellow dealer based in Manchester, while we were racing our SS at a Cadwell Park club event in June 1974. He was competing that summer on a similar bike for the first time. Steve was later to win fame through his involvement with Mike Hailwood's great TT return of 1978 – Ducati-mounted of course.

As a production racer, the 750SS was to prove competitive throughout the 1974 season, its only serious challengers being the Triumph Trident and the Norton Commando. On short circuits the Commandos were the ones to watch out for – the pukka 'yellow peril' Norvil production racer being extremely quick and light. Formula 750 events were another story, with the Trident and its BSA sister, the Rocket 3, being the most difficult to beat. But a well-ridden SS was capable of taking on all comers under any conditions.

In the year from October 1973 to October 1974, the retail showroom business of Mick Walker Motorcycles, as opposed to the spares distribution arm, enjoyed record sales of Ducati machines. However, all this was about to change drastically when the Bologna factory decided to axe its entire existing range at a stroke. This meant that there were to be no more of the now-popular 750cc round-case V-twins (in SS, Sport or GT form) or, for that matter, the long-running single-cylinder machines.

The 750SS was eventually to be followed by a new 864cc model, the 900SS. As a result, I was able to buy back my original 750 in 1975 when Marc Wigan decided to trade it in for the new, larger model, which was later shipped out to his new home in Australia. I kept the 750SS for a short time before selling it to Pete Fisher, who went on to become Secretary of the British Ducati Owners Club. Pete still had the machine when I wrote *Ducati Twins* ten years later.

The immediate replacements for Ducati's existing range were a 125cc two-stroke enduro bike, a couple of parallel twins (with chain-driven overhead-cam engines) and finally the new square-styled 860GT. Ducati design chief Fabio Taglioni had taken the logical step of seeking more power from the existing 750 V-twin engine and produced a larger version, with a displacement of 863.9cc (achieved by increasing the bore of the 750 from 80 to 86mm, with the stroke remaining unchanged). The 860's debut came at the Barcelona 24 Hour endurance race in July 1973. Taglioni was on hand to witness Ducati's Spanish arm, Barcelona-based Mototrans, run the new prototype, which was ridden by Benjamin Grau and Salvador Canellas. The result could not have been better, for it scored a record-breaking victory in this prestigious event.

The ugly, angular Giugiaro-designed bodywork of the 860GT, as displayed on the prototype at the Milan Show, November 1973.

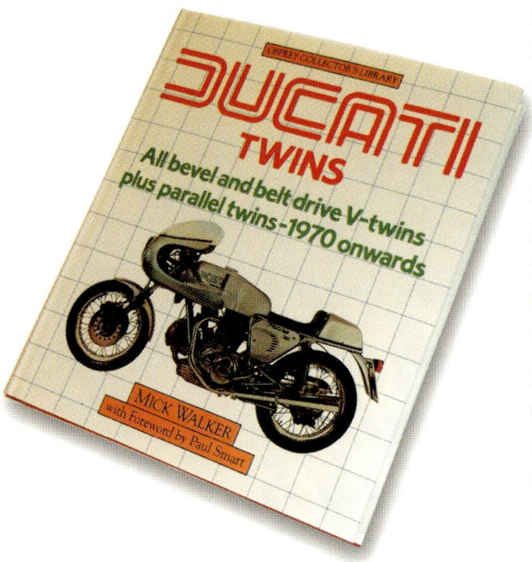

As far as the racing prototype was concerned, 'new' was not entirely accurate. Except for the increased bore, it was a combination of parts from the 750SS and Imola works racer – the dry clutch coming from the latter, for example. The Barcelona 24 Hours winner even retained the contact-breaker points and condensers of the 750 series; eventually this stone-age system was ditched for a more modern electronic ignition on the production models.

In November, four months after the Barcelona triumph, a pre-production road-going prototype made its début at the biennial International Milan Show, in the shape of the 860GT. Sadly, this was in stark contrast to the exciting 24 Hours endurance race winner. Instead of the expected sleek racer, there was a bike that I described in *Ducati Twins* as, 'an ugly touring mount with angular, apparently futuristic styling'. The production version that followed some 12 months later had lost the headlamp fairing and the Borrani aluminium wheel rims, had re-angled louvres in the side panels and featured a different colour scheme, but otherwise it was essentially the same bike.

The new '860's' initial development was sound; unfortunately its progression to market was not. At considerable cost, the Ducati factory had commissioned a design job from the well-known car stylist Giorgetto Giugiaro of Milan-based Italdesign (who had, amongst other projects, penned the original VW Golf). Wrapping up their new, bigger V-twin in contemporary bodywork would, the senior management reasoned, add to its mass-market appeal. Unfortunately, the result was to prove exactly the opposite, and is a stark reminder that motorcycles should be designed by motorcyclists. The result of Giugiaro's work was a mish-mash of sharp lines that did not echo the machine's function and were the antithesis of the compact, racing lightweight style so beloved by Ducati's traditional customers. The reason why customers eagerly purchased the final batches of singles and 750s was because they were raw, sporting machines with not an ounce of surplus fat on them. This created the style that gave them their appeal – it was not something that could be tacked on afterwards. As events were to prove, if Ducati thought that by ignoring their traditional customers they could attract a mass of new buyers, they were sadly mistaken.

I well remember my own first impressions of the 860GT, and the immediate gloomy feeling which it left in me that the factory had made a serious error of judgement. During a visit to the Bologna works in February 1974, in the company of Ray Elliott of Coburn & Hughes and journalist John Nutting, I was the first Englishman to try the 860 – still a pre-production prototype at this stage. Although John raved on about the newcomer's improvements over the 750 (such as its switchgear) I just could not come to terms with its styling – or lack of it – compared to the smooth, sporty lines of the then-current 750GT, Sport and SS. To me the 860GT was just damn bitty and downright ugly.

This feeling was reinforced at my company's annual show, which we used to stage at the Wisbech showrooms every November. The day before the 1974 show, Coburn & Hughes took delivery of the first production 860GT in the UK. At the time, we were selling large numbers of singles and 750s, but many potential customers travelled from all over the country to view the new machine. From their reactions when it was unveiled, I could tell that they didn't approve either, and this was something which was quickly reflected in our sales – or lack of them – over the next twelve months. We sold just six new Ducatis, against a previous high of almost 200.

The tragedy of the 860GT was that while the styling was abysmal, it featured a number of improvements in the engine department. Outwardly, the latest engine was instantly distinguishable by the outer casings, which had adopted some of the model's angularity in contrast to the smoother curves of the smaller models. Inside, however, there was much that the 750 owner would approve of. Besides the larger bore size, a 9.3:1 compression ratio and 32mm Dell'Orto carburettors and the electronic ignition system (with Ducati Elletronica transducers), there were other real improvements, one of which was a car-type disposable oil filter cartridge (this being mounted in the space left by the removal of the 750's points and condensers. The cartridge supplemented the long-running nylon gauze filter/drain plug used on all previous bevel-driven ohc designs from Ducati since the late 1950s.

Another significant redesign was an improved method of supporting the bottom bevel gears. On the 750 series, a lot of stress had been placed on the gears themselves, with the consequence that shimming and bearing wear became a critical factor, and if either was not absolutely perfect, this would inevitably result in the bottom bevel gears becoming excessively noisy. This problem was rectified in the 860 engine by mounting the bottom bevel gears on a support plate which itself contained a trio of bearings. A second major difference between the 750 and the 860 series concerned the gearchange where, on the latter, the foot pedal had been transferred from the right to the left. This was clearly due to Japanese and American influences.

The first batch of 860GTs were kickstarter-only, although later an electric starter variant was offered. The kickstart lever was still the curved 750GT component – guaranteed to bruise a shin if one attempted kicking whilst astride the motorcycle. To quote a Stateside tester's view, 'Without electric starting, it was a rogue of the first degree to bring into life. Every possible combination of setting the starting lever and throttle was tried, but it still depended more on luck – or the humour of the gods – to get any response.'

The 1973 860GT

Stamped control card and medal from the 1975 ACU National Rally, completed on an 860GT.

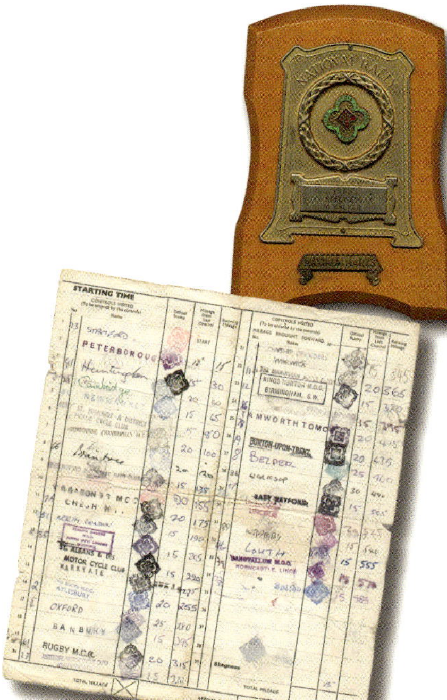

A couple of technical glitches were encountered on early 860GTs. The first was excessive valve guide wear. The 'official' cure was to remove the valves, fit new guides, polish the valve stems, grind in the valve and rebuild. This worked every time. Although the factory never admitted it, my own theory is that they had produced a batch of faulty guides. The second problem was a tendency for the clutch to judder and snatch when taking up the drive from cold. This was traced to the thrust washer in between the two support bearings in the clutch housing. Later the two (identical) bearings underwent a design modification, with the rear bearing being increased in size from 25 x 47 x 12mm to a larger 25 x 52 x 15mm type (from engine number 852177).

As far as the running gear was concerned, the major difference between the 750 series and the 860GT centred around the swinging arm. The 860GT featured an eccentric cam system, for the first time on a Ducati V-twin. Instead of the Seeley-conceived swinging arm of the 750, the 860 had a couple of aluminium eccentric blocks in the pivot area of the arm.

Even with the addition of an electric starter, getting going was still an issue, which from cold with the electric button was virtually impossible. Another major failing was the poor waterproofing of the electrics. Believe me, it's no joke at 2 o'clock in the morning having ridden since early morning the previous day (while taking part in the 1975 ACU National Rally), to stand in a downpour on the deserted A5 trunk road north of Birmingham with the tank off, trying to dry out the transducers in order to regain a spark. Amazingly, later that day I finished the event (in Skegness on the Lincolnshire coast) rounding things off by returning to Wisbech, after having spent over 30 hours in the saddle. Events of this nature are no longer allowed – partly due to the Health & Safety regime and also due to common sense.

The 860GT I used in the 1975 ACU National Rally completed the event, despite some serious problems with the electrics in heavy rain.

1976 860GTS

To round off the 860GT story, during late 1975 I compiled a detailed report concerning this machine's lack of sales, detailing the reasons for this situation, the weak points and the general decline in Ducati's UK sales over that year. This report was sent to the management at the Italian factory but I received no reply, not even an acknowledgment. Years later (in 1981, to be precise) I did receive a reply, which came from someone recently appointed to the management team, who told me that he agreed with every single point I had made. But six years on, this was of little use!

By the time I sent my report, Ducati had produced its replacement for the 750SS. Confusingly, while the touring GT model used the '860' moniker, the Super Sports (SS) version was called a 900 – although both were 863.9cc and shared the same square outer engine cases. The new 900SS arrived in the UK in mid-1975; there was also a new 750SS, but this was intended mainly for the Italian home market. The new bike was not simply a continuation of the existing model, as it, too, had the new-style square-case engine. Both the 1975 900SS and 750SS models retained the 40mm carburettors, gearbox and clutch from the old round-case 750, but benefited from the other technical changes already described and introduced on the 860GT.

The 1975 900/750SS models followed the previous year's round-case 750SS in having polished, webbed con-rods, with 20mm small-end bushes and a straight 36mm crankpin, each rod having its separate cage, with twin side-by-side hardened steel rollers. Having retained the earlier gearbox, unlike the GT model, the 1975 SS retained the right-hand gearchange lever. As for the colour scheme, gone was the distinctive Imola-derived duck-egg green, and in its place was an overall silver finish with blue decals. The only visual difference between the two square-case SS versions was the colour mix of the fairings; the 750s were silver with a 3-inch-high blue decal in the middle, while the 900 fairing was blue with a silver decal.

1975 GTL 350 at the factory track, with an SS under test

Although the frame was similar, the GTL's single front downtube had been replaced by twin tubes (braced at the mid point), running to the steering head. The rear of the frame was also modified, whilst the suspension was uprated and the wire wheels of the GTL were superseded by 12-spoke cast-alloy items. The most noticeable change was to the bike's appearance – Tartarini's restyling exercise dramatically altering what had been a mundane commuter/tourer into a sleek sportster. In fact the Tartarini styling was to be used when Ducati created the Darmah model, which was to become a best seller for the Bologna marque in the final years of the 1970s.

Despite the changes, Ducati's new sporting parallel twins were no more of a sales success than the GTLs had been, for much the same reasons. The larger version of the Sport Desmo was imported into the UK in 1977, but although only one batch of 50 was shipped (plus one previous special import) to the concessionaires, the majority of these machines took some time to move, with many still unsold two years later. These machines were both praised and vilified by the Ducatisti, so I felt that the only way to settle the argument was to find an as-new example and test it for as many miles as possible. As Assistant Editor of *Motorcycle Enthusiast* I was finally able to do this in July 1983. My friend Bernard Adey (the owner of Spares GB) and I travelled to Italy in his van to commence the test.

A 1981-registered 500 Sport Desmo in completely standard trim had been located in a small town near Bologna. Thanks to Bernard's kind offer of a lift (he was going to Italy on a 'spares expedition') I was able to collect the machine and begin the adventure of riding back to England, where I used the bike for several months thereafter. Upon my arrival at Dover, however, British customs impounded the machine, together with a Rolls-Royce car that was being brought into the UK for servicing. The customs official told me that the Italian-registered Ducati would not be released until the VAT had been paid. This, of course, was prior to the Eurocrats getting their act together and opening up the borders of the member states. As far as I'm concerned, the EU has expanded, not for reasons of brotherhood, peace and co-operation, but because an expanded EU means more VAT. With the 500 Sport Desmo impounded, I was left with no means of getting home – and I had to return to Dover several days later once *MCE* had paid the duty.

Although registered in 1981, the Desmo had originally been constructed in 1977, and was thus identical to the motorcycle imported into the UK officially by the Coburn & Hughes organisation. I have to say that in many ways the 500 Sport Desmo was unquestionably a real Ducati, with a character quite unlike a conventional parallel twin. The 180-degree engine was just the opposite to, say, a Triumph, for the Duke vibrated at low revs, but above 70mph everything levelled out and it became really smooth. I discovered that the worst area of vibes was between 55 and 65mph, but on the journey back from Italy to England I chose a steady cruising speed of 70 to 75 mph – an easy speed to maintain for lengthy periods on the continental motorway network. At this pace, fuel consumption averaged out at around 50mpg.

The handling was on a par with the best of the bevel-drive Ducati V-twins except at very low speeds, when it became excessively heavy and awkward. At first I thought this might have been due to tight steering-head bearings, but it proved precisely the same when they were readjusted on the slack side. Having consulted other riders this situation appeared to be quite normal, although, strangely enough, the touring GTL model did not show this trait. I had imagined that the riding position would be really uncomfortable for such a long journey, but was favourably surprised when, even with clip-ons and a hard seat, I managed the trip in under two days, on one day covering in excess of 600 miles. One of the factors that contributed to this high mileage was the beautifully light clutch, particularly in traffic, a real one-finger touch job and the lightest Ducati clutch action I had ever experienced up to that time. If only a similar action could have been obtained on the bevel-drive V-twins.

The journey also tested the 500 Sport Desmo under extremes of climate, a heat wave where it was almost too hot to ride, and a cloudburst with torrential rain to test the electrics. Perhaps the most surprising aspect was that the machine seemed completely unaffected by water. In fact the electrics were in stark contrast to my similar experiences with the 860GT. The one area where the water did have an adverse effect was on the really poor finish of the black-painted exhaust system, without doubt the worst feature of the machine.

Another area that could have been improved was the gearbox. Its action was good, but because of the engine's relatively narrow power-band, the conclusion I quickly formed was that it needed a six-speed box to utilise the power available. The five-speed one was just not able to cope, and surely the smaller 350-engined version would be at an even bigger disadvantage. Sadly, even today the 350/500 Sport Desmo models are largely shunned, which is a pity as they are a better bike than their reputation would have you believe.

MCM ROAD TEST

DUCATI'S LITTLE DICTATOR

Ducati Desmo Sport 500

by John Robinson

THE UNDENIABLE good looks of Ducati's 500 Sport have all the finely-styled contours you'd expect of a thoroughbred. It's sleek, slightly aloof, and nothing quite so vulgar as a cafe racer . . . and that's the first hint you get of the character locked up inside the closely-finned engine.

It most certainly isn't a cafe racer in the sense of a street bike dressed up to look like a refugee from some grand prix. In fact, the engine behaves more like a real racer tuned to a fine pitch and it doesn't miss a chance to let you know that it isn't an ordinary roadster.

When things go well, the desmo twin howls along perfectly with a crisp response which makes you want to ride along with one hand protectively clutching your driving licence. When it's good, it's very, very good . . . But push the 500 into doing something it doesn't want to do and the highly-strung engine will throw an instant tantrum.

It dictates its own terms. Play along with it and the Ducati co-operates; go against the grain and it behaves like it's ready for a new owner. The logo on the side panel should read "Ducati rules, OK?"

The uneven firing of the 180-degree twin makes it sound lumpy and rough at low speed, turning into a hard snarl as the motor picks up. Passing through a sharp spell of vibration the 500 gets into its power band at 7,000, packing in a hard wedge of horsepower before it peaks out at 8,500. The performance is there all right, but that is a narrow rev range even for a racer and explains why the Ducati demands a sympathetic rider. Keep it in this narrow band and the motor thrives, delivering exciting surges of performance which have made people addicted to big twins. Grab an arbitrary handful of throttle at lower speeds and it will just gasp and die. On the 500 Sport you don't just open the throttle when you want to go faster.

JULY 1978 73

Powerful Brembo brakes kept up their performance in the wet.

Soggy rear brake, firm suspension but excellent damping.

The neat lines of the 500 were marred by the rapidly-corroding exhausts.

MCM ROAD TEST

DUCATI SPORT 500

Like the motor, the chassis is set up for high speed. The bike feels slow at 70mph and like it has almost stopped at 30mph; everywhere you go the Ducati wants to go faster. Dual carriageways become more boring than ever. Anywhere else the buzzy motor, the tight handling and the nice exhaust note blend perfectly to make you want to keep on riding.

The 500 Sport could have any number of faults but they'd be pushed aside by the bike's overwhelming ability to get where it's at. It focuses your attention sharply on just why you're riding a bike and not travelling on the bus. You're out on your own, making your own choices and the Ducati makes you live it to the full. It lets you turn ordinary road riding into a craft, the level of which I've only experienced on competition bikes.

If all this makes the 500 a bit special, it also makes it specialised. When you make the effort to appreciate the bike, it rewards you; if you don't want to make the effort, it's the wrong bike for you.

The philosophy behind the bike is single-minded, its scope about as narrow as the engine's power band. Handling and roadholding are the bike's strongest features and the harder you go the better it gets.

Low-speed steering is pretty heavy, emphasised by the low bars which put a lot of weight on the rider's arms. This doesn't get balanced out until the bike is up around 60mph, cutting down on agility and comfort in heavy traffic.

We found the 500 had a long, rolling weave at very low speeds and felt edgy in slow turns, especially in the wet. Later, when the back wheel was removed for the dyno test, we discovered that although there was no play in the swing-arm, there was about 1.3mm end float between the arm and the frame. This may have let the wheel move enough to affect low-speed handling, while at higher speeds the greater wheel loading would keep it pushed across to one side. There wasn't any adjustment provided at the spindle, although it could presumably be shimmed.

But as the speed went up, the handling and the ride got better and better. Front and rear the suspension is a bit hard, giving a fairly rough ride at low speeds although the dampers made a good job of keeping the bike stable and on line. As the Ducati hit bumps, the first shock could be felt but instead of the pitching or skipping that usually follows, it felt like the dampers had just locked on to the forks, holding the Ducati firmly down.

Over 50mph the bumps and ripples started hitting the wheels hard enough to encourage the springs to play their part and the ride smoothed out. The 500 could be cranked through long fast turns, flicked through S-bends or laid down hard into sharp corners and it stayed as steady as a rock. The steering was heavy, but it responded instantly to the lightest pull on the bars, the heaviness only being a resistance to anything that wanted to get the bike weaving. The rider could make the Ducati change course, but nothing else would. In a straight line, at top speed, the Ducati wouldn't weave or wobble even when I tried pushing and pulling on the handlebars — it would go where and when I pushed and as soon as I stopped, it straightened up.

And every time it came out of a bend, the 500 felt like it could have gone through just a bit faster. It certainly demands tyres as good as the Red Arrows which were fitted — the only feel they transmit is one of grip, no twitching or slipping, no insecurity of any kind. The combination worked so well that I frequently found ways of making my journeys longer than necessary.

In the wet the only problems were on very slow corners, at junctions or in-town roundabouts — possibly caused by the strange endfloat in the swing-arm. At open road speeds and again at the track, where it rained, and it rained . . . the Ducati felt as stable as many other bikes do in the dry.

Braking was barely affected by rain — there was enough of a lag to be perceptible but neither front or rear brakes lost any appreciable power. The twin front discs had a heavy operation but there was ample power and my only criticism is that the span from twistgrip to lever was too large. The rear brake, in contrast, was soggy and insensitive but at least it wasn't prone to lock up the wheel or make the back end hop under heavy braking.

We didn't take any braking figures at the test strip, because of the bad conditions, but I don't think the Ducati would have given much better than average figures, from our usual 30mph. Like the rest of the bike, the brakes didn't come into their own until it was being used at speed — there was nothing startling about its performance in the 30mph bracket. Double this speed, or treble it, and the brakes were just what was needed; strong and reliable, with plenty of feedback to the rider.

No matter what the road conditions, the Ducati needed to be worked up and down through the gears, buzzing the motor for the odd burst of acceleration. Pushing it through to a higher gear usually made life more difficult — the twin didn't like plonking along and wouldn't respond to the throttle. In traffic it was easy to be caught out in the wrong gear, with a spluttering motor that was about to bog down. Just before it gets into its power band, between six and seven thousand, it runs through a patch of vibration but you don't really notice it, in the same way that you don't notice the hard seat or the riding position, which could get uncomfortable in slow traffic.

Obviously it's not a bike for trotting around the West End all day — once you're on the open road it all clicks into place, the wind takes the weight off your arms and you forget the minor discomforts.

The motor is something else. It demands sympathy and concentration. All the time. It comes down to the twin's inability to pull full throttle below 7000rpm. You can accept this as something which goes with the nature of the bike and trade the inflexibility for the power that kicks in at the top end. Or, you may think it's the result of cams and carbs that are a couple of sizes too big for the engine. It's two ways of spelling out the

74 MOTOR CYCLE MECHANICS

MCM ROAD TEST

DUCATI SPORT 500

same thing, depending on whether you are likely to become a Ducati owner, or not.

The motor fires up and idles quite reliably, helped by an air control lever on the handlebar (which is quite a relief in itself compared to the fiddly levers worn by some Dell'Orto carbs, plus the fact that all you see of the carbs is the fuel lines disappearing from the twin taps).

As you pull away, balancing the clutch against the high bottom gear, the motor still feels tractable enough. But once you're through second gear you need either the rev counter or a very sensitive seat to your pants. If you want the 500 Sport to go faster, you don't just open the throttle.

Cruising at 60mph, the natural thing to combat headwinds or hills or to overtake is to lean on the throttle. In top gear the 500 would usually slow down, give it still more throttle and the twin would run rough and start to misfire. Often, just holding a steady speed, I found I'd used more throttle than necessary and as I backed it off the bike would gently accelerate. The only way to get performance would be to drop down a gear or two and as soon as the motor got close to 7000, the throttle could be cracked open and the motor would fly up to its 8500 redline. It would rush up to a true 100mph with indecent haste and, then at the top the power disappeared as quickly as it had come in.

The motor was very sensitive to part-throttle at low speeds — a point which was exaggerated by the full-throttle dynamometer tests. There was a region around 3000 rpm where it would hold full throttle under protest, and then nothing but misfires until just below 7000 where it came in with a vicious pick-up. Between here and 8500, the motor shot up to 40 bhp — enough power to make 110mph a feasible proposition. At the track, we ran a fraction over 100mph, easily and quickly. But despite experiments with gearshift points and so on, the best we managed was 103mph. This is because the gearing is about as wrong as it could be for top speed — in top gear the motor is not far enough into its stride to pull the bike any faster, in fourth gear it's stretched out to beyond the power peak.

The motor really needs a six-speed box, with a ratio in between the present fourth and fifth. Just lowering the overall gearing would solve the top speed problem, but would spoil the bike's high-speed cruising.

On the existing gearing it will hold 70 to 90mph with a long-legged easiness and without the feeling that the engine is screaming its heart out.

This sensitivity to gearing and low speed reaction to throttle is typical of the Ducati's behaviour but there's no getting away from the fact that it is great fun to ride. The biggest drawback, for a bike which encourages you to ride it so much, is the tiny fuel tank. With two gallons between reserve and full, its useful range is about 80 miles. I dragged out a further 25 miles on reserve once, which got the 500 up to around 50 mpg. Normally it would run in the low 40s, and dropped to 34mpg at the track. The fuel consumption is not particularly impressive but it would be tolerable if the tank gave anything like a decent range.

In other aspects of its detail design, the Ducati is an improvement over other Italian models. The electrics seem improved and more reliable. There's a powerful headlamp, steady indicators and an electronic voltage regulator built in to the circuitry. The switches, particularly the tumbler type used on the dipswitch and indicators could be better.

The Italians still seem to have a lot to learn about basic preparation — especially for our climate. The importers, Coburn and Hughes, are trying to do something about the exhaust finish — the matt painted pipes were rusting after one week. The throttle cable also started sticking after our wet session at the track. Basically I think the bike just needs a thorough going-over before it is used, adjusting and routing cables, tailoring the riding position and controls, lubricating linkages, and so on. I found the fat handlebar grips didn't add to the comfort, and made the brake-span problem worse, and there would probably be a few other detail changes individual owners would want.

The only work we had to do on the bike — removing the rear wheel and adjusting the chain — was straightforward enough, although the engine looks as if it might be less accessible.

You could go through the machine and produce a list of faults and imperfections which wouldn't look good at all. On one of the bland Japanese models they would attract far more criticism than I've aimed at the Ducati. This is solely because the Ducati isn't bland and isn't aimed at a rider whose sole contribution is to wind open the twistgrip. It contrives to put character into both the motor cycle and into motor cycling which, in my view, is worth a lot.

Apart from saying that the 500 Sport is far from an everyday workhorse, I see little point in criticising the machine. You can be fully aware of its problems and still think it's a great bike.

JULY 1978 77

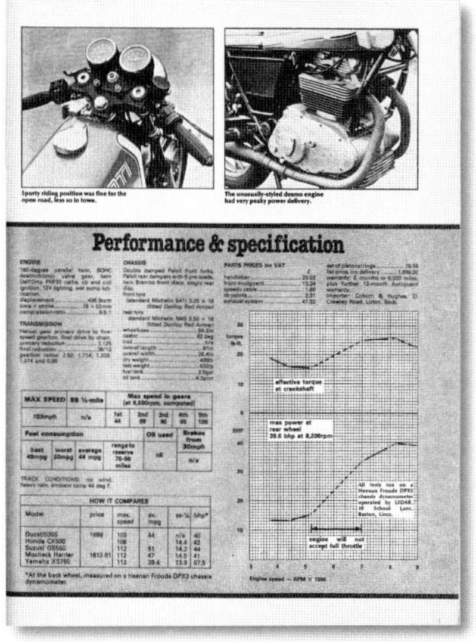

Sporty riding position was fine for the open road, less so in town.

The unusually-styled desmo engine had very peaky power delivery.

Performance & specification

ENGINE
180-degree parallel twin, SOHC desmodromic valve gear, twin Dell'Orto PHF30 carbs, cb and coil ignition, 12V lighting, wet sump lubrication.
displacement ... 496.9ccm
bore × stroke ... 78 × 52mm
compression ratio ... 9.6:1

TRANSMISSION
Helical gear primary drive to five-speed gearbox, final drive by chain.
primary reduction ... 2.125
final reduction ... 38/13
gearbox ratios: 2.50, 1.714, 1.333, 1.074 and 0.90

CHASSIS
Double damped Paioli front forks, Paioli rear dampers with 5 pre-loads, twin Brembo front discs, single rear disc.
front tyre
(standard Michelin S41) 3.25 × 18 (fitted Dunlop Red Arrow)
rear tyre
standard Michelin M45 3.50 × 18 (fitted Dunlop Red Arrow)
wheelbase ... 55.2in
castor ... 62 deg
trail ... n/a
overall length ... 81in
overall width ... 26.4in
dry weight ... 408lb
test weight ... 432lb
fuel tank ... 2.6gal
oil tank ... 4.3pint

PARTS PRICES inc VAT

	£
handlebar	20.02
front mudguard	13.24
speedo cable	1.80
cb points	2.31
exhaust system	47.02
set of pistons/rings	39.59
list price, inc delivery	1,699.00

warranty: 6 months or 6,000 miles, plus further 12-month Autoguard warranty.
importer: Coburn & Hughes, 21 Crawley Road, Luton, Beds.

MAX SPEED	SS ¼-mile	Max speed in gears (at 8,500rpm, computed)				
103mph	n/a	1st 44	2nd 69	3rd 90	4th 95	5th 105

Fuel consumption				Oil used	Brakes from 30mph
best 49mpg	worst 33mpg	average 44 mpg	range to reserve 70-90 miles	nil	n/a

TRACK CONDITIONS: no wind, heavy rain, ambient temp 44 deg F.

HOW IT COMPARES					
Model	price	max. speed	av. mpg	ss-¼	bhp*
Ducati500S	1699	103	44	n/a	40
Honda CX500		106		14.4	42
Suzuki GS550		112	51	14.2	44
Mocheck Harrier	1613.61	112	47	14.5	41
Yamaha XS750		112	39.4	13.9	57.5

*At the back wheel, measured on a Heenan Froude DPX3 chassis dynamometer.

350 Desmo Sport

Nineteen seventy-eight was a milestone year for the 900SS. Not only did it get an entirely new colour scheme (black and gold), but also it switched from wire wheels, with the flanged aluminium Borrani rims, to the solid-spoke cast-alloy variety. However, to begin with, this was a major problem area. The original wheels were of Campagnolo manufacture, and both these and the Speedline replacements suffered various weaknesses in one way or another, it not being uncommon to discover cracks or other defects on a regular basis. It was not until Ducati began to fit the FPS type that these failings were finally eradicated.

Many other detailed changes were made at this time. There was a dual seat with a fibreglass base (replacing the single racing saddle previously fitted to all SS models), featuring a lockable compartment at the rear. The engine and electrics were uprated in line with the new Darmah model (which effectively replaced the poor-selling GT/GTS series). The new clutch cover featured two hexagonal blanking plugs, one of which enabled the ignition advance settings to be made. Other changes meant getting rid of the Aprilia electrical equipment previously used (this is not the same company as the bike builder of today) and substituting with components manufactured by Bosch, Nippon Denso and Lucas, whilst a CEV headlamp replaced the original Aprilia unit. There was also a new rear light, as the original small, round CEV assembly was replaced by the larger one that was first used on the 860GT, GTS and Darmah. The switchgear was also changed to items of Nippon Denso manufacture. It is worth noting that in the same year Aprilia (nicknamed the

Italian Prince of Darkness) went out of business. This company had been a major component supplier to Ducati since the early 1950s, notably providing such items as lighting equipment and switches.

June 1978 saw, of course, the triumphant return of Mike Hailwood to the Isle of Man TT, where he pulled off a dramatic victory aboard a factory-prepared NCR racing special version of the 900SS, entered by Sports Motorcycles. For the 1979 model year, the Bologna factory decided to cash in on the success of the TT win, and the MHR (Mike Hailwood Replica) was born, and became available to the buying public. In reality it was little more than a lightly customized version of the existing 900SS, the main difference being a full fairing and a colourful red, white and green paint job. The MHR was destined to become Ducati's top-selling model in early 1980, and was to be offered in several versions, the final limited production batch being built in 1986.

1978 900SS with dual seat

Mike Hailwood
a personal view

Never in the history of motorcycle racing has there been a more popular champion than 'Mike-the-Bike' Hailwood. His long racing career on two wheels began aged 17, at Oulton Park, Cheshire on 22 April 1957, where he rode a borrowed 125cc MV Agusta, and ended at Mallory Park riding a 1000cc Suzuki in a Formula 1 event on 10 June 1979.

Mike was one of the most experienced riders ever. In the course of his competitive career, he probably rode in more races than any other rider, and not only this but he was effective on any make or any size of machine. In his time, he straddled everything from a 49cc Itom single-cylinder two-stroke to a 1000cc Dunstall-Suzuki GS1000 four-cylinder four-stroke superbike. He could switch engine sizes and types at the same meeting on the same day and give breathtaking, winning performances regardless. Among his many achievements Mike could count 14 TT victories, 10 world titles and 76 Grand Prix wins.

There is no doubt that Mike was put on the path to early success thanks to his larger-than-life father Stan, a multi-millionaire who could ensure his son always had access to the best bikes, but it soon became evident that Mike had more than enough talent to hold his own at the highest level of motorcycle racing. In person, Mike was a real contrast to his in-your-face, brash and overbearing father, Stan. A modest, even shy, man – never motivated by money or power – he shied away from the massive publicity attracted by his on-track performances. I think that it was this down-to-earth approach that made him such a huge favourite with his many fans, and today some three decades after his death, his memory is cherished by all those with an interest in the sport.

Funnily, although I had witnessed his racing exploits over the years – even competing against him occasionally – I did not really get to know Mike until he went into partnership with fellow racer and world champion Rod Gould. In my role as a roving ambassador for the Ducati and Moto Guzzi factories, as their official British spare parts distributor, I visited the dealer network during the late 1970s and early 1980s. The network for both marques was nationwide and for a period included Hailwood & Gould in Birmingham, England's second city.

After living abroad for a number of years, Mike moved back to the UK in spring 1979. Straight after that year's TT, he got stuck into the task of arranging his future, as he now had family responsibilities (he and his wife Pauline now had a daughter Michelle, born in 1971, and son David, born in 1974). The Hailwood & Gould business was situated at 60-98 Tyburn Road, Erdington, Birmingham B42 8LA. At the time of its opening in the summer of 1979 Mike commented, 'Getting the business off the ground has taken a lot of time and concentration – and the time has come when motorcycle racing, for so long the main love of my life, will have to take a back seat. I have a wife and family to look after and a totally new way of life to organise. Rod and I both have a lot of work to do before we can call ourselves a successful business.' When asked how he saw the Hailwood & Gould dealership progressing Mike continued, 'Expansion? It's a little too early just yet – but my father set our family's precedent in that field. He built up King's of Oxford until it was just about the biggest chain of motorcycle shops in the land and it would be terrific if I could do the same.' Unfortunately in this last respect Mike did not have his father's talent (or ruthlessness for that matter), and, as I know only too well, the motorcycle trade was just about to enter a crippling recession that was to last well into the 1980s. It not only destroyed many previously prosperous businesses, but also took its toll on newcomers such as Mike and Rod.

There were a couple of bright spots in an otherwise gloomy picture. The first was the undoubted value of the Hailwood name. I know of several customers who purchased bikes from Hailwood & Gould purely because they were able to tell their mates, 'Mike sold me my motorcycle.' The other was the arrival that same year of a new Ducati production model, the MHR (Mike Hailwood Replica). In many respects this was perhaps Mike's greatest tribute. How many people can say they have had a motorcycle named after them?

Even though the machine which customers could buy bore little resemblance to Mike's 1978 TT winner, except for having a V-twin engine and a green, white and red paint job, it still proved to be a big commercial success for the Italian factory. With this bike and Mike's name, the dealership of Hailwood & Gould benefited from a mini sales boom. However, it didn't last, and by spring 1981, things were looking bleak for H & G and the motorcycle trade in general. I visited the dealership and met Mike on several occasions, but never felt that he was that happy with the routine of the day-to-day business. After leading a life filled with excitement and success on both two and four wheels, who would? The first time I arrived at the Tyburn Road emporium, Rod was busy with a customer, so I introduced myself 'officially' to Mike. He immediately suggested a visit to the local cafe, and I soon realised that he was glad of an excuse to, as he put it, 'get away from it'. On a later visit, he told me that at times he felt little better than 'a life-size cardboard showroom display'. There is no doubt that Mike intensely disliked being 'the silent salesman'.

Our short trips away from his showroom were probably some sort of relief to him. In fact, he once told me, he looked forward to my visits. All these years later, I think perhaps I could have made slightly more of these visits than I did. They were largely innocent and enjoyable meetings, and in Mike's case just a bit of an escape, but they did give me some insight into the workings of the real Mike Hailwood, the man behind the name. Of course, this was long before I had any idea of becoming an author, but again I feel this was an advantage. There was no other motive than simply enjoying each other's company, and in Mike's case a chance to be able to 'unwind'.

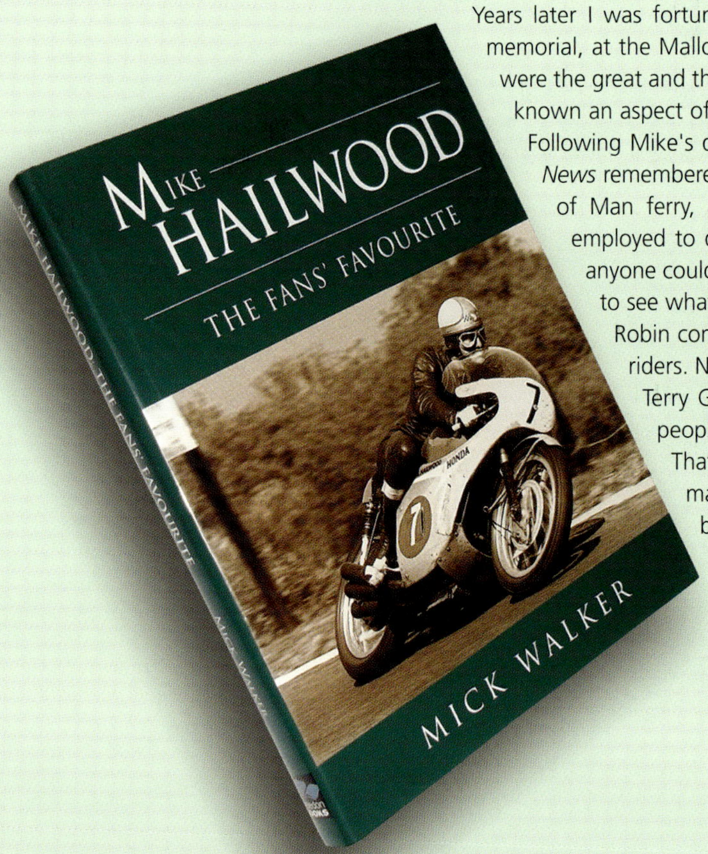

Years later I was fortunate enough to attend the unveiling of the Mike Hailwood memorial, at the Mallory Park race circuit in the summer of 1998. Assembled there were the great and the good of the motorcycle world, but somehow I felt that I had known an aspect of Mike that very few of the others had seen in the great man.

Following Mike's death in 1981, Robin Miller, the former editor of *Motor Cycle News* remembered the man: 'He had a boyish grin, wide as the back of an Isle of Man ferry, and a marvellous sense of humour and barbed wit, often employed to deflate paddock poseurs.' Certainly Mike was the last person anyone could describe as a poseur himself – if anything he found it difficult to see what all the fuss was about.

Robin continued: 'The greatest tribute, however, comes from his fellow riders. Not just the Agostinis and Reads, but the Mick Chattertons and Terry Grotefelds. They speak a common language in a sport where people live for the day.'

That was exactly how, I am sure, Mike saw things – enjoy yourself, make every minute count, life is too short. Mike-the-Bike has become a true legend in motorcycle history, for all the right reasons. As for myself, I feel privileged to have known the man, however briefly.

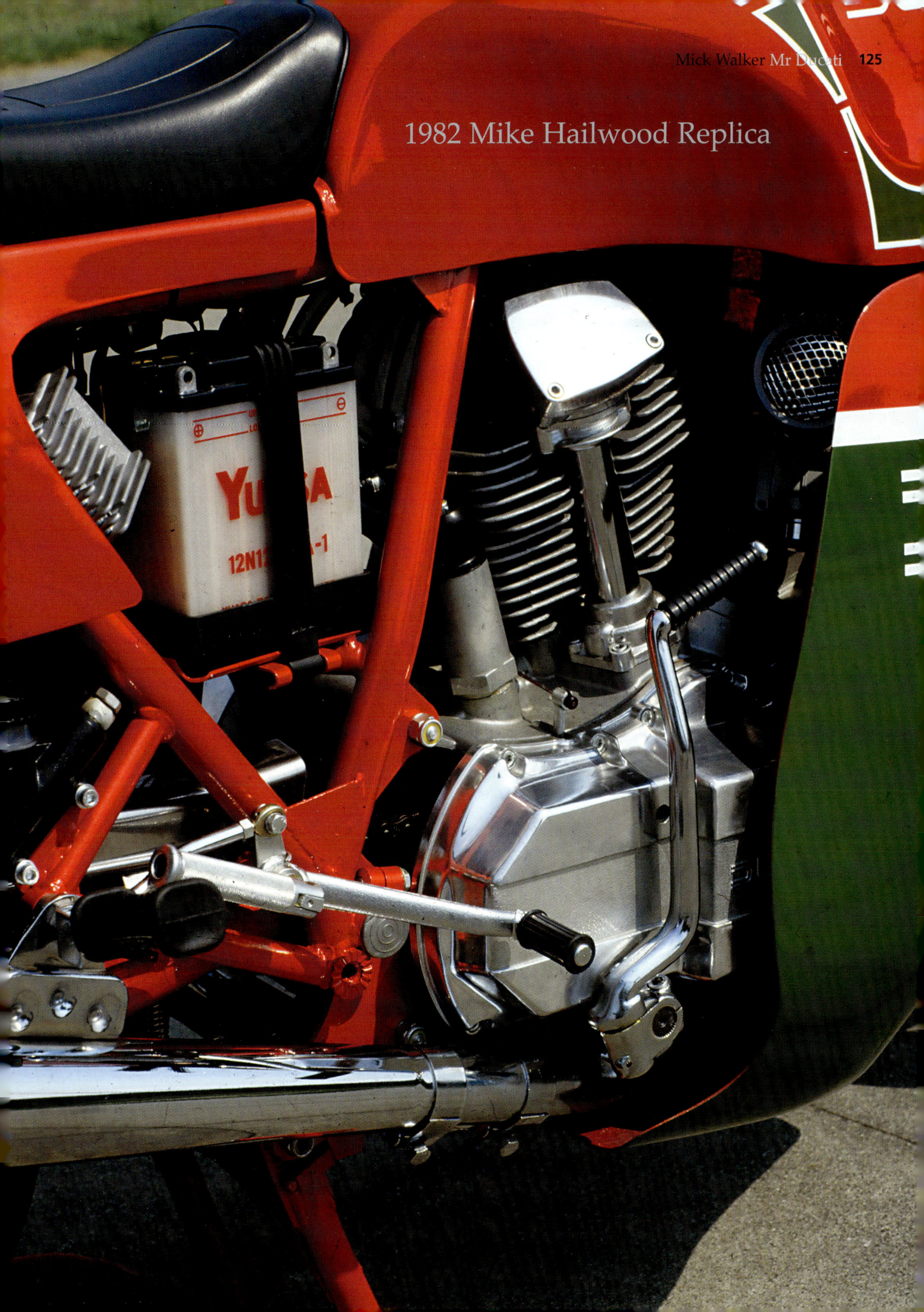

1982 Mike Hailwood Replica

The 1986 MHR Mille brought the bevel-drive V-twin story to a close.

That first 1979 MHR variant (at the time intended as a one-off batch) featured a fibreglass cover over an inner separate steel fuel tank, which was later to give way to a full-size steel tank. Early models had no side panels, but these were added to provide a tidier appearance. Seat designs also varied, but on most there was a combined single/dual racing type in fibreglass. Originally, the MHR had Conti silencers like the SS, but the post-1981 machines sported more restrictive Silentiums. As on the SS, various wheels were fitted, including Campagnolo, Speedline and FPS. Unlike the SS, the replica used exclusively Darmah instruments and switch gear of Nippon Denso manufacture. It should also be pointed out that all Hailwood Replicas and 900SS models from 1979 used the Darmah engine as a basis.

The fairing of the MHR was always a full dolphin type, and until 1983 had oblong indicators fitted integrally. At first, the fairing was a one-piece affair, which was an absolute pig to remove and refit. In fact this job could not be accomplished without first removing the front wheel. It might have looked good, but it wasn't practical. When 'mass'-production of the MHR began for the 1980 model year, one of the changes was a revised fairing that featured detachable side panels, making servicing and general access much easier. Mass-production, in Ducati terms, of course, was nowhere near Japanese figures.

In 1981, a new 900SS was launched, which, sadly, had lost the performance edge of the original – the factory finally giving way to ever stricter legislation from Brussels. This meant ultra-restrictive Silentium silencers, and of course air filters to quieten the intake roar. It also received a silver/blue paint scheme, but with decals more likely to be found on an American Harley-Davidson than an Italian Ducati! Other changes included longer clutch springs and cups, a successful attempt to finally cure the clutch slip that had blighted the more sporting Ducati V-twins up to that time. Previously, an owner's only recourse had been to fit springs from the 450 single.

For 1983, things got even worse when the S2 replaced the 900SS. *Motor Cycle News* referred, correctly, to the S2 as a 'dog'. And in truth, it must rate as one of the worst Ducatis ever. The example I tested in August 1983 had several glaring faults. With a restricted performance, it still came with the gearing of the real 900SS, so that it was seriously over-geared. Indicating the restrictive nature of the previously mentioned silencers, they were both equally badly discoloured, exactly halfway along their bodies. The combination of handlebars, seat and footrests gave a riding position that had obviously never been tested before production began. It was the most uncomfortable Ducati that I have ever ridden – even the fairing-mounted mirrors were in the wrong position. To add insult to injury, the foam-block saddle (similar to the Moto Guzzi Le Mans) was quite literally falling to pieces – and this on a new motorcycle. I can only describe the S2 as a mere shadow of a once truly great motorcycle, which showed just how far Ducati's creative powers had slipped.

NCR 900 as raced by Hailwood in his 1978 Isle of Man comeback

Ducati SD 900 Darmah

Several detail changes distinguished the S2 from the earlier models. The engine was identical to the Darmah of the same year, but included a new gear cluster. This was a stronger three-dog type instead of the original six-dog affair. The six-dog gearbox ran up to engine number 092919 with the three-dog internals starting at engine number 092920. The three-dog components were capable of being retro-fitted to the earlier bevel-driven V-twins. The cycle parts were based on a mixture of Darmah and Pantah components, with very few true 900SS items – the swinging arm was about the only genuine SS bit remaining. The machine's most obviously Pantah-based influence was the fairing, although it also borrowed the excellent folding lifting handle first fitted to the 500SL Pantah.

Towards the end of 1983, a modified MHR made its entrance. This new model featured an engine with remodelled crankcases and outer covers, together with a hydraulic clutch. To go with this unit, a master cylinder and hoses were mounted leading from the left-hand clip-on. The MHR also gained a completely new fairing and screen, with the front indicators being taken out of the fairing body and relocated on arms that formed part of the indicator body. There was also a new warning light and switch mounting panel to replace the earlier Darmah assembly, and a new rear light and indicator assembly in place of the original one inherited from the 1978 900SS. Other detail changes included the replacement of the stainless steel chainguard (first seen on the 1971 750GT) with a black painted one, and alterations to the rear-brake linkage and master cylinder. But probably the biggest change was a switch to electric starting, with no kick-start lever provided – nor even a shaft for fitting one.

New Silentium silencers were adopted for the Replica; they had been designed expressly for it and the 1984 S2. The latter machine continued, however with the old engine assembly, its only changes for 1984 being to the colour scheme, now all-black with a red frame, in place of the original gun-metal grey and orange finish. The MHR's colour scheme remained the traditional red, white and green with white striping, although black mudguards (adapted from the previous season's S2) replaced the original red items. By 1984, these two machines were the only models above 750 in Ducati's range, the Darmah series having eventually been discontinued.

For 1985, the engine's displacement was upped to 973cc (88 x 80mm) and at the same time the opportunity was taken to replace the anachronistic oiling system with one offering greater output, together with a plain bearing crankshaft. The Replica was now re-branded as the 1000 Mille, and the same mechanical changes were introduced for the 1000 S2 Mille.

LA MOTO ITALIANA

Then, on 1 May 1985, Cagiva took over Ducati. The S2 Mille was axed immediately but the Mille Replica survived. However, this was short-lived, as the new owners axed the by-then ageing bevel-drive V-twins early the following year. The design was not only dated, but production costs far exceeded those of the belt-driven engines which had been introduced at the end of 1970s via the Pantah model. And so, early in 1986, the last Mille Replica rolled off the production line to bring to an end the era that had begun with the 750GT back at the beginning of the 1970s.

My association with Ducati had continued beyond the closure of my own motorcycle business, and in the Autumn of 1998 I was invited as one of 50 individuals who had had an important connection with the Ducati factory over the preceding half-century to celebrate the Bologna marque's 50th anniversary of motorcycle production. The idea was to stage a dinner with 50 tables that would be hosted by one of the 50, together with a guest. My wife Susan didn't want to attend, so I took along my long-standing friend, Norfolk man George Paget. George, small in stature and something of a practical joker, had always been a Ducati fan.

Long-standing Ducati fan George Paget was my guest at the factory 50th anniversary celebration, where he kidded Phil Read that he was fellow Yamaha works rider Bill Ivy's brother.

We arrived at the venue to be greeted by the organisers, who explained that before being seated at our table, each personality would be introduced to the gathering. We were to go up on stage in alphabetical order, and it turned out that I and Phil Read (who had ridden for Ducati during the early 1970s) would be among the last to be interviewed. I had known Phil for many years and Mick Walker Motorcycles had even sold his Premier helmet range and branded clothing line during the 1970s. While I was chatting to him up on the stage, George was beside me, and suddenly introduced himself to Phil as Bill Ivy's brother.

The significance of this is that when Phil and Bill were Yamaha works riders together during the late 1960s, there was a major and much-publicised falling out between the two stars. This centred on the Yamaha team orders for the 1968 season. Phil was to be the 125cc world champion, with Bill taking the 250cc title. Everything had gone well to start with, with Bill assisting Phil to take the 125 crown. However, once this had been achieved, Phil conveniently forgot the second part of the agreement and did everything to stop Bill's title aspirations. Eventually, at the final race, the Italian Grand Prix at Monza, it was Phil and not Bill who became the 250 champion. This did not go down well with the public, and my friend George never forgave Phil for it. Three decades later he had decided to exact his revenge.

Phil must have had a guilty streak about the incident, as he fell hook-line-and-sinker, believing that George really was Bill's brother. (In fact, Bill only had two sisters, Sue and Marie.) Phil told George just how much he loved Bill, including the fact – true – that it was he who was responsible for getting Bill into the Yamaha team in the first place. By now the gag was going down really well, but I felt that it was time to tell Phil the truth. When I broke the news, I could tell that Phil was not amused and what's more, he thought that I had organised the joke. A few years later, when reminded about the incident, Phil said that he couldn't remember it.

One of my great experiences of 1998 was riding the 916 SPS Fogarty Replica. Costing a cool £20,500, the limited-edition UK-market-only Replica was the ultimate factory-built collector's motorcycle of its generation. Its introduction was down to my friend, the then-British Ducati importer Hoss Elm, Managing Director of Northampton-based Moto Cinelli.

The man the motorcycle was named after, Carl Fogarty, had wanted an official Ducati factory ride following his sensational victory on a privately entered Ducati at Donington Park in the World Superbike Series in 1992. A suitable deal was only finalised in January the following year, and Hoss Elm had been instrumental in organising it, with Carl riding under the Moto Cinelli banner in the UK during that season, alongside his WSB duties.

1998 Foggy Replica

Interviewing Carl Fogarty, Cadwell Park, 1999

Carl then joined the Virginio Ferrari team for 1994 and went on to make history and win the WSB championship titles in both 1994 and 1995. As Hoss recalled: 'I had always remained in close contact with Carl and considered his link with the factory to be vital to Ducati's success in the UK. Certainly Moto Cinelli's advertising campaign in 1997, which featured Carl and his family, proved to be the most popular in our history and helped us to achieve record sales. When discussing the 1998 contract for Carl with the factory, I had an idea of a replica. In the following months, I agreed the final specification with Ducati. The total build quantity of 200 units (plus an additional two – one for Carl and one for Moto Cinelli) ensured that the model was one of the most exclusive ever produced in Bologna. I felt that we had produced a fabulous machine that was a fitting tribute to one of Britain's greatest-ever motorcycle racers.'

With only 202 examples (all built in 1998) the 916 SPS (actually 996cc) Foggy Replica was right from the start and, as a limited edition, virtually guaranteed to retain its value more than any other road-going 916/748 series model. I was able to get my leg over one of the very first examples in August 1998. Of all the motorcycles I have been fortunate enough to test from manufacturers all around the world, the Foggy Replica has to rate as one of the handful of true classics. My first impression – and a lasting one – was of the truly awesome linear power delivery, a seemingly flat torque curve that allowed the rider to tap instantly into real power. This is unlike many modern high-performance machines, which only give their best in the upper regions of the rev range. One could easily lift the front wheel in almost any gear, such was the dynamic power that was instantly available by way of the rider's throttle control.

Of course the basics of the machine were closely related to the less glamorous (and less expensive) but still very usable 916/748 series. Where the Foggy Replica scored was on its additional abilities in terms of power, suspension and braking performances. You really felt that you could do almost anything. Of course, all this was fine in the controlled environment of a race circuit, but what about out on the public highway? As I said in my 1999 book *Ducati 4-valve Twins*: 'There's no need to worry – this is a bike that is incredibly easy to ride despite its scintillating performance. That word performance again, I hear you say, but with the 996cc (although officially labelled as the 916) there is a claimed 123bhp at 9,500rpm (at the crankshaft).'

The overall look of the Foggy Replica mirrored that of the 1998 works racing machines with red paintwork and white 'race number' sections on the seat tailpiece and fairing frontal cowling. 'Ducati Performance' graphics (in white) were to be found on the sides of the lower fairing and the sides of the fuel tank. There were Moto Cinelli logos in white on the fuel tank and the upper part of the seat tailpiece between the race number areas. A Carl Fogarty signature was on the top section of the fuel tank, with the famous 'Foggy Eyes' on the windshield. These graphics were all lacquered over as part of the overall finish of the machine. In addition, a sponsor's graphics kit was also provided, for the customer to apply as he chose. Other goodies included a racing-type paddock stand, special key holder, a matching cloth motorcycle cover, certificate of authenticity and an individually numbered production plate (located on the machine's top steering yoke).

Unlike any other Ducati models of the period, the Foggy Replica was never sold as a 'grey import'. This was because it was a UK-only project. And with such small numbers produced there was simply no need for dealers to offer discounts.

As with the legendary Mike Hailwood Replica (MHR) bevel V-twin of two decades before, the Foggy Replica was a celebration of a racing star and the part Ducati had played in the success the rider had enjoyed. It is interesting to note that only 199 examples of the Foggy Replica were eventually sold. Besides the two bikes already mentioned, an additional machine was retained for display at the Bologna factory museum.

Ducati Experience Race School

One dry but cold February day in 1998, together with several other Ducati personnel including World Superbike Champion, Carl Fogarty, and British Ducati importers Moto Cinelli's boss, Hoss Elm, I attended the official launch of the Ducati Experience Race School at Brands Hatch. Run jointly by the Brands Hatch Leisure Group and Moto Cinelli, the school quickly proved itself one of the very best in Europe. The first year of operations saw a squad of 748/916 models ready for customers to sample at three of the top British circuits (Brands Hatch, Cadwell Park and Oulton Park) backed up by a team of leading instructors.

For 1999, the Ducati Experience School introduced one-to-one tuition by some of the top British racers of the day. I was invited by Hoss Elm to take part in a special track day organised by the school at Cadwell Park on 15 March 1999. Having attended the Brands launch the previous year, I was immediately able to see the benefit of the new one-to-one tuition instead of the 1998 multi-rider/instructor set-up. Before being let out onto the track, a briefing took place, which included topics such as riding techniques, track-craft, flag signals, safety and how cones were positioned at peel-off points around the circuit. As only one pupil rode out with each instructor, it meant that there were fewer people out on the circuit at the same time. Race school customers had the choice of using their own riding gear or having it provided. As I said at the time, 'whichever you opt for, the important issue is being comfortable on a motorcycle – a 748 normally, or a 916 for more advanced pupils'.

When your track time came around you followed your instructor out onto the circuit. For the first part of the session you followed him. Later, you were pulled in, points discussed with him and then you resumed your riding, but now you were in front, with him noting your progress (or otherwise). My session on a 748 with Gary Dickinson lasted 40 minutes, which is quite a long time to be circulating a race track. A year later, I took in another session, this time on a 916.

No practice needed - the flattering verdict on my performance at the Ducati Experience, Cadwell Park 1999.

CADWELL PARK

DUCATIEXPERIENCE

This is to certify that

Mick Walker

rode a

Ducati 748

around

Cadwell Park

on the 23rd of Oct 1999

DUCATIEXPERIENCE

ANALYSIS FORM

Riders Name: (16) Mick Walker Date: 23-10-99

1	**Braking**	9 out of 10
2	**Throttle control**	9 out of 10
3	**Line**	10 out of 10
4	**Riding position**	8 out of 10
5	**Body Position whilst cornering**	8 out of 10
6	**Ability to look and plan ahead**	9 out of 10
7	**Awareness**	9 out of 10
8	**Consistency**	10 out of 10
9	**Speed**	8 out of 10
	Total Marks	80 out of 90

Areas most needing practice NONE!

Instructor comments WHAT CAN I SAY MICK, ABSOLUTLY SPOT ON EVERYWHERE, MAY BE YOU SHOULD THINK ABOUT A COMEBACK

Instructors name Gary Dickinson (GARY DICKINSON)

Recommended for 916 experience **YES/~~NO~~**

Brands Hatch Leisure Group Limited use and recommend Ducati Motorcycles.
Bookings and Enquiries: Cadwell Park 01507 343555
Call Centre 0990 125 250
The Ducati Experience is operated by Brands Hatch Leisure Group Ltd.
Registered office: Fawkham, Longfield, Kent DA3 8NG. Registered in England No: 515994

CADWELL PARK BRANDS HATCH OULTON PARK

My close association with the Ducati marque had spanned the 1960s, 70s, 80s and 90s, and for the majority of this time I was also the spares specialist for the Italian firm, with satisfied customers all around the world. However, at midnight on 31 December 1999, Ducati set up its own import company, Ducati UK, and my friend Hoss Elm, owner of Moto Cinelli, lost the contract to operate as Ducati's official British agent. This coincided with a change in ownership of the Bologna factory itself, from Italian to American hands. The original, government-owned Ducati Meccanica had been bought out by the Castiglioni family-owned Cagiva concern as far back as May 1985. But the Cagiva company suffered financially during the 1990s, and in September 1996, TPG (Texas Pacific Group) purchased a slice of the company. Finally, in March 1999, Ducati was floated simultaneously on the stock markets of Milan and New York.

Writing my book *Ducati 4-Valve V-Twins The Complete Story* gave me the opportunity of testing virtually every model from the 851 to the limited-edition Fogarty Replica. As I stated then, 'Another of TPG's stated aims was greatly increased production. This could well pose another problem. Lots of Ducati clientele like the idea of a product that is not only appealing, but is not to be seen on every street corner. Maybe Ducati are not Ferrari, but they could well learn from their Italian auto brothers, in that Ferrari have a production limit of 3,000 cars per year. Will the Ducati customer base want to be more Ford than Ferrari? I doubt it very much.'

During the 1990s, Taglioni's successor Massimo Bordi, together with the gifted stylist Massimo Tamburini, had been largely responsible for that most classic of all modern Ducati series, the 748 and 916. But very soon after the Americans gained full control, both men left. South African Pierre Terblanche, who had worked as Tamburini's assistant at CRC (Cagiva Research Centre) was entrusted with future Ducati designs. One only has to look at what has come in recent times to see that he has not been entirely successful. Terblanche carried out his design work by using a computer, rather than passion. A Ducati definitely needs the latter.

After the end of 1999, my dealings with Ducati became less productive. For a start, Ducati UK's attitude was that as I didn't sell their bikes, I could not deal directly with them – even though I had faithfully represented Ducati for many years. However, every time they got an unwanted enquiry, for diesel engine spares or an obscure two-stroke part, they would tell the customer to contact me. Needless to say, I was not pleased. Over the next few years, the enthusiasm built up over four decades steadily drained away. Finally, one Monday morning in April 2005 I decided that I had had enough, and within days ended my connections with the marque by selling my remaining spares stock, a sad end to my association with an iconic Italian design that I had cherished for so many years.

For this Ducati enthusiast, the Ducati of today is not the one of yesterday. The charisma is no longer there – how can it be, when big business has become involved, and the end product is now relegated to become a mere commodity and might just as well be a baked bean can as a motorcycle? For me, the 748/916 series was the last of the really iconic Ducati motorcycles, a view which I believe is shared by the vast majority of other genuine Ducati enthusiasts.

DUCATI 2000
an icon for the century

Ducati 2000 Expo

The Ducati 2000 Expo scheduled for 22 July to 16 September 2000 was originally discussed as early as 1998 by the Ducati Owners Club of Great Britain, but problems with obtaining machines meant that close to the event's opening the staff at the University of Northumbria Gallery were very worried that they would have nothing to show. Redline Books suggested that I could help, so I flew over to the Ducati works on a begging mission in the company of Mara-Helen Wood, the Gallery Director. The Ducati Museum director Marco Montemaggi was extremely helpful, and agreed to lend ten bikes, which included the brand new prototype Hailwood Evolution that had never been outside the Bologna factory before.

On the first day of the Expo I gave a talk about the Bologna factory from its conception to the present. I also compiled a catalogue of the machinery on show. Mara-Helen Wood kindly said she was 'indebted to Mick Walker, Ducati author, historian and consultant, whose involvement was crucial to the success of the Expo'. Little did anyone know just how close it had been to being a failure.

Ducati 2000
an icon for the century

The University of Northumbria is currently hosting a unique exhibition which traces the history of Ducati – the greatest of the superbikes.

Ducati 916

916
brembo
SHOWA

6

Moto Guzzi

my commitment to Guzzi was on the same level

Inside the wind tunnel at Mandello del Lario. Built in 1950, it gave Moto Guzzi a massive lead in the science of motorcycle aerodynamics.

My first experience of the Moto Guzzi marque came during the spring of 1975, when I agreed to become the British Guzzi parts distributor, in a similar way to my existing Ducati arrangement with Luton-based dealership Coburn & Hughes, which had replaced the existing British Guzzi importers, Barretts of Redhill. The official launch of the new C&H/Mick Walker tie-up was in Luton on 8 May, where the model line-up included not only the 850T that Barretts had already brought into the UK (albeit in extremely small numbers), but also the new 850T3 and T3 California, neither of which had been seen in Britain, and had only just been launched at home in Italy. The other models were the 250TS and the 750 S3.

Both the T3 and the California were clearly based on the 850T, with the biggest technical difference being the brakes. Whereas the T had featured a single disc at the front and a full-width drum at the rear, the T3 and California (and the S3) were equipped with Guzzi's exclusive, patented integrated triple-disc set-up. With this system, applying the brake pedal not only operated the 242mm rear disc brake in the conventional way, but also applied the left 300mm front disc. The braking pressure was automatically balanced to produce the correct front-rear bias needed to bring the rider to a steady, even halt. For extra braking in emergencies, or simply to hold the bike whilst stationary, the front brake lever could be used to apply the right front disc only.

'The Europeans taught the world how to make good motorcycles.
Today one country produces one of the world's finest machines: the Italians'.

Moto Guzzi

Of the leading Italian marques, Moto Guzzi has been around considerably longer than Ducati, tracing its origins back to the meeting of three motorcyclists in the Italian Air Force towards the end of the Great War in 1918. Two pilots, Giovanni Ravelli and Giorgio Parodi and their young driver/mechanic Carlo Guzzi talked of little else than an advanced design of motorcycle that Guzzi had sketched during his off-duty hours. Sadly, Ravelli never saw Guzzi's design reach fruition, as he was to lose his life during a flying mission shortly after the end of the war. However, Parodi and Guzzi went on not only to produce the dream machine but also a myriad of other designs – both production roadsters and racing models.

From the 1920s until the late 1950s, Moto Guzzi was a major player in Grand Prix racing, winning a host of championship titles and TT victories. During the 1960s, Guzzi made the transition from road racing to off-road sports, notably the ISDT (International Six Days Trial). The mainstay of its customer road bikes remained the company's trusty singles until, in the middle of the decade, it débuted the first of the now-traditional Guzzi V-twins, the V7. However, towards the end of the 1960s, Guzzi finances hit the rocks and, in 1972, the company was ultimately saved by the industrialist, Alejandro de Tomaso, who was a big name in both the Italian car and motorcycle manufacturing industries during the latter part of the 20th century.

De Tomaso was born in Argentina in 1928 and was only 15 when his father, a leading politician, died – leaving him the most likely successor to the family's large estate just outside Buenos Aires. However, young De Tomaso had other ideas. He planned a future in car racing, which he began in 1951, quickly progressing to become one of his country's leading drivers. In 1957, he made Italy his new home, partly because of the stance he had taken against the dictator Juan Peron. Italy was a logical choice for his new home, as both sides of his family had Italian blood, but his love of motor sport also played a key role.

That same year, he began an association with the Osca team (run by the Maserati brothers) as a works driver. Then, in 1959, he realised a personal ambition when he began construction of his own cars in Modena. The first De Tomaso cars were purely racers, but by 1963 he had decided that his future lay with the manufacture of production sports cars. Later that decade, he became involved with the automotive giant Ford. By now De Tomaso was well established, and his financial clout meant that he could consider future investments. In the two-wheeled world, this meant Benelli, which by 1971 had fallen on hard times, and was ripe for acquisition. Little over a year later, in a joint venture with the Italian government in December 1972, a much bigger name was added – that of Moto Guzzi.

In a very short space of time, one man had gained a major slice of the Italian motorcycle industry. The new combine began its operation in early 1973, and right from the start, Benelli and Moto Guzzi were considered as parts of one giant corporate body, despite the factories being over 300 miles apart. Soon De Tomaso streamlined the operation, with a scheme that was to result in all four-stroke engines being built in the Guzzi facility at Mandello del Lario in the north, while the Benelli plant at Pesaro on the Adriatic coast provided only two-stroke power units. This meant that the exotic Benelli four and six-cylinder superbikes of the 1970s were effectively built by Guzzi, while the 250cc Moto Guzzi two-stroke was constructed by Benelli – very confusing.

De Tomaso's attitude towards the Japanese motorcycle industry seemed ambivalent. In public he expressed a violent dislike of their business practices, but paid their designs the ultimate compliment by basing his multi-cylinder Benellis on them. The 350 and 500 fours were virtually direct copies of Hondas – even to the point of using cross-head screws on the engine casings – while the 750 and 900 sixes were logical extensions of Japanese four-cylinder technology.

Rick shows how to rebuild the Guzzi's car-type clutch in the Wisbech workshop for *Motorcycle Mechanics.*

strip

is removed.

As the clutch plates were removed on our machine, the extent of the damage was fully realised, the first friction plate had the centre completely ripped out and the second plate had no teeth inside the boss — it had been ground completely flat, almost as if it had been in a lathe! It's a tribute to the strength of the clutch drive components that they had suffered only minor damage which could easily be cleaned up.

When checking parts generally for wear, the clutch spring free length isn't given, the only way this can be checked is to see whether it exerts a pressure of 20kg at 20mm compressed length.

The final free play adjustment is very easy, just twiddle the clutch arm setting so that the arm doesn't make contact with anything at either end of its travel and make sure there is about ½in free play at the end of the handlebar lever.

Our thanks to Mick Walker Motorcycles of Norwich Road, Wisbech, for their help in the preparation of this article.

The very first Moto Guzzi to arrive at my Wisbech dealership was actually an 850T. We enthusiastically uncrated the machine in our workshop, and according to our usual practice, stripped it down to its component parts – including the engine, transmission and final drive. By doing this we not only had every single spare part on the shelf, but also had the first-hand experience of the Guzzi V-twin. So from day one, my staff and I could relate to both the Guzzi design and our customers' needs. I had introduced this procedure with the Ducati range, which without doubt gave us an advantage over our competitors. In my opinion, success in the motorcycle business is down to genuine enthusiasm as well as product knowledge and real old-fashioned after-sales service, whether that be expertise in the workshop or parts availability in the stores. In fact, in the 1970s when sales were buoyant, lots of British dealers would only service bikes that had been purchased from their dealerships; this to my mind was a very short-sighted approach in terms of attracting new customers.

My view was entirely different, if we were capable of servicing a machine or supplying a part we were happy to help anyone. In the late 1970s, when quite widespread discounting became popular, many dealers were only interested in 'getting rid of units'. The problem this attitude caused is best illustrated by an incident I witnessed early one Saturday morning. A machine had been booked in for a first service, and the owner asked if we could help him unload it from his van, which was parked outside. Upon opening the van doors we saw that the bike was actually still in its crate! It emerged that the owner had purchased it from Midlands-based dealer Davick Motique, which ran flashy adverts and had coffee-making machines, bright lights and music in their showroom. However, his confidence was so low in the dealer's ability on other fronts that our visitor didn't want his machine touched by their workshop! He would only allow Mick Walker Motorcycles to assemble and service his new bike. We did as we would have done with any other customer and serviced his bike. This policy, I'm sure, was and still is a valid one. As a mark of customer satisfaction, when Mick Walker Motorcycles floundered in the recession of the early 1980s, I received hundreds of letters from patrons imploring me to carry on.

850T, the first Guzzi to arrive at Mick Walker Motorcycles

I owned two long-legged 850 T3s like this 1975 example.

Even though I had been a Ducati enthusiast for many years, my commitment to Guzzi was on the same level. In fact, I owned – at various times – two 850T3s, a model that in my opinion was the best all-round Guzzi of its era. My wife Susan was equally enthusiastic about the T3 and we travelled many thousands of miles, including trips to the Isle of Man and to the Isle of Wight, the latter for the annual Two-Day Trial.

My favourite Guzzi of all was a rather special 750S3. We had taken this as a part exchange early in 1977. Its engine had been blueprinted by a former Rolls-Royce (Derby) engineer, and compared to a standard S3, it was immediately obvious that it was quite different – crisper, smoother, more responsive and certainly possessing an additional 10mph on its maximum speed.

One Sunday later that year, several members of staff, me included, were invited to form a team to do battle with one from a rival dealership. The location was a large tree-lined parkland on the outskirts of the Norfolk market town of Swaffham. When we arrived we discovered that the contest was between our team of six riders and six riders from the local dealership, headed by the Swaffham-based road racer Greg Page. With hindsight the whole escapade was pure madness. Our task was to charge across the grass field at speeds approaching (and possibly exceeding) 70mph; making sure that we missed the opposing team's rider, who approached us from the side, White Helmets display team-style. I was riding the Guzzi S3 and Greg was aboard his road-racing Yamaha TZ350, so you can imagine that this type of event

The Moto Guzzi Museum, Mandello del Lario

Motorcycle Politics

An interesting insight into what drove Moto Guzzi's boss Alejandro de Tomaso (and his wife Elizabeth) came at a meeting over dinner early in 1976 at the luxurious Canalgrande Hotel in Modena – owned, incidentally, by De Tomaso. I was there with Ray Elliot and Clew Hughes from British importers Coburn & Hughes to discuss various ideas for importing Italian motorcycles into Britain. What I remember most from the two-hour discussion was the strong personalities of both the De Tomasos, and Alejandro's strident dislike of the Japanese industry, together with his clear willingness to involve politicians in his business ventures.

At this time, Britain's remaining motorcycle industry was split into two factions: Norton Villiers Triumph (NVT), which had been backed by Britain's previous Conservative government; and the former Triumph factory in Meriden, which had formed a workers' co-operative, sponsored by Harold Wilson's current Labour government. De Tomaso expressed his strong distaste for the management of NVT and its board of directors, headed by chairman Dennis Poore. I later discovered that De Tomaso had approached NVT, hoping to set up a co-operative agreement between the Italian and British motorcycle industries in an attempt to limit Japanese expansion into Europe, but was turned down flat.

He went on to talk about arranging a meeting with Harold Wilson, the British Labour Prime Minister, with a view to arranging a link – or at least co-operation – with the Triumph Meriden workers' co-operative. This would eventually founder, as related in the main text, and most of the British industry of the time sank into oblivion. In my view, the politicians were largely responsible for the eventual demise of both NVT and the workers' co-operative. NVT was the first to go, bled to death as a result of the actions of Labour Industry Minister Tony Benn. The men at Meriden received a series of government handouts totalling many millions of pounds before finally calling it a day in 1983.

Argentine industrialist Alejandro de Tomaso (right) won a Gold Mercury Award for industry.

would never be allowed today. There was no insurance for the event, which was attended by several hundreds of spectators. Our efforts on that day certainly made it a colourful interlude, a far cry from the flower-arranging and jam-making usually found at local fairs! Amazingly, there were no problems – not even the odd near-miss. I don't know if this was down to skill or just plain luck, as there were no practice runs beforehand.

At around the same time, I was asked to build a prototype Moto Guzzi police model, based on the existing T3 California. The initial request came from the Norfolk police, and although not a particularly profitable enterprise, I still considered it to be important – and prestigious. So we set to and constructed the machine. It was a success and resulted in an order for a fleet of bikes for the Norfolk force. Word soon spread, and before long the Sussex police copied their brothers in Norfolk and placed a substantial order. This could have been taken much further, but the Guzzi importers Coburn & Hughes were lukewarm. We needed help with sensible discounts to enable us to build the model at a decent profit. Instead, the likes of BMW and Yamaha took what could have been Guzzi police sales. Both these firms made major efforts in terms of factory support, something that Mick Walker Motorcycles alone could not match. Even so, for several years afterwards both Norfolk and Sussex were extremely pleased with their Guzzis – and the efficient parts backing they received. I visited both police forces (as I regularly did with the official dealer network), and these visits seemed genuinely appreciated by all concerned.

The original prototype T3 California modified for the Norfolk police force.

One of Tony Divey's Guzzi-powered Triking three-wheelers, a homage to the Morgan Aero.

Another interesting side project that used the Guzzi V-twin power unit was the Triking three-wheeler. This sold in small numbers during the late 1970s and much of the 1980s, and represented a modern-day take on the pre-war Morgan three-wheeler, constructed by the Norwich-based company Triking Cars headed by Tony Divey. In place of the classic JAP and Matchless power units of the original, the Guzzi twin offered a fine combination of power characteristics, and looked stylish in this application, too.

Of all the series-production bikes to have left the Guzzi works at Mandello del Lario on the shores of Lake Como in northern Italy during the 1970s, the Le Mans was unquestionably the best known. It was also to enjoy one of the longest production runs of any Guzzi model. Named after the legendary French endurance-racing venue, the original 850 Le Mans (retrospectively given the Mk1 tag) was clearly aimed at the enthusiast with a desire for fast road work, or production machine racing. Its debut was at the Milan Show in late 1975.

During this period, I spent a considerable amount of time in Italy working closely with the Moto Guzzi and Ducati factories. It just happened that I was on hand to test the very first production example of the Le Mans for myself in early 1976. I quickly discovered that there was more to the Le Mans than extra performance. Yes, it was good enough to attract the sporting rider who might have been considering a Ducati or Laverda, but it also had the added advantage of being civilised enough to double as an everyday ride. Unlike rivals such as the 900SS or the 3C, the Le Mans could be a sportster and a tourer all in one. In fact, in my dealership days, I was frequently asked by customers which bike I would choose, the Le Mans or the 900SS. My reply was always that they were both great bikes, 'But if you want to ride the bike every day, pick the Guzzi. For Sundays only, go for the Ducati.'

Many dyed-in-the-wool Guzzi enthusiasts would argue that the Le Mans' predecessor, the original V7 Sport had the real heart and soul of a sportster, and that its sporting character had been successively diluted through the 750S, S3 and Le Mans. This is true, but the Le Mans Mk1 had a clear advantage in terms of its customer appeal – and by the time it appeared, one has to take into account that under De Tomaso's ownership, Moto Guzzi had been forced to become much more commercially aware. It is an undisputed fact that the Le Mans enjoyed not only a vastly superior number of sales, but also a much longer production run than any of the earlier models.

I was frequently asked by customers which bike I would choose, the Le Mans or the 900SS. My reply was always that they were both great bikes, 'But if you want to ride the bike every day, pick the Guzzi.

Moto Guzzi 850 Le Mans Mk I

The 1972 V7 Sport, precursor to the Le Mans.

The V7 Sport – and, for that matter, the 900SS and 3C – offered raw, animal appeal, keeping the rider constantly extended. The Le Mans may have lacked this sharp edge, but instead possessed an infinitely more subtle charm. With the other three models you instantly fell in love, but that first love was never improved upon. With the Le Mans, and most other Guzzi V-twins for that matter, it was a more subtle process; the more you rode the bike the more you loved it.

Even on that initial ride, on what was, after all, a pre-production model, I was impressed with the performance, handling and perhaps most of all the styling. I must say that the Le Mans Mk1 was the pukka version; somehow, looks-wise the subsequent versions took a backward step. There is a famous credo in design 'If it looks right, it is right' – and this was certainly true in the case of the Mk1. It looked fast even standing still, and once I swung my leg over the saddle, pressed the starter button to fire up the engine, selected first gear, let the clutch out and left the confines of the factory yard at Mandello, I really began to enjoy myself. Leaving the town behind, I headed north on the road to Switzerland. This route from the factory follows the lakeside with a succession of sweeping bends, real motorcycling country. On the way back I took a different road climbing much higher into the hills.

The road I chose that day is known in Guzzi folklore as the TT of Italy, the Circuito del Lario and follows the route of a 24.8-mile event staged between the wars. This circuit, just like the Isle of Man Mountain course, presented some breathtaking scenery and some truly difficult going with many climbs, descents and hairpin bends. Running through the eastern hills bordering the lake, it swept through the difficult bends of the Valbrona Valley, made even worse in those pioneering days by another hazard, as the event was run over dirt roads. By the 1970s, the surface was of a decent grippy tarmac, thank goodness. Before I returned to the factory, the Le Mans and I had covered almost 100 miles, and I had loved every minute of it. I had also formed a pretty good idea of the bike's capabilities, and I was impressed. I couldn't wait to sell the bike from my Wisbech showrooms.

When it was finally launched onto the British market in June 1976, the Le Mans cost £2,000, some £400 more than the standard 'cooking' T3, but there was no shortage of customers. The legend had been born and lives on to the present day, as the Le Mans Mk1 is still a popular choice with classic enthusiasts, who appreciate its unique combination of speed, style and stamina.

John Sear of Sports Motorcycles,
racing a Le Mans Mk1 at Cadwell Park, 1977

In the mid-1970s, the workers' co-operative at the former Triumph factory at Meriden was struggling for survival, and the British concern believed it needed a line of entry-level motorcycles to supplement its traditional parallel-twins. To solve this problem quickly, a deal was struck whereby Moto Guzzi would supply Meriden with consignments of the Moto Guzzi 125 Turismo commuter motorcycle in kit form. This comprised the complete engine unit (a five-speed, two-stroke single), frame, front forks, rear shock absorbers, wheels complete with tyres and disc front brake, carburettor, tinware, saddle, lighting equipment and other smaller components. The idea was that the bikes would be finished and assembled at the co-operative works, and sold in the UK as the Moto Meriden Co-Uno. Originally, the deal called for some 2,500 sets of parts to be shipped to England. However, only the initial batch of 500 was eventually delivered. The whole episode was a dismal failure, and what had been intended as a promising beginning to Anglo-Italian co-operation became the complete reverse.

None of that was anticipated on 17 April 1976 when *Motor Cycle News* ran the headline 'Moto Meriden bikes start rolling soon'. *Motor Cycle* reported, 'Co-operative chairman Dennis Johnson met Signor Alejandro de Tomaso, chief of the Benelli and Moto Guzzi companies in Modena, Italy, last week to finalise the deal whereby he would buy 2,500 machines in kit form and assemble them here'. Johnson was also reported as saying, 'It's all agreed, we are purchasing an initial batch of 2,500 125cc single cylinder Moto Guzzis, and hopefully the first crates will arrive by the end of next month, subject to the availability of parts. We will be painting and distributing the bikes, and Coburn & Hughes will supply marketing, advertising and field sales assistance.' No mention was made of the spare parts backup, which was due to be my responsibility.

Later that year, at the London Earls Court Show in August, the Co-Uno 125 was displayed on the C&H stand, alongside its Ducati and Guzzi ranges. Dealers were signed up, and Mick Walker Motorcycles had received and binned the initial stock of spare parts. Everyone – distributor, dealer and customer – was ready. The missing link in the chain was the workers' co-operative at Meriden, where the bikes were to be built. From then until the following March, not a single 125 Co-Uno reached dealers' showrooms.

The kits supplied by Guzzi included all the completed sub-assemblies, so the construction job was pretty straightforward. Besides the basic assembly, the only other considerations were producing the decals and printing an English-edition rider's handbook. I visited Meriden on more than one occasion but no one really seemed interested, so perhaps it was little wonder it took the co-operative over nine months to produce the first machine. By then, both dealers and potential customers had virtually forgotten about the Earls Court launch.

Needless to say, there were no more overtures from Alejandro de Tomaso to the British industry. I might also add that a similar situation arose from a venture between the Austrian Puch concern and the co-operative, when a contract to assemble the top-selling Maxi moped was not followed through by the Meriden men (I refrain from using the word 'workers'). I had invested a considerable amount of time and money in the Co-Uno project, so to recoup some of this, I purchased the remaining stock of kits from Meriden in September 1978. We built these up in Wisbech and sold the Co-Uno for the bargain-basement price of £299. No wonder that by then I had little or no faith in the co-operative set-up.

While all this had been going on, Moto Guzzi had declared its intention to double the factory's output from its 1975 figures by the end of 1978. It was realised that if this was to be achieved, there were several gaps in the model range that would need to be plugged. The most noticeable gap was in the middleweight (350 to 600cc) sector. Although, in theory, the Nuovo Falcone single and the four-cylinder 400GTS should have plugged this, these models had proved to be poor sellers. Guzzi's owner Alejandro de Tomaso was quick to order his design chief Lino Tonti to produce a smaller V-twin that would capitalise on the factory's existing reputation for this engine configuration. The newcomer had to be suitable for mass-production, and modular in concept, to enable a series of alternative engine sizes. 'Middleweights for the masses', was how I described the situation in *Moto Guzzi Twins*.

Tonti began his design work in 1975, and by the following spring, prototype 350cc and 500cc models were being road-tested following a successful series of bench tests. The result was everything that De Tomaso could have wished for, centred on the tried-and-tested Guzzi formula of a 90-degree V-twin, with pushrod-operated valves, car-type clutch, five-speed gearbox and shaft final drive. Completion of the first of the new machines, coded the V35 and V50, was scheduled for the German show at Cologne in September 1976. De Tomaso felt, correctly, that the new middleweight V-twins, on which so much depended, demanded the top treatment. Luckily, he had chosen the major motorcycle exhibition of the year to launch the newcomers, with only Yamaha (XS250/360) and Honda (CB125T) showing any new models. Guzzi's far more exotic offering enabled the company to grab the major headlines: 'Cologne – Guzzi's smell success'.

As De Tomaso had intended, the début of the two new models caused considerable interest both in Italy and abroad. The smaller-engined V35 was originally destined for the home market, offering Italian buyers a unique opportunity to purchase a shaft-drive machine that had the advantage of falling into the low-taxation category offered to bikes of 350cc and under. In export markets, the V50 offered a competitive alternative to Honda's recently introduced CX500, also a transverse V-twin with shaft final drive.

First impressions indicated a great future for the middleweight Guzzi, but there were two major threats to series production. Both stemmed from the same cause – the limited manufacturing and assembly facilities at Mandello del Lario. At the end of 1976, the plant was almost at full capacity, unable to cope with the additional facilities needed for the V35/50. This led to very few of the new bikes actually being built during 1977, which was when volume production should have begun. The limited numbers also meant that manufacturing costs were higher than originally budgeted for.

However, Alejandro de Tomaso solved the problem by acquiring the Innocenti plant in southern Milan. My continuing involvement with the Moto Guzzi marque (as the UK parts distributor) had meant that I had taken an interest in De Tomaso's career. He had recently added the legendary Maserati supercar brand to his portfolio, but the news about Innocenti was of far more interest to my two-wheeler involvement. The home of the Lambretta scooter during the boom years of the 1950s and 1960s, Innocenti had made the switch to four wheels, building BMC (British Motor Corporation) cars under licence. These included the best-selling Mini, Mini Cooper, the earlier A40 and the second series Austin Healey Sprite, together with Innocenti's own Mini-engined model.

By the time the company's founder, Ferdinando Innocenti, died in 1973, the firm had been swallowed up by the British Leyland group (successor to BMC), but when Leyland hit financial problems, one of the first of its offshoots to feel the squeeze was Innocenti, with the result that the entire operation was sold off to a partnership consisting of De Tomaso and the Italian government industry body GEPI. By utilising his contacts, De Tomaso also acquired a large consignment of American machine tools with which to re-equip the Milanese production lines. This would enable the intended number of the smaller Guzzi models to be manufactured with a significant saving in unit costs. Finally, it looked as though the Italian dealers and the overseas importers would at last get their hands on supplies at the right price.

Alejandro de Tomaso was a dynamic man, always looking to move forward, and like many top industrialists this probably meant at times sailing pretty close to the wind. He was not averse to getting into bed with politicians to advance his cause, so Innocenti became ripe for government funding under the watchful eye of De Tomaso. Once again he used his bargaining skills, and within a few months of transferring the entire V35/50 production from Guzzi's Mandello del Lario facilities to the Innocenti plant in Milan, De Tomaso's Seimm Moto Guzzi parent company was able to purchase no less than 76.6 per cent of Nuova Innocenti shareholdings from the Italian government at a knock-down price. As a result, Innocenti, now widely seen as the most profitable sector of De Tomaso's fast growing empire, was placed firmly in the hands of Il Supremo.

Moto Guzzi V35 Imola

With so many prominent parts of the Italian car and motorcycle industry under his control, and his avowed hatred of the Japanese, it was perhaps pretty obvious that De Tomaso would bring his power to bear on his business partner, the Italian government, to introduce a policy of protection against the 'enemies', as he saw them: Honda, Suzuki, Yamaha and Kawasaki. On 26 May 1977, the Italian government imposed a complete ban on the import of all Japanese motorcycles. Observers of Italian politics saw this as De Tomaso's handiwork, rather than of the nameless officials who had rubber-stamped the document.

Of course, the Japanese manufacturers could hardly be expected to take this lying down. They brought pressure to bear on their own government, resulting in the matter being put before the European Court in Luxembourg for alleged infringement of Common Market regulations. Eventually, in 1978, the Italian market import quota for Japanese motorcycles was raised from zero to 18,000 units, although it was stipulated that there should be no bikes under 400cc. This was not total victory for the Japanese, but better than it had been. And although De Tomaso had won a small victory, it would ultimately be the Japanese who won the battle. To bypass the under-400cc rule, Honda simply set up its own manufacturing base in Italy, building large numbers of their popular 125cc four-stroke and then the two-stroke singles (albeit with a percentage of Italian-sourced components).

Meanwhile, on one of my frequent trips to Italy, I was able to sample both the V35 and V50 models and I must say that I was impressed. These models ticked every box – even though neither the chassis nor the engine unit offered anything really innovative, there was nothing wrong with the fact that the newcomers relied on engineering traditions established by their older, bigger brothers in the Guzzi V-twin family, developed over the previous two decades since the V7. The world's motorcycle journalists were similarly full of praise for the new models, which were even commended in countries without a Moto Guzzi importer. In Britain, *Which Bike* voted the V50 top of a four-machine test, against the Yamaha XS500, Moto Morini 500 and Honda CX500. The magazine concluded, 'So for the moment, the likes of Yamaha, Morini and particularly Honda should be seriously worried'.

The V35 and V50 were excellent machines to ride but there were two factors that potentially made them highly competitive in the middleweight stakes: the price (after production began at the Innocenti plant); and the incredibly low dry weight of only 303lb (152kg) – which was particularly good for a twin-cylinder model with shaft final drive. Compared to the opposition, the Guzzi weighed in at some 100lb less than the CX500 and 80lb less than the XS500 (which had a chain final drive). The new Guzzi was even lighter than any of the Japanese 250cc twins of the era, which endeared it to many potential new owners and was particularly liked by the new breed of lady riders.

So the design was an instant success, both at home and abroad. There is absolutely no doubt that Moto Guzzi could have – and should have – turned this into the biggest-selling Italian motorcycle of all time, but marketing, quality control and the general economic climate of the early 1980s were to prevent this. Marketing has never been a particular strength in the Italian motorcycle industry, which has characteristically been unwilling or unable to match the effectiveness of the Japanese 'big four' or the German BMW concern in this area.

Guzzi 350 and 500cc engines at the Milan Innocenti factory

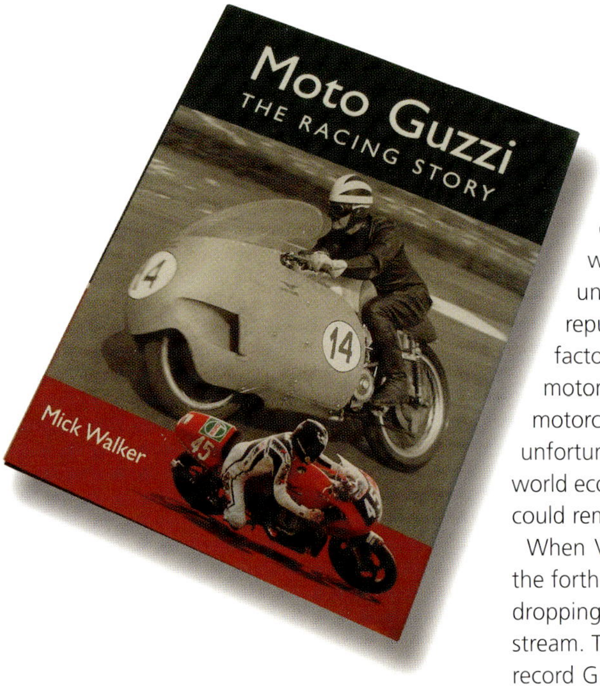

First came a spate of reliability problems, indicating that the design was not as bullet-proof as the larger models. These problems were by no means insurmountable, as Guzzi went on to prove, but, unfortunately the damage had been done, and the machines' reputation was tarnished. However, in my opinion, by far the major factor was not Guzzi's fault, as the global recession was to affect the motorcycle industry probably worse than any other sector. Worldwide motorcycle sales simply fell off a cliff from the end of 1980. This was an unfortunate fact: a mere motorcycle producer was unable to influence a world economic slump, and no improvement in the quality of the end product could remedy it. Even Yamaha lost £80 million in 1983 alone.

When V50 imports to Britain began in April 1979, there were no signs of the forthcoming economic storm and the first models were priced at £1,475, dropping to £1,299 in August when production at Innocenti really came on stream. The reduction in price reflected the confidence inspired by what were record Guzzi sales in the UK and, of course, the lower production costs. But dealers and customers were far from happy, and the V50 (Series II) was generating a large number of warranty claims. The only good thing that could be said was that these claims were restricted to a small number of components, but each of them was annoyingly common. These included failure of the flanges and oil seals in the final drive, the front fork oil seals, and the ignition switch. Also, the finish of the motorcycle was poor and could be truly appalling, with whole flakes of paint falling off the plastic side-panels (self-coloured in red!). None of these panels appeared to have been prepared for painting in any way and, when they flexed, the paint simply lost all adhesion to the shiny surface underneath; a very basic error, which should have been foreseen. All this contrasted sharply with the continuing rave press reviews. Yes, there was no doubt that the V50 (and V35) remained a joy to ride – providing they didn't break down and that the owner didn't mind if the paint fell off, which unfortunately happened far too often.

By the middle of 1980, these problems were beginning to affect sales; word had got around. In an attempt to counter the by-now drastic drop in sales and update the machine, a new version was introduced later that same year. Known as the V50 III, it had a much superior level of finish, both in terms of paintwork and plating. The front mudguard (which had previously been in steel, and thus rust-prone in northern climates) was replaced by a plastic component. A new headlamp with a quartz bulb was also specified. The cable-operated front brake master cylinder was moved from its original location under the fuel tank to a more conventional position on the handlebars, adjacent to the lever, which now operated it directly. There were lots of other cosmetic changes, including indicators, brake discs, saddle, fuel filler cap and many detail points. More importantly, there were changes to rectify the existing weak areas. The V50 II had suffered from an annoying flat spot, which might have been put down to carburation, but was in fact a design failing within the German Bosch electronic ignition system. To cure this. Guzzi resorted to replacing the electronic module with a pair of ancient-technology contact breakers and condensers.

The various modifications vastly improved the machine, gave superior reliability, increased overall performance and even, in my opinion, improved handling. The maximum speed had risen from just over the ton to a genuine 105mph, but more importantly, and more usefully, the level of acceleration was better.

Strangely, the latest V35 was coded II, not III, but was just as improved. When testing a V35 II in late 1984, I found it slightly quicker than the original, with a maximum speed of 93mph (2mph up on the original model) and although no faster than many touring Japanese 250 twins, it nevertheless offered an almost ideal lightweight sports/tourer for the mature rider who had no need for excess power. In fact, I have to say that the V35 II is my personal favourite of the entire range of middleweight Guzzi V-twins.

Sadly, however, the damage had been done for the V50 III (and its V35 II brother). In the UK, at least, (where only the V50 version was imported officially), sales of the revised machines were a mere fraction of what had been achieved by the ill-fated V50 II, and in my opinion this was a great shame, for these were very attractive motorcycles. One of my customers had purchased a second-hand Honda 400F four, but he soon brought it back, complaining that it had no performance. My staff could find absolutely nothing wrong with the Japanese bike, even though they eventually stripped the engine – but the complaints kept coming, which in due course reached me. I agreed to visit the customer and test the machine. I made the journey on a Guzzi V50, which the customer rode out with me while I tested his Honda. I couldn't find anything wrong with the Honda, so I asked a lot of questions and discovered that the trouble lay with his last mount, of many years ago. This had been a heavyweight AJS single and he was trying to ride the Honda like his old British bike, putting it into top gear at 30mph. The poor Honda was suffering from transmission snatch and a decided lack of power at this engine speed. Meanwhile, the customer found that he simply loved my Guzzi, its power characteristics being very similar to his old AJS. He didn't want the Honda back and part-exchanged it for a new V50 – job done.

With their potential for modular development, Guzzi's new middleweight contenders were ultimately to spawn a larger 650cc V65 and, later still, the 750cc V75 series in touring, sports, custom and even off-road guises. By this time, I had been forced to close down my dealership. However, my association with Moto Guzzi continued – as almost as many of my early books were on the marque as they were on my first love, Ducati. Later, due to demand, I produced more literature on these Italian classics, including the various editions of the *Illustrated Buyer's Guide, Moto Guzzi V-Twins: The Complete Story* and *Moto Guzzi Twins Restoration*, while I remained involved with Guzzi through its excellent UK Owners Club. I was their guest of honour at the May 2010 Rally in Shropshire, where I gave a talk to club members followed by a question-and-answer session. It's always enjoyable to share an enthusiasm with like-minded people – and what a fantastic group of people the brotherhood of motorcyclists really is. This wonderful day was one of my last public engagements before illness prevented these activities.

Moto Guzzi V7 Sport

SPORT

7

A New Breed

I was proud to say that I had been there at the start of it all

Schiranna factory, Lake Varese, Northern Italy

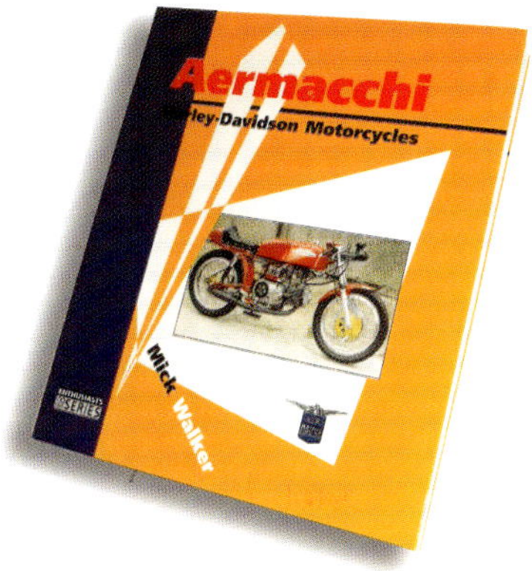

In 1974, I added a new brand to my company's stable, forging a link with the long line of motorcycles made in Varese, a small provincial town near the Swiss border in northern Italy. Dating back to 1912, the factory in Varese was the home of one of the great pioneers of the aeronautical industry before the emphasis changed to making motorcycles, after the Second World War.

The company Società Anonima Nieuport Macchi was set up by Giulio Macchi to build French Nieuport aircraft under licence, but would later change its name to Aeronautica Macchi, or 'Aermacchi', when it branched out into more general aircraft construction. Virtually all its early aircraft were seaplanes; hence the famous lakeside Schiranna works on the outskirts of Varese, which became the home of the Schneider Trophy-winning seaplanes and world speed-record breaking MC72 of the inter-war era.

In the aftermath of the Second World War, Aermacchi, like other firms in Germany and Italy, was banned from building aircraft. As far back as 1943, the Varese company had taken its first step towards motorcycle manufacture with the construction of a prototype two-wheeler, which surprisingly, was electric-powered. Anticipating a postwar motorcycle boom and keen to have a share in it, Aermacchi decided that they needed to offer an attractive lightweight. They offered the job of designing it to Lino Tonti, who had worked on aircraft engines during the war years and also had experience at Benelli. The Aermacchi site, with its massive aircraft hangar and slipway, would be the headquarters for motorcycle production.

Tonti's first design, which appeared in 1950, was decidedly unorthodox, being a strange mixture of scooter and motorcycle with a 125cc two-stroke engine. A few years later, Tonti was replaced by Alfredo Bianchi – whose first design, called the Chimera, featured a single-cylinder ohv four-stroke power unit with a horizontal cylinder and a built-in gearbox, wrapped up in enveloping bodywork. It was launched in a blaze of publicity at the International Milan Show in November 1956, but by 1958 Aermacchi had concluded that the staid-looking roadster would never sell in sufficient quantity. So Bianchi 'undressed' the Chimera to reveal the 175cc Ala Rossa and 250cc Ala Verde ('red wing' and 'green wing') sportsters, which shared many of the Chimera's technical features. These sold well and were extremely successful, going on to spawn a successful line of racers.

The next development was one of the strangest of all motorcycle company marriages, involving Italian Aermacchi and American Harley-Davidson as partners. At first, this seemed an unlikely pairing, with Aermacchi's reputation being built on small, lean, lightweight machines, while Harley-Davidson was famous for its heavyweight, large-capacity cruisers. However, the motorcycle division of Aeronautica Macchi sold half its share capital to the Americans for $247,209 in April 1960, with the first motorcycles being delivered to the States in September of that year, well in time for the 1961 season. (Aermacchi's aircraft division, which had got back into production when the post-war ban was lifted, was not part of the deal, and continues making aeroplanes to this day.)

The first Italian-built Harley-Davidson model was the Sprint C, named the Wisconsin, after HD's home state. Essentially this was the European Ala Bianca ('white wing') 250 touring bike, which itself was closely based on the Ala Verde sportster and the Ala d'Oro ('gold wing') road racer. By the end of the decade, the Aermacchi range stretched from a 50cc two-stroke to a 350cc four-stroke. A range of competition bikes was also on offer in 125, 250 and 350cc guises. Although the horizontal-cylinder ohv single was still being built, the factory was mainly concentrating on two-strokes. 1972 saw Harley-Davidson purchase the remaining shares to gain 100 per cent ownership of the Varese plant, with the motorcycle output being subsequently badged as AMF HD. The AMF stood for American Machine & Foundry, which was principally a manufacturer of bowling alley equipment.

The new parent company soon realised that besides its American base, it needed to mount a serious sales push into Europe, and so AMF International established its marketing headquarters in Switzerland. This division operated separately from the manufacturing facilities in Varese. In late spring 1974, a British base was set up in London, with a spares warehouse in Whitstable, Kent doubling-up as the storage depot for AMF's bowling alley operation.

'Harleys in Britain!' exclaimed *Motor Cycle*, on 29 June 1974. It went on to explain: 'The first of the new Harley-Davidsons to emerge from the Italian factory, formerly Aermacchi, is a stylish 250cc two-stroke single, the SX250, first examples of which are just reaching this country'. Harley's full range, including the American-made V-twins, now ranged from tiddlers to the mighty V-twins: X90, Z90, SX125, SX175, SX250, SS350, XLCH 1000, FX 1200 Super Glide and the 'Big Daddy', the 1200cc Electra Glide. AMF International's new UK operation split the country between seven dealers: Fred Warr (Central and West London), Pratt's Vintage Motorcycle Co (South East London), Park Motorcycles (North London), Peters of Luton (Bedfordshire and Northamptonshire), Dawson's of Scarborough (North East England), Knotts of Manchester (North West England) and my own company Mick Walker Motorcycles (East Anglia).

The 1974 X90 mini-bike, smallest of the Harley-Davidson range built by Aermacchi.

A 1974 SX250 trail bike, the first Italian Harley model to enter Britain.

So why had I become one of AMF's dealers? Well, there is more than one answer. To begin with, in spring 1974 I had only one major agency: Ducati. Secondly, during my road racing days I had always aspired to own an Aermacchi, although I never got around to it. Thirdly, AMF's representative came to visit my Wisbech showroom riding an SX350, and I loved that bike. Unfortunately, it was to be the one model of the Harley-Davidson range for 1974 that was not imported. The SS350 street bike was, compared to the Aermacchi horizontal singles of old, somewhat heavy and ugly, whereas the SX trail bike was much better designed, with a lusty four-stroke engine that was ideal for its task as a green-lane mount. Also, in the black, chrome and polished aluminium finish of the rep's bike, it shone out as something of a style icon, meeting the Italians and the Americans halfway. After a blast round the back roads of Wisbech, I was hooked. I reckoned that the Italian flair mixed with the HD quality had to be a winner. How wrong I was. Yes there were bright spots, notably the tiny X90 mini-bike, but unfortunately most of the Italian-made bikes' quality was simply not good enough in service, even though all of them (except the X90) had 12-volt electrics and all the two-stroke engines employed a Japanese-made Mikuni oil pump. At that time, every other Italian-made lightweight 'stroker relied on a messy petroil mixture and feeble 6-volt electrics.

I sold a fair number of the HD lightweights, plus a handful of the big, lumbering 'tractor division' V-twins. But soon two problems emerged; poor finish and, more importantly, an appalling lack of spare parts. This caused major difficulties, because we were often unable to fix a warranty claim quickly, sometimes for many weeks. Finally, after around nine months, I reluctantly decided to chuck the agency in – not because the bikes didn't go well and handle well, but because of AMF's terrible track record on spare parts.

Three years went by, and in late 1977 my company was having problems with Coburn & Hughes over the exclusive nature of our agreement and the general retail cost of Ducati and Moto Guzzi parts. AMF International had long since withdrawn from the British market and my company had been approached to take over the UK import of the Varese factory's model range. This now consisted exclusively of two-strokes: 125, 175, and 250cc models in roadster and trail guises. We were also told of the forthcoming motocross and enduro version of the larger-engined machine. Were we interested? After visits to the works in Italy, I decided that we were. The old chestnut of the spare parts deficiencies was looked into and soon scotched. A check of parts availability – my prime concern – showed up as virtually 100 per cent in stock, while the machines themselves appeared to be better finished.

Next came the question of how to set up the operation. This was ultimately achieved by building a duplicate parts centre at my 22,000 sq ft Wisbech premises. Essentially, this was a second floor put in on top of the existing Ducati/Moto Guzzi warehouse. Actually the local council planners forced us to build a mezzanine lined with asbestos as a fire retardant. I was dead against this, but the authorities were adamant. In the long run I was proved right and just to mention the word asbestos today is enough for the current generation of planners to throw their arms up in horror.

So, in 1978, the Mick Walker Harley-Davidson operation began trading, with the appointment of the first dealers. Most of these I picked myself, and as with the Ducati and Moto Guzzi dealers, I visited them on a regular basis. They included Geoff Monty (Edenbridge, Kent), Len Bayliss (Coventry), John George, father of racing star Alex George (Glasgow), John Harris (East Sussex), and Eddie Cordle (Ipswich). Even today, decades later, the principals of these and other companies still tell me how they appreciated my personal attention to their needs. It was also a way of keeping a finger on the pulse of the operation. If a dealer had a problem he could tell me. I know I'm not alone in my frustration when things go wrong and I'm told, 'refer to our website'.

I felt the Harley-Davidson name was an asset that would help market the range of motorcycles successfully – and with the 'Volkswagen-type backup' (as *Which Bike?* described the Wisbech spares operation), we should have been OK. Vicki Michelle, star of television's 1982-92 comedy series 'Allo 'Allo!' was an employee of mine during the late 1970s and early 1980s, and she featured in our Harley-Davidson advertising campaigns. She also made several appearances for me at shows, which included the annual big one at London's Earls Court.

Vicki also featured in my 'Harley-Davidson leathers' campaign, which was particularly successful. Run in 1978 for a limited period, every buyer of a new Harley Davidson Varese-built model received a full set of one-piece leathers, manufactured by Ketts of Northampton. Vicki later presented me with a 6-piece table mat set, with six different colour photographs of her with a Harley model; I still have these today, almost 35 years later. The only problem I had with Vicki was dealing with her fan mail. One particular guy was an absolute nuisance. I finally got rid of him, but I'm not prepared to repeat what I said to do it.

Badge engineering? HD Cagiva prototype based on a 350 Aermacchi flat-single, sleeved-down to 250cc.

The famous table mats

Things had started well but, unfortunately, only six months after signing a five-year agreement with AMF, they dropped a bombshell: they were to close the Varese operation. The first I heard about it was via the press in May 1978. I had invested heavily in the operation – a quarter-of-a-million pounds, in fact – and I should have withheld the payment of any outstanding AMF debts, as the Americans had conned me into an agreement that they almost certainly knew would never run its full term. We had a few months instead of the promised five years. So what was I to do? Not only did I have a problem with the actual investment, but I had 50 employees relying on the operation, which included the Guzzi/Ducati parts business, the Mick Walker Motorcycles retail company, together with the sale of various Italian makes which included Ducati, Guzzi, and the HD lightweights, plus the recent acquisition of the Suzuki franchise.

The Varese factory was put into liquidation in late July 1978, when the whole of Italy traditionally closes down for the four weeks' annual holiday. During this time, an ambitious new company, Cagiva, emerged as the clear favourite amongst the interested bidders, which included me. When Cagiva became the new owners that autumn, one of the first projects mooted was a couple of horizontal singles based on the old Aermacchi design. There was a touring model as well as a sportster, which featured enclosed disc brakes and Campagnolo alloy wheels. Neither got past the mock-up stage, and even in that form, the saddles were actually made of wood.

Although the switch to the Cagiva name didn't seem to affect sales in Italy, it most certainly did in the UK. Customers and dealers were familiar with Harley-Davidson, but most could not even pronounce the name of the new marque properly – being unsure whether to say 'cadge-eva' or 'cag-ivor' and all sorts of other variations. The first Cagiva UK dealer meeting, held at Mendi's Restaurant in Wisbech didn't get off to a good start either. The Italian factory's sales manager Luigi Giacometti presented the new company logo, which was a white elephant. I explained to Luigi that in Britain, this was an emblem of failure and not a very good idea. Since that meeting, the Cagiva elephant has always been a shade of grey! Vicki Michelle would switch from the Harley-Davidson campaign to advertise Cagiva, and today her best-remembered ads are the Cagiva 'Elephant' series.

At the time, however, the name remained a problem. In an attempt to improve matters, and for one year only, the tank decals were revised to read HD Cagiva. Even so, several UK dealers simply replaced them with Harley-Davidson decals from our spares stock. As the machines were still known as Harley-Davidson by the DVLA licensing authority, and the HD name continued to be used on the V5 registration document, we got off to a somewhat shaky start, but there was some light at the end of the tunnel. 1978 had seen the first of some new models, the 350 SST roadster and the SX trail bikes. These were an attempt to offer a wider range and bridge the gap left by the departed SS/SX350 four-strokes. However, although the pre-production handbuilt prototypes showed an excellent turn of speed (over 90mph) and a high level of reliability, production versions were a disappointment. They vibrated and were prone to engine seizure, something the smaller models would never do.

Announcing the lightweight with the heavyweight back-up...
HD CAGIVA
HD CAGIVA
-it's the new name in Italian lightweights. And
ame you'll choose – for its exciting and stylish
s the name you'll choose too
vyweight back-up of
e parts and spares service,
r twenty six appointed
s.
Cagiva . . . say it KA-GEE-VA. And just say it once. Cagiva
will be your choice from then on. And your choice will be
from the exhilarating range of trail
bikes – 125's to 250's, and the rugged
'fuel miser' road bikes from 125's up
to the powerful 350 model.
Cagiva and you. It's a natural.
Mick Walker Group
236 Norwich Road, Wisbech. Tel: 61523 and 65291

LA MOTO ITALIANA

During the early days of Cagiva in 1979, several dealers would simply tell the customers who had a complaint to phone the importers – in other words, to ring my company in Wisbech. A typical example came when I was sitting at my office desk one fine morning and my secretary informed me that she had a lady on the telephone who had a problem. Her young son Jimmy – who owned a Harley-Davidson/Cagiva SXT125 trail bike – had seized it. Knowing that this problem was either down to using an incorrect oil or no oil at all, I asked her to find out what lubricant Jimmy had been feeding his engine with. A couple of days later, the lady phoned again; she had found out – it was Fairy Liquid. After a moment, with visions of bubbles frothing from the exhaust, I said that Fairy Liquid might be excellent for washing dishes, but the same could not be said for its lubrication properties in a motorcycle engine. I felt sorry for the by-now tearful lady on the other end of the telephone, so I agreed to go halfway on the cost of parts and labour to rectify the problem; another satisfied customer...

Mick Walker, of Cagiva importing fame, has launched an extensive new advertising campaign and whenever possible it will include the lists of dealers — at no cost to the dealer! Several top riders are being talked to about competing on Cagivas for 1982 to supplement existing sponsored riders. Assistance is also given to dealers wishing to race enduro or motocross machines; next year such dealers will be known and publicised as Team Cagiva dealers.

All new models are to have names rather than alpha numeric designations. Space (Rocket, Red- Flash, Silver Streak) will provide names for off-road models while classic aircraft names will be attached to street and trail models. Some examples are Gladiator, Hunter, Fury and Hurricane.

The new range consists of four street and trail bikes from 125-350 cc, two fully street legal enduros (125 and 250 cc) and three motocrossers (two 125's and a 250).

John George

The father of 1970s/80s racing legend Alex George, was a great character in his own right. The first time I visited him at his dealership in Glasgow I was a bit shocked, as his premises were in the middle of a major redevelopment programme and looked more like a bombsite. When I was editor of *Motorcycle Enthusiast* I carried out an interview with Alex, only to discover that he had started his racing career illegally – when he was just 16 – with the Ducati 175 Formula 3 that I had traded in to Vic Camp in January 1966. Alex never had any trouble with the machine, but could not remember who the next owner had been.

Eddie Cordle

Best described as a piece of living history, Eddie Cordle's business would not have been out of place in the 1930s. It was the reverse of the glossy, soulless modern motorcycle supermarkets. One had to clamber over bikes, spares, accessories and heaven knows what else inside Eddie's 'showroom', but Eddie was a character, and I greatly enjoyed every visit. He was also a leading trials rider in the Eastern Centre.

Team Cagiva Dealers

Geoff Monty

During my own racing career in the 1960s, I had some dealings with Geoff Monty and his Twickenham shop in West London. Ten years earlier, Geoff and his friend (and later business partner) Allen Dudley-Ward were well-known racers – not only in Britain but also in the Continental Circus. By the time I encountered them, they had become the legendary Monty & Ward, with Geoff running the retail side of the business and Allen, who specialised in race tuning, the engineering division. Besides focusing on sports and road racing machines, Geoff also sponsored a number of riders, notably Tommy Robb and later Bill Ivy. Monty & Ward became the first British Yamaha agents, dealing with the roadsters and the TD1 and TD1A road racers. In the early 1970s, Geoff closed the Twickenham shop and moved to Edenbridge, Kent, but he and his wife continued to trade as Monty & Ward.

Len Bayliss

Len was a great guy. Because of his experiences during the war, he would have nothing to do with Japanese bikes: instead he stuck to British and Italian products. I knew him through his connection with Ducati (as a dealer), but he wanted some smaller bikes, so he became an HD (and later a Cagiva) agent for me. Sadly, at the time I hadn't realised that Len had been one of the leading 250cc class racers on British short circuits in the immediate post-war period, with his Elbee Special. Len was a modest person and would never have boasted of his racing successes, which is why I didn't know about them.

John Harris

John Harris Motorcycles has been at Whitehill Road, Crowborough, East Sussex for 36 years and John is very much one of the old school (like myself I suppose), always happy to meet customers and have customers know who he is, rather than being a faceless wonder. John phoned me in January 2011 about some spares he needed. Afterwards, he sent a letter that contained these memories of the Cagiva days, and one of racing's all-time greats:

'Restoring this HD Cagiva had me thinking back to the days when you imported them and I became one of your dealers. The motorcycle world was then so different; those were happy days – such a contrast to the retail motorcycle world of today.

'The Cagivas, apart from the electrical problems, were fine machines, handling and performing well, whilst the Cagiva dealerships were an enthusiastic bunch; it was like being part of a large motorcycle family, again so different to the retail world now.

'Let me bring you up to date; in the mid 1980s we became Honda dealers and in 1987 sponsored Ray Knight with a CBR 600 Supercup machine in the production events at the Isle of Man TT. We helped Ray for a number of years and then in 1991 we were asked by Honda UK if they could loan our CBR 600 Supercup machine (then being ridden by Gary Weston) for none other than Joey Dunlop to ride at the TT that year. And so began a beautiful friendship with Joey until that fateful day on 2nd July 2000. I had flown out to Estonia to give him a helping hand – he raced our 600 on Saturday, won the race, and then on the Sunday – the unthinkable happened. Joey lost his life in the 125 event. You know, many people have asked me what Joey was like. I have always replied that if ever one wanted a role model in life there could be no better person; a thoroughly honest, decent individual, totally without an ego despite being a superstar. It's ten and a half years since that tragic day and I still miss him terribly.

'So there you are Mick, I hope these words have been of some help; it has indeed been a pleasure to write this letter. Thank you for the Cagiva days. And I do hope that you get well again soon.'

When Cagiva first came into being, no one could have predicted that in little over three years it would become Italy's largest motorcycle manufacturer, or that in 1981 the SST125 (derived from the old HD model) would become the top seller in the all-important 125 class of the domestic market. Meanwhile, Cagiva's engineers had designed a brand-new 125 motocross bike, which in 1980 became the world's first liquid-cooled production dirt-bike racer. This became my introduction to the world of Schoolboy Motocross. Before then, I had little experience of the motocross scene, other than a few outings on a Velocette 500 scrambler back in Aden during the 1960s. But Cagiva already had a good reputation based on the excellent MXR 250 dirt racer, and early in 1980 my company imported a single example of the newly released 125cc Cagiva motocrosser, which had first appeared in prototype form late the previous year.

It's now clear that Cagiva had stolen a major lead over the entire Japanese industry in the highly competitive 125 motocross market. However, at that time, the Cagiva name was little known – and even less so its new offspring, the WMX125 motocrosser. But I had one sitting in its crate awaiting collection by a customer from Elgin in northern Scotland and eventually, to satisfy our curiosity, we decided to have a look in the crate. What a surprise awaited us. Here was the sleekest dirt-bike racer I had ever seen. It was soon uncrated, assembled and taken for a test session, and it immediately became apparent what a truly superb little bike it was, going on to cause a sensation everywhere it went during the final two months of the 1980 racing season.

Schoolboy Motocross was entirely different to any other form of motorcycle competition in which I had been involved. As the name implies, this was a sport for young lads, but what I did not fully appreciate was the heavy involvement of the parents or, indeed, other family members. One of the first and lasting impressions I got when first arriving at the venue (on the side of a mountain it seemed) was of a grandmother running alongside a 6-year old cadet, screaming advice (abuse?) at the youngster, using words that would have been embarrassing in a rugby changing room.

My involvement was restricted to the 125 class of the Senior and Expert divisions – the top two disciplines in the sport – where I watched many fathers becoming very vocal and ambitious for their sons. What we had here was the birth of 'Schoolboy Motocross Syndrome' – a phrase I coined to describe the situation. I quickly realised that Schoolboy Motocross was very fashion-conscious, and that money was no object to the Dads, many of whom were successful businessmen in their own right. Winning was all that mattered to the vast majority of these well-off parents. Obviously there were exceptions to the rule, and it was sad to see the talented kids who had less well-heeled parents going to waste, so I sponsored two riders that year: Mathew Skeets in the Experts category and Steven Jones in the Senior division.

For the last two months of 1980, we simply could not get enough bikes. The demand for them was totally unexpected, but not surprising. Firstly the machine's liquid cooling made it revolutionary; secondly, it was a race winner in the right hands. But of course things move quickly in competitive bike developments: Honda, Yamaha, Kawasaki and Suzuki all débuted liquid-cooled production 125 motocrossers for the 1981 season, making things much harder for the Italian marque in terms of sales. Even so, because of the victories of the previous year we managed to do reasonably well. In little over a year, Mick Walker Motorcycles managed to sell around 350 WMX125s, but although Cagiva won the top award in Schoolboy Motocross in 1981 – much to the surprise of the big Japanese factories – the factory's inability to produce anything other than a 125 for the schoolboy sector was a major issue and after I quit the scene in 1982, Cagiva was caught napping. That year the Italian company stood still – a year is a lifetime in the rapid development world of off-road racing. I had told Cagiva that the next development needed to be an improved rear suspension system with a single shock, but they ignored my advice, and in 1982 the Japanese offered single-shock rear suspension, while Cagiva stuck to what was by then considered to be the old-fashioned twin-shock swinging arm.

Next season, Cagiva fought back with their intriguingly titled 'Soft Damp' rear suspension system, a reaction to the new Japanese products: 'Mono-shock' (Yamaha), 'Full Floater' (Suzuki), 'Pro-link' (Honda) and 'Uni-trak' (Kawasaki). Also in 1983, Cagiva began to take a serious interest in the 125cc World Motocross championship and the factory machines were painstakingly developed throughout the next two years in the intensely competitive atmosphere of Grand Prix racing. In 1985, Cagiva won the 125 crown for the first time, and in the process scored a major publicity coup. I was proud to say that I had been there at the start of it all.

As the 1980s unfolded, Cagiva began swallowing up other marques, including Moto Morini, Husqvarna, CZ and, its biggest scalp of all, Ducati. It even purchased the rights to the legendary MV Agusta brand name. In the 1990s everything started to go wrong, and with debts mounting, Cagiva was forced to sell off Ducati and cease production of both Moto Morini and CZ. However, by the end of the 1990s it had managed to reorganise the company and relaunch the MV brand, with its magnificent new four-cylinder engine, financed by the sale of Ducati to the Americans.

The MV Agusta F4

In spring 1999, I became the first person outside the staff of the British importers Three Cross to ride the new MV Agusta F4 on British roads. This came about because of my past involvement as race-team manager for Three Cross, and because its boss Keith Davies was a long-standing personal friend. I had already seen the limited-production, ultra-expensive F4 Serie Oro and the series production F4S at shows, so knew what to expect visually – or so I thought. However, meeting a Serie Oro in the flesh so to speak, outside a show hall, was an altogether different experience. I thought it was a truly magnificent piece of engineering that made every other street-legal motorcycle seem old hat – even the Ducati 916 Fogarty Replica, which I had tested a few months earlier.

But what would the MV be like to ride? Having been an MV dealer in the 1970s, I was absolutely certain that the F4 would be nothing like the old air-cooled models of over two decades earlier, and I was fully expecting that the visual experience would not be matched by the riding one. However, I was not disappointed, as the F4 proved to be as good in practical terms as it was from the styling and technical viewpoint.

What I discovered immediately was that here was a motorcycle designed and built by motorcyclists. Everything was in exactly the right place and it all worked. Massimo Tamburini (the man who created the Ducati 916) had got things right, with a capital R.

Accelerating away from rest, the engine struck the heart with its smoothness, useful power and the wonderful noise it made – while the six-speed cassette gearbox was truly superb, like a hot knife through butter. The brakes were powerful, yet exceedingly safe in their operation. The handling and roadholding gave the rider supreme confidence. It immediately felt that if racing tyres were fitted, the lights taped up and the sidestand removed, you could actually go racing with it – the MV felt that good. I also found myself downshifting the gears just to experience the glorious howl from the free-revving engine. But the biggest surprise was just how flexible the engine was, for I was fully expecting it to need constant cog-swapping. However, it was possible to drop the liquid-cooled unit down to 30mph in top and accelerate cleanly away (full throttle at this speed is not advised).

Most of the day-long test session took place in Dorset on relatively traffic-free minor B roads. The F4 was quite at home, and even at these relatively low speeds, the riding position was comfortable. Obviously, it did not have the armchair ride of a Honda Gold Wing or even a CBR1000, but by the standards of a single-purpose sports bike, it was excellent. All the ancillary equipment, including the instrumentation, switchgear and electrical components seemed to be top-class – an area where past Italian sports bikes have been sadly let down. As for attention to detail, this could only be described as breathtaking, and it took photographer Vic Bates and me at least three times longer than usual to record all the F4's features. The quickly detachable front and rear wheels, the sculptured lines, the superb aluminium castings, the curvaceous exhaust, the star-like wheels and the ultra-clean and precise welding of the steel frame; there were even a couple of coloured buttons on the swinging arm to adjust the ride height. Perhaps the only area where I thought an improvement could be made was that I was worried that the side stand (there being no main stand) might dig in and the F4 would fall off its perch. As I was riding the £25,000 limited-production F4 Serie Oro, damage was always uppermost in my mind, not helped by a 'bring it back as you took it' warning from Keith Davies. Compared to the standard F4S, the Serie Oro featured a gold instead of grey finish for the swinging arm and rear subframe assemblies; carbon-fibre bodywork instead of heavier fibreglass; aluminium floating-disc flanges for the front brakes (instead of steel); and magnesium wheels replacing the aluminium ones. There were some less-noticeable differences, such as the colour of the front mudguard support and adjustable foot controls. But the mechanical specification of the engine unit together with the suspension package were the same for both versions. Back in 1999, I posed the question was the near-double price of the Serie Oro over the F4S really worth it? 'The truthful answer is no, but of course someone who can afford £25,000 instead of £13,000 will probably not notice the difference. He will also be able to boast that his MV is identical to the ones owned by Claudio Castiglioni (the company boss), Giacomo Agostini and King Carlos of Spain.'

8 A Writing Career

I never intentionally set out to be a writer

It all started by chance in spring 1982, when I had some spare time on my hands (something that hadn't happened for many years). However, shortly after my company had folded, I decided to attend the Ducati Owners Club Rally for the first time. That year, it was held in the showrooms of Manchester-based Sports Motorcycles, where I was soon recognised by John Fairclough, then a journalist for *Motorcycle Enthusiast* magazine. John approached me with the idea that I could help him with material for a series of articles on Ducati to appear in *MCE*.

Over six months passed before I heard any more about the project. Then Howard Lindley, the owner of *MCE*, called to inform me that John was no longer working for the magazine, but as he was still interested in the Ducati features, would I be interested in writing them? This was a surprise, as the nearest I had ever come to anything like this was being interviewed by Bill Haylock a few years earlier for a Ducati singles article in the very earliest days of *Classic Bike*. Other than that I'd last written stories at primary school. Had Howard asked me to do something on any other marque, I would have said no – but because it was about Ducati, I agreed.

Howard visited me in Wisbech and proceeded to read my handwritten manuscript. I fully expected him to say it was a load of rubbish and disappear. Instead, he was genuinely enthusiastic, and so began a completely new stage of my life. Nevertheless, I certainly never envisaged what result this series of articles would lead to. Mick Walker the author has a lot to thank John Fairclough and Howard Lindley for.

The puny 6-volt flywheel magneto that let down my *MCE* road-test Suzuki GN400.

My first Ducati article appeared in the February 1983 issue of *MCE* and the series ran for 20 issues. Then Howard asked me to do a road test on a Suzuki GN400. As I owned an example myself, this was to be no 'round-the-block' effort, but a proper test report. In many ways, the Suzuki was an excellent bike, its engine being based on the thoroughly well-sorted DR400, which originated from its older brother – the SP370. Both the DR and SP were off-road bikes, but the GN was a pure roadster. What spoiled it was the continued use of the puny 6-volt flywheel-magneto electrics that might have been just about acceptable on the trail bikes, but were simply not good enough for a serious touring machine – a very non-Japanese omission. It also had another glaring fault – a bad habit of refusing to start when hot, which could be extremely embarrassing after refuelling at the pumps.

The second bike I tested for the magazine was the Moto Morini 500 V-twin, which I collected from the importers Harglo (Wilf Harrison and Peter Glover) in Dorridge, near Solihull in the West Midlands. Actually, I tested two Morini 500s, the Touring (known as Strada in Italy) and the Sport. Both machines had six-speed gearboxes, a first for me. Personally, I preferred the Touring, as it did everything the Sport would do, but in more comfort. In the test I said, 'At the moment I would give the Touring version my vote, although it has to be said that the Sport outsells it at present, which says a lot for the clip-ons and the badge.' Over the next few years, I tested many more bikes for *MCE*, including models from all the world's great motorcycling nations.

Moto Morini 500 Sport

An Italian job

Mandello del Lario, home of Moto Guzzi, formed part of an itinerary organised by the Italian Trade Commission.

Although my new career as a writer led to me working on a huge variety of topics, I maintained particularly close connections with the Italian industry. On one occasion, I was invited by the Italian Trade Commission in London to take part in a two-week adventure with a total of 12 guests from various countries, to visit the Italian motorcycle factories and a selection of accessory manufacturers. We travelled by minibus, staying in a different hotel every night. Among others, we visited Moto Guzzi, Benelli, Gilera, Aprilia and the exhaust manufacturer Lafranconi, at all of which we were wined and dined at lunch and dinner. I was used to the Italians so I paced myself, unlike one of our team, who 'retired' after a few days due to an over-indulgence of the irresistible and plentiful food and wine.

The trip pointed up the contrasts in the Italian industry of the era. One night, we stayed in Venice to visit the nearby Aprilia works – at that time a young, thrusting concern, on the wave of a sales boom. We were all impressed by its modern plant, stylish motorcycles and youthful workforce. By way of contrast, although I'm sure it was not intentional, our next visit was to the sprawling, old-fashioned and rather dingy Moto Guzzi works at Mandello del Lario, where a factory tour was arranged. Leaving the manager's office there was a narrow passage with a few new Guzzi models. It was a cold wintry day and the light was poor. Our American representative asked, 'Gee, are these part of the museum?' He was deadly serious, but as you can imagine, this did not go down too well.

It was a shock when a copy of the May 1983 issue dropped though my letterbox to see that I had been 'promoted' to Assistant Editor. This was totally unexpected, but it did mean that I had to commute monthly to *MCE's* office in Wakefield, where I often had to stay overnight. My role of Assistant Editor and chief road tester for the magazine even saw me venture abroad, bringing back the Ducati 500 Sport Desmo vertical twin in the summer of 1983. However, not long after this came news that Howard was in the process of selling the magazine to another Yorkshire company. I was sorry because I felt, and I still do, that Howard Lindley had played a major role in my career.

I met the new owners in Newark and discovered that my contact was to be Stephanie Hapgood, who lived in St Albans, Hertfordshire. However, before the official takeover there was a major hurdle to be negotiated. The deal would not go ahead unless I agreed to become the Editor. I accepted, mainly, I must say, because I didn't want to see *MCE* disappear. At around the same time, I was offered the editorship of nothing less than *Classic Bike*. It was obvious that *CB* was in the Premier League compared to the Wakefield-based magazine, but I never seriously considered the offer, because it would have meant working in Peterborough full-time. Not only did I have the responsibility of a partnership with my brother Rick in our ongoing Ducati spares business, but something else had happened just before the *MCE* takeover.

In July 1983, after returning from Italy with the Ducati, I was confronted by a heap of mail, and a number of telephone calls to return. One was from Tim Parker, a name I wasn't familiar with at the time, although that would change very soon. When I called the number back, it turned out to be Osprey Publishing, where Tim was the Commissioning Editor, and I quickly discovered that he wanted to send me a contract for a book entitled *Ducati Singles*.

I had no inkling that this would be a historic day, and that this one call would lead to so many other books. Osprey was producing a series entitled the 'Collector's Library', and Tim explained that his problem was finding 'quality' motorcycle authors who could write definitive histories. It appeared that he didn't rate conventional bike journalists who had come up through the mainstream press, so had decided to approach knowledgeable marque specialists instead. Actually, this policy was only to achieve limited success, and Tim was to discover that although all the specialists had the knowledge, many of them could not transfer it into a presentable manuscript. After Tim Parker crossed the Atlantic to join the Motorbooks organisation, Tim's successor, Lydia Greeves, asked me to read a manuscript written by another marque specialist (who will remain nameless). Suffice it to say that it was absolutely dreadful. Instead of splitting the story into chapters with an obvious narrative structure, and including the relevant models where they fitted in to the chronology, the author had included every model in every chapter. The story darted all over the place and was virtually unreadable. Lydia asked me if I could lick it into shape, but I reported back that the only way to do this was to start again from scratch.

At Cadwell Park, 1988, with a racing 250 Desmo

During the summer of 1984, Tim Parker came to Wisbech to take delivery of the manuscript of *Ducati Singles*. I had written 12 chapters, and had invited Bruno Spaggiari, the ex-Ducati works rider from 1955-74 (who, at that time, had probably more victories than any other rider on the Bologna machines) to write the foreword. I had also prepared a detailed appendix that included specifications, colours, carburettor settings, prices and model recognition – very much in Osprey's 'house style' pioneered by Roy Bacon.

At that time, Roy was Osprey's main author as far as motorcycles were concerned, although he concentrated mainly on British bikes, plus the odd Japanese title. Roy was a well-established author, having been writing since the late 1960s, where I was very much the beginner, and learning from his approach gave me confidence in those early Osprey days. Roy later moved from London to the Isle of Wight, which distanced him from the mainstream motorcycle and publishing worlds, but maybe this did not matter, as he had decided to branch out and begin to publish his own work as Niton Publishing. However, possibly because of expense, he rarely updated any of his works, so that by the 1990s many of his books were considered out of date.

I first met Roy back at the annual BMF (British Motorcyclists Federation) Rally held at the Peterborough Showground in May 1984. *Motorcycle Enthusiast* had taken a stand with shelves displaying all the remaining past issues of magazines, and I was there in my capacity as editor. I had noticed someone thumbing through the back issues with more than the usual interest, and was just about to go over and talk to him when he came over and introduced himself to me as Roy Bacon. He explained that he was due to meet me (along with Tim Parker) the following day at EMAP (East Midlands Allied Press) headquarters in Peterborough.

My part in this would be to find photographs to illustrate the *Ducati Singles* book. In those days, the old *Motor Cycle* and *Motor Cycling* archives were owned by EMAP (not Mortons, as they currently are), and Tim Parker had an arrangement to use photographs from their library for Osprey titles. Each author would select the images he wanted, and the financial arrangements were taken care of by the publisher.

After accepting the manuscript and picture package for *Ducati Singles*, Tim Parker presented me with a contract for *Ducati Twins*. I had not expected this, but, obviously, Tim felt I had potential as an author. For a while, Andrew Kemp (who was to become a good friend) edited my work, but after half a dozen books, I was to be left to my own devices. While at Osprey Tim commissioned not only the two Ducati titles, but *Spanish Post-War Road & Racing Motorcycles* and *Moto Guzzi Twins* (both published in 1986) together with *Moto Guzzi Singles* and *MV Agusta Production Road & Racing Motorcycles* released in 1987.

At the beginning of 1986, *Motorcycle Enthusiast* had been taken over again, this time by a company headed by Mark Williams, founder of *Bike*, and then the owner/publisher of *Motor Cycle International*. Mark was based in East London, and I visited once a month. The journalists on *MCI* included Julian Ryder, now a TV presenter, and Chris Dabbs who became the chief road tester for *Motor Cycle News*.

Tim Parker

Tim on his 1975 Laverda 750 SFC.

Mick Walker is the nicest man on earth in my opinion. It's both his saving grace and thorn in his side; people take advantage of you when you are like Mick. I first met him in 1973 or '74 when I went to his shop in Wisbech to look at a Moto Guzzi V7 Sport. I didn't buy it but I remembered Mick, smiling and waxing lyrical. I liked him there and then, and often wished I had bought it.

I next 'met' Mick on the pages of Motorcycle Enthusiast. I liked his raw simple prose on bikes I thought I might like. My work at Osprey Publishing in the late 1970s demanded that I source a Ducati book, so I called Mick. He agreed to terms – the most unusual of which was that he would hand write the whole thing – so I fed him the book's specification. Reams of paper soon turned up. He hand-delivered this first manuscript on time, as I recall, riding a Ducati Paso(?) to my office in Covent Garden. I had it typed and Andrew Kemp edited the whole thing with the clear remit 'not to take the Mick out of Mick'. All of a sudden Mick had reinvented himself as a writer.

There has been much criticism of Mick's books over the years. Most of it is hogwash. Mick's service to the motorcycle community is huge. The 'collective we' of the motorcycle enthusiasts at large owe him big. Informative and entertaining. And always smiling. Thank you, Mick.

Tim Parker, publisher of Mick's very first book, Osprey, London.

Andrew Kemp

1953 ALK and 1929 AJS near Montreuil, France.

I feel privileged to have contributed to a handful of Mick's 130+ titles, although I believe I can also claim a unique honour, since I was involved with Mick's first title as well as his most recent.

Mick Walker Motorcycles was part of my motorcycling experience long before I met the man himself, so I was surprised to discover that the founder of such a landmark business had learnt all his technical and entrepreneurial skills along the way, driven purely by his passion for motorcycles. As I quickly learnt when we started working together, Mick's enthusiasm was unequalled, his knowledge was impeccable and his integrity was unquestionable – so it was no surprise that he had reinvented himself as an author and expert whose views are respected worldwide. Mick quickly became a friend who gave freely of information so esoteric it was almost impossible to find in those pre-Internet days. Who could you ask to identify the hot cams for a Ducati Mark 3, find parts for an obscure Harley X90 or a one-off 1930s/1950s Inter hybrid – and much more besides? Mick, that's who.

Mick's unequalled breadth of practical experience means that his books will be avidly consulted as long as people ride and restore motorcycles. Many enthusiasts have gone on to race bikes, others to sell and service them, some have run spares operations, a few have imported motorcycles, a handful have managed a race team… but Mick is perhaps the only one who did all this before even starting on a writing career that has few (if any) parallels.

It is often overlooked how entertaining Mick's stories are. I suspect this is partly due to his modesty (and feeling that his first duty is to satisfy his reader's quest for information), and partly to his desire to protect the feelings of others. I am pleased that telling his own story has allowed him to reveal the lively background to anecdotes touched upon in earlier titles, and that he has felt free to share some tales that might otherwise never have appeared in print. Mick, thanks for everything…

Andrew Kemp, editor of *Ducati Singles*…

For my own part, I had assembled a great team of writers at *MCE* – Frank Westworth, John Fernley, Rosemary Swindells, Barry Hickmott and Phillip Tooth, who became Editor of *Classic Bike*. I felt that *Motorcycle Enthusiast* offered exactly what it said on the strapline: 'For enthusiasts, written by enthusiasts', but in 1987 I decided that the time had come to step down as editor. My workload had increased and there just weren't enough hours in the day. Not only was I looking after *MCE*, but I was writing several books a year, and still running the motorcycle business with my brother Rick. I was also working a day a week as a consultant at Harston Motorcycle Centre, a Cambridge firm.

My final edition of *MCE* was the October 1987 issue, in which I told readers, 'It may come as a surprise to many of you, that I have never been anything more than a "caretaker editor"– even though my stint at the helm has lasted some four years. Even more surprising will be the fact that I never wanted to be the editor in the first place!' But it was not to be a clean break – as I told readers, 'But just in case I, or you, thought that MJG Walker Esq was being put out to grass, publisher Mark Williams has asked me to become the Senior Editor.' I ended my editorial piece by saying, 'The magazine has always had an informality and friendliness about it and the large number of letters received that began "Dear Mick" has only served to reinforce this.' I was to carry on for several more months in my new role, before quitting *MCE* for good. Sadly, not long after, the magazine (by then renamed *Silver Machine*) ceased to exist.

One of the closest friends I have made through my writing career is Rob Carrick, who lives a half-hour drive away. We have completed several books together and his input has been really valuable. Rob's writing career began when he compiled a manuscript on the restoration of the Greeves trials machine that no one was interested in publishing. Osprey said they might be interested in a complete Greeves story but, as Rob put it, 'At that time I considered that a task of this magnitude was beyond my capabilities'. Then, 'A chance meeting with Mick Walker in 1987, at a Snetterton Classic Club meeting, via mutual friend Stu Rogers resulted in me being taken on as Mick's apprentice to co-write the Greeves story for Osprey. The initial meeting between Mick and myself resulted in a draft chapter list, and with Mick's wide road racing experience, he looked after the road and racing chapters together with the illustrations from his extensive archives, with myself completing the off-road chapters and the appendix. This pairing became a co-authorship success which led to other titles also being written together. The next project was the *International Six Days Trial* book for Osprey, a very interesting and informative work that was unfortunately ten years too late, for by this time British interest in the event had sadly waned. This was followed by *British Performance Two-Strokes*, which suffered from the publisher's appalling reproduction.'

Rob also played a key role in *BSA Gold Star*, published in 2004, and when he retired we were able to complete the long-awaited *Villiers – Everybody's Engine* book. Rob explains, 'As this was one of my favourite subjects it was agreed that I should complete the text under the watchful eye of my mentor, with Mick being responsible for the illustrations, captioning and editing. With the publication of this book may I be bold enough to say that Mr Ducati is now a two-stroke fan.'

Rob Carrick

With Rob Carrick - Greeves and Villiers specialist, and off-road enthusiast.

Rob was brought up on motorcycles, but while his father was a Francis-Barnett man, he started riding a pre-war Coventry Eagle 150 on the fields. At the local 10-mile Wansford scrambles track, where the centre of attention was usually Brian Stonebridge's factory Greeves, Rob recalls, 'I always wanted one of those Thundersley flyers with a Villiers engine, but had to be content with a lesser breed… a James K7 Captain'.

In 1958, Rob joined the RAF and was posted to Ballykelly, Northern Ireland, where 203 Squadron flew Shackletons tracking Russian submarines off Norway and Iceland. Rob kept a Dominator 88 and AJS M18CS on the base, and was a regular customer at Campbell Donaghy's motorcycle shop in Limavady. Posted to Akrotiri, on motorcycle-friendly Cyprus in 1963, Rob switched to a Matchless G12CSR. He also rode a Norman 197 off road, and when the original twin-cylinder Anzani blew up, he replaced its engine with a 6E Villiers from a decrepit James. After some time in the Far and Middle East, he was posted back to Norfolk in 1966, purchasing a Vincent Black Shadow for fast roadwork.

Rob was now working as a technical author, writing Canberra service schedules, but found time to gain qualifications in offshore sailing. In 1972, when he moved to RAF Wildenrath, Germany for a tour on Harriers, motorcycling had to take a rest, 'until my return home to Marham in 1974, when I acquired my very first Greeves – this was to start an obsession with the marque'. Rob took a post at Marham's Victor Servicing School, then became a training manager at Upwood, Cambridge. After a final tour in Belize, Central America, he was demobbed in December 1981.

Rob retrained as a teacher, but with no local jobs, he and old RAF buddy Dave Thacker started a motorcycle workshop at Snetterton, which he recalls was '…colloquially known as Honest Rob & Dodgy Dave's'. They specialised in Japanese commuter machines, but Rob never lost his passion for the bikes of his youth, and it was his interest in Greeves that first brought us together professionally.

After 19 years trading, Rob closed his workshop, and until 2006 was a part-time lecturer in Automotive Systems at the College of West Anglia. During the 1990s his interest in Villiers engines – particularly performance versions – saw Rob road-racing a 197 Greeves at events throughout East Anglia, before he switched to a more sedate trio of Greeves trials machines. A long-term member of the Greeves Riders Association, he is now a technical specialist, answering members' queries about Villiers engines.

Rob's many 'outside' activities included founding the well-known Fenman Classic Bike Show with three other enthusiasts in 1989, and he was its chairman for 16 years. All proceeds from the August Bank Holiday event go to local charities and the Fenman has gone from strength to strength, due to its open, friendly atmosphere. In 1992, *Back Street Heroes* called it: '…an event enjoyed by everyone… the entire village of Wimbotsham is overcome with bikes. It does not matter what you arrive on, as long as it's a bike. No one has anything to prove…'

The spirit of the show hasn't suffered as it has grown. I was roped in to judge the concours at the first event and only relinquished my role in the early 1990s when I was heavily involved in my son Gary's racing. When my replacement, trials star Don Smith died, I was recruited back, greatly enjoying the job until I became ill in 2010. The Fenman is unique; where else does an annual motorcycling event involve the whole community for a day?

Doug Jackson of the World's Motorcycles News Agency, an old friend who supplied many wonderful images for my books.

The 1990s was a new era for me. I had left *MCE*, and my consultancy post at the Harston Motorcycle Centre had also ended. Up to that time, Osprey had been my only book publishers. Even though I had received offers from rival firms, loyalty, rather than monetary gain, has always been important to me, and in the early 1980s – thanks in no small part to Tim Parker – Osprey had been at the top in the motorcycle book league and their Collector's Series were best sellers. However, by the end of the decade, Osprey, previously owned by old-established map specialists George Philip & Sons, had been taken over by Reed International, who were not doing too well. This coincided with several publishers approaching me to write for them, and I reluctantly decided that the time was right to move on.

During the 1990s, a busy decade for me, I had a total of 53 titles published by an increasing number of companies. After Osprey, I wrote a couple of titles for Aston and Haynes, and eventually went up to a total of eleven publishers, after the addition of Bison, Crowood, Hamlyn, Millers, Motorbooks (MBI), Redline Books, Transport Source, and Windrow & Greene. Best of all, I never had to chase after any of these companies – they all approached me.

Towards the end of the decade, I received one of my most prestigious commissions of all. From June to September 1998, the world-famous Solomon R. Guggenheim Museum, on Fifth Avenue, New York, staged its most popular exhibition ever: The Art of the Motorcycle attracted over half a million visitors. Spanning over 100 years of the motorcycle, the display included 95 machines, the oldest being the 1894 Hildebrand and Wolfmüller and the newest the 1998 MV Agusta F4.

I was deeply involved with the exhibition and wrote the histories of approximately one third of the machines on display. Most flatteringly of all, I was told I was 'the only person who could have written both the first and last entries'. In truth, I was fascinated by them equally, and by what a century of progress can mean. When one considers that the Hildebrand and Wolfmüller needed 1489cc to generate 2.5bhp at 240rpm giving a top speed of 28mph, while the MV Agusta F4 only needed a displacement of 749cc to achieve 126bhp at 12,200rpm and attain a maximum speed of 171mph, what will the next hundred years bring?

The Art of the Motorcycle was so successful that it was transferred to the Field Museum of Natural History in Chicago from November 1998, before showing at the newly constructed Guggenheim Museum in Bilbao, Spain, in 1999. Later it transferred to Las Vegas. The exhibition was impressive, but so was the catalogue, a heavyweight 432-page hardback that I was proud to have worked on. The photographs, in colour and black and white, were all stunning, reproduced and printed using techniques and materials of the finest quality.

In 1989, on the publication of the 50th Mick Walker book

Friends and Associates

Mick is a man with a huge passion for motorcycling and road racing in particular, and within the sport Mick can take direct credit for the success of many a young rider. His love of all things Italian, especially Latin motorcycles is legendary, as is his special affinity with Bologna's finest, Ducati. And his appetite for writing, with well over 100 books to his name, is without equal. For many years Mick was the Ducati importer and spares distributor. For a time I worked for Ducati importer Moto Cinelli. Mick raced Ducati motorcycles, and so did I. And we have faced personal tragedy and serious illness head on. But the greatest thing we have in common is a love of the best hobby in the world and a passion for a sport without equal. I'm proud to have been able to make this small contribution to your autobiography Mick, and even more proud to call you a friend.

Malcolm Wheeler, Associate Director Mortons Media Group Ltd, Editor *Classic Racer*

Malc Wheeler captured in action aboard the Moto Cinelli Ducati TT2 in the 1984 Isle of Man Formula 2 race

Mallory Park 1971 - Rod Gould, Barry Sheene and Phil Read with Walter Gruber and his 1972 Grand Prix Calendar

Writing 130 books in longhand is a phenomenal achievement. An unrivalled historian of all aspects of motorcycling, Mick's archives are all neatly filed in his amazing memory. Mick, as I did, witnessed first-hand the last great classic era of motorcycle racing, so when he used one of my photographs as the cover picture for his BMW book this was the beginning of a great friendship. Mick is a great expert, but humble and unassuming too. Even though motorcycling resulted in the tragic death of his son Gary in an accident at Brands Hatch, he never lost his love and enthusiasm for the sport. He also continued to write, making a massive contribution to all enthusiasts of our sport.

Wolfgang Gruber, motorcycle photographer

As someone who has had a lifetime of interest in motorcycle racing, I must admit that it was very late in my life that I got to know Mick. I had started the 'I Gotta Gilera Owners Club of Britain' in 2006, I had also purchased some Gilera related books from Mick and thought that maybe he would be able to assist the club in our marquee at the 2007 Festival of 1,000 Bikes at Mallory Park. To my delight Mick accepted and he certainly brought a lot more visitors to our display than we could have hoped for without him. That was my first meeting with Mick and just talking to him made me aware of his total dedication to motorcycle racing. This dedication comes through clearly in his various books and I have learnt a lot from reading them.

I have read various comments regarding the style in which Mick writes and my own view is that he writes from the heart, with knowledge accumulated through his many varied interests within the sport and that he is primarily writing with enthusiasm. This shows abundantly in his various books and to me it gives the impression that Mick was actually present at the events he is writing about. His passion is there for all to see and he shares with his reader the good and the bad that this sport throws up at people. I too am an enthusiast, but there is no way I would be able to transfer that enthusiasm into words and I think Mick deserves the recognition that his prolific writing has given him.

As for Mick the human being, I would like to add that he has had some enormous setbacks of which losing his son must have been the worst possible thing. Mick, however, carried on after that tragic event and now unfortunately has another problem. His deteriorating health is not good, but it certainly hasn't curbed his enthusiasm for the sport and he is again meeting this latest challenge. Mick I salute you.

Paul Tipler, founder of the 'I gotta Gilera' club

The legendary John Surtees, the only man to have won world championship titles on both two and four wheels

The 21st century saw the demands on my services showing no signs of relenting. Because of this, I had to limit the number of publishers I dealt with. I chose a very simple formula: keep the ones I get on with best – in other words, those who made a good job of the finished article, and those with the nicest people. Strangely, the two usually went together. In particular I must mention Alan Wilson of Redline Books, who I met while I was manning the trade stand for Three Cross, the Laverda importer, at the 1996 NEC Birmingham Show. Alan has become one of my closest and most trusted friends and his books are widely recognised as amongst the best for their design and quality.

Crowood Press ranks a close second, and I must mention my original publisher Osprey, for the sheer quantity of my titles that they have published. Then there is Breedon (now trading as Derby Books) with whom I have written the biography series that began with *John Surtees*, as well as *British Racing Circuits Since 1907* (one of my personal favourites) and the Reg Everett story, *From Rocker to Racer*. Several of the editors for the various publishers have also become friends, as have other members of staff.

Early in 2001, I had a phone call from Rupert Harding that would lead my writing in a whole new direction. While working for Sutton Publishing, Rupert had commissioned *Ducati: Taglioni and his World-Beating Motorcycles* (published jointly by Sutton and Motorbooks in 2000). Although the book charted the Italian engineer's life story, it was equally a book about the motorcycles he had created, and the factories he had worked for – not just Ducati, but also Ceccato and FB Mondial). Rupert wondered if I'd consider writing a biography of a well-known motorcycle racer. I had never written a biography before, and my suggestions of either Bob McIntyre or Arthur Wheeler were rejected. Instead Rupert gave me a shortlist: Mike Hailwood, Barry Sheene, Giacomo Agostini or John Surtees. I opted for Surtees, on the basis that, in my opinion, John had had the most varied and interesting career, as a rider, driver, mechanic, engineer, team owner, sidecar passenger and specials builder.

Rupert duly organised a meeting between the three of us, at John's business address in Edenbridge, Kent. I arrived some time before Rupert and took a seat in the outer office. John's premises was relatively small (he dealt with commercial properties) and besides himself there were three ladies, one of whom was his secretary Sharon. Anyway, John soon beckoned me into his office, where I straight away noticed that he had a copy of the second edition of my Manx Norton book (which had just been published by Redline Books), sitting on his desk.

I soon discovered that John and I had lots in common besides our mutual love and enthusiasm for motorcycles and mechanical things. We had both grown up in a world far removed from today, where happiness didn't mean having money as it was possible to enjoy competing on a shoestring, and maybe even have a chance of success. Sadly, John and I now share another special bond, as we both lost a son to motorsport in accidents at Brands Hatch: Henry Surtees (Formula 2) 2009 and Gary Walker (250 GP) 1994.

Eventually, Rupert arrived, but for the best part of the next three hours John and I swapped stories about bikes. Rupert hardly got a look in; in fact he barely got around to asking John what it would take for him to co-operate in the compilation of the biography, to which John replied that all he wanted was 'a few books'. Actually, we'd already had the same conversation before Rupert arrived. John had showed me another biography (featuring four instead of two wheels) and he'd said, 'Your book has to be considerably better than this one'.

Limited Editions

John Surtees had figured heavily in my original Manx Norton book (published by Aston in 1990), and when Aston's owner Anthony Pritchard commissioned the production of 100 leather-bound special editions (on sale at £100 each), John was invited to sign them. Geoff Duke was also asked, as was Phil Read. Then Anthony telephoned me to ask if I had received the books, as I was next in line to sign – but I knew nothing about it. I contacted Phil Read to enquire as to the whereabouts of the books, only to find out that he was sitting on the consignment, angling for an increase in his fees. I contacted Anthony, who got back on to Phil Read. As if by magic, the books turned up the next day. I don't know what Anthony said, but his call achieved the desired result.

At the end of the meeting John invited me to his home, a mansion near Lingfield, in East Sussex – so I visited a month later, in early December 2001. We spent a day discussing the book and going through the collection of photographs he'd assembled during his lifetime. These documented his motorcycle racing career, plus his four-wheel racing as a driver and then team manager, together with many family photographs. John was keen that I should use as many of these pictures as possible, so we selected approximately 200 images. I began to list these, but John asked me what I was doing. I replied that I was making a list of what I was about to take away, but was surprised when he said, 'There's no need to do that – I trust you'. As a novice biographer, it was wonderful to know that John was not only enthusiastic about the project but also, right from the start, showed great faith in me.

John Surtees grew up in a close-knit family and his parents had played a pivotal role behind the scenes in his rise to the top – not by bankrolling their son, but by helping him to gain the experience and enthusiasm for his chosen sport. Certainly, John's father (more commonly known as Jack to avoid confusion) was a hard taskmaster, but his heart was in the right place and John would be the first to relate just how close he was to his parents. As I said in the preface to the book, 'Being responsible for writing *John Surtees – Motorcycle Maestro* has been a real challenge – I feel the man has achieved so much in his life. The book is written in the same way as I see John myself, truthfully recording the facts without in any way making it all sound more glamorous than it really was. Certainly anyone aspiring to reach the top in any sport could learn a lot from John Surtees's life – the combination of talent, commitment, enthusiasm and professionalism is a winning formula. Second best is not good enough.'

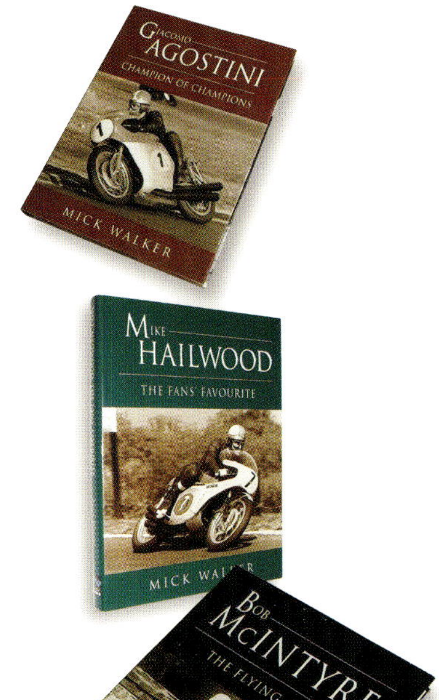

When the book came out in 2003, I viewed it as no more than a one-off title. However, it was well received and even won 'Book of the Week' award in *The Independent* newspaper. As a result, the publishers decided to make it the first of a series of motorcycle biographies. Several followed: *Giacomo Agostini* (2004), *Mike Hailwood* (2005), *Bob McIntyre* (2006), *Geoff Duke* (2007), *Derek Minter* (2008), *Bill Ivy* (2009), *Sammy Miller* (2010) and the latest, more general *Sidecar Champions* (2011).

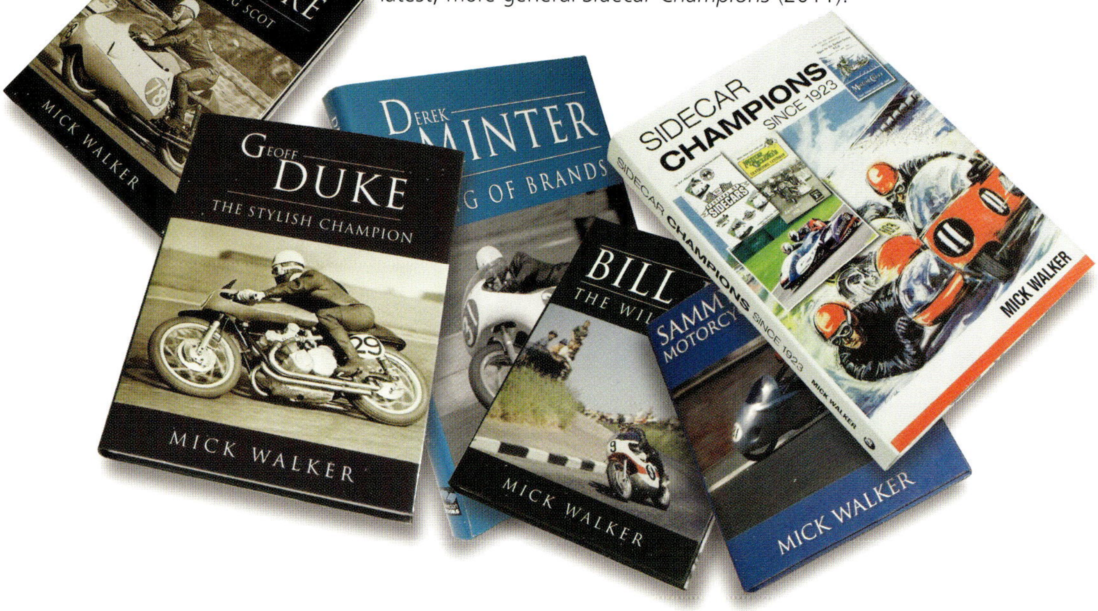

Surtees would probably still be my number one choice as the greatest motorsports competitor when all aspects of his career are considered. Apart from his unique double first – the only man to be World Champion on both two and four wheels, who else has achieved such a wide range of success? Each competitor should be viewed with respect to his own time, but there have always been those who stood head and shoulders above the rest. Geoff Duke probably marked the end of one era, that stretched back before him through the greats such as Stanley Woods and Jimmie Guthrie. The modern age arguably began with Agostini and Hailwood, since when there have been the likes of Barry Sheene, Kenny Roberts, Eddie Lawson, Mick Doohan and, most recently, Valentino Rossi. But to me John Surtees is truly the maestro.

Reg Everett on the Ted Broad TD1C Yamaha special at the 1967 French GP.

I was soon able to share my newfound experience of writing about motorcycle racers' careers with a rider who wanted to write about his own. I had watched Reg Everett's early races as an enthusiastic spectator and, in the mid 1960s, I rode against him on several occasions. Later still, when compiling my Greeves book with Rob Carrick, Reg told me the story of his Silverstone road racer. Although he had started competing on an ex-Derek Minter BSA 500 Gold Star, Reg went on to ride not only the Greeves, but also Kreidler, Velocette, Ducati, and, most of all. Yamaha machinery from the well-known dealer/entrant Ted Broad of Ilford, Essex. Reg finished runner-up in the British 250 championship on no less than three occasions, with a string of victories against the likes of Minter, Read and Bill Ivy. Besides the British short circuits, he rode in the Isle of Man, the Thruxton 500 and the legendary Spanish Barcelona 24 hours marathon.

We kept in touch, and after Reg was taken ill in the autumn of 2004, he asked me to visit him at his home in Galleywood, Chelmsford, Essex. In November that year, we spent several enjoyable hours talking about many things – including Reg's idea of writing his life story. I explained what I thought was the best way to go about it, but I also advised that it could end up in disappointment if his manuscript wasn't good enough. Modestly, Reg told me that if this happened he would simply 'put a rubber band round it and put it away in the filing cabinet'. For my part, I said that I would help as much as I could, and so the project began.

The manuscript was finally finished, and dropped through my letterbox in May 2007. I thought that Reg had really got a story to tell, and I particularly liked his 1968 Barcelona 24 Hours story. I was able to help with extra details, general editing, sub-headings, finding illustrations of the right quality, captioning and generally tidying up the text, and I also suggested a title. Together, we approached Derby-based Breedon Books (now Derby Books) and Reg's *From Rocker to Racer* was published in October 2009. To me, Reg's story charted the era, the social change and the honest fun that a generation of youngsters like myself had experienced growing up in post-war Britain. As I said in the foreword, '*Rocker to Racer* is something special, I am sure reading it will make you appreciate why I so enthusiastically embraced the project'.

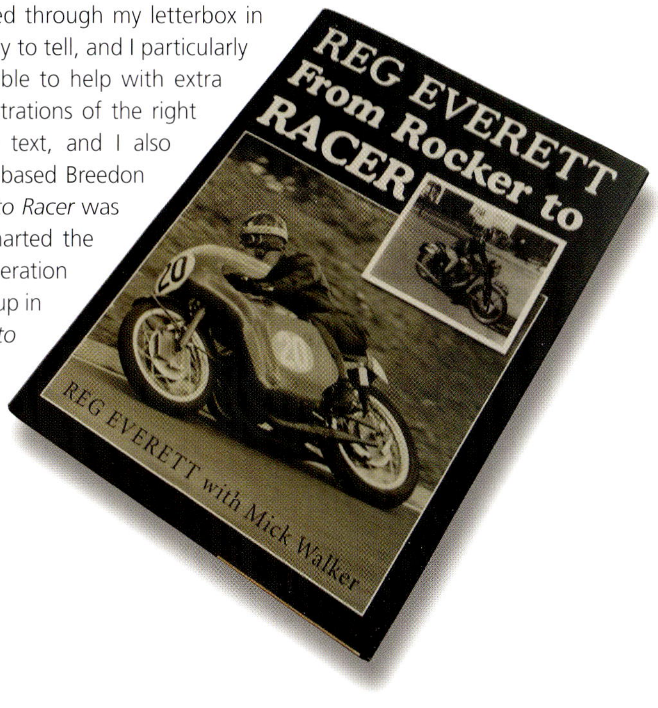

When the second edition of *The Manx Norton* book came out in 2001, I was just beginning to sell direct – offering signed and numbered copies to the public. A copy of the book was bought by Isle of Wight enthusiast Colin Pascoe, who contacted me about the 1956 350 Manx featured on page 173 (191 in the 2005 third edition). He was the current owner of the bike, which had been purchased new from the Norton factory, then ridden by Alan Trow and spannered by Peter Goodman.

Colin kept in touch, and was always good for a laugh, but then he had some terrible news: he had terminal cancer. So far, I had only spoken to Colin on the telephone, but I visited him (staying at his home for a few days at a time), and arranged for the ex-Trow Manx to be displayed on the Redline Books stand at the Stafford Classic Motorcycle Show in April. I later enjoyed an extended stay at Colin's cliff-top home at Yaverland on the Isle of Wight in July, and even rode Colin's bike at my son's memorial race meeting at Mallory Park in August.

Colin was still able to drive at this time, so we toured the island and attended some motorcycle-related activities. The two most notable were a visit to the Sammy Miller Museum just across the water at New Milton, Hampshire, and the monthly meeting of the Isle of Wight Classic Motorcycle Club in Newport. We visited the Sammy Miller Museum on a truly superb English summer's day: a cloudless blue sky, hardly a breath of wind, warm without being too hot – perfect.

Although I had known Sammy for many years, this was my first visit to his museum. As anyone who has been there will know, the premises is on the site of an old farm, with a central courtyard with tea rooms and gift shop, the museum itself and finally the workshop in which the famous Miller restorations are carried out. On the way over, Colin mentioned that when he contacted Sammy requesting some information regarding his Manx, Sammy had been rather abrupt. So when we arrived, Colin went to the workshop and said, 'Could you please tell Mr Miller that Mick Walker is here to see him'.

When 'Mr Miller' appeared, I introduced Colin as my personal assistant, and witnessed Sammy's evident confusion that he had virtually told my valued aide to get lost. However, Sammy said he would give the two of us a guided tour of his museum and offered me a free museum guide. The half hour or so spent with Sammy was really enjoyable, not only seeing his motorcycles and associated material, but also swapping stories. Finally, Sammy said he had to go back to work and we spent more time looking around before making our departure. As we left, the staff member on duty said, 'I don't know who you are, but that is the first time Mr Miller has ever given anyone a free copy of the museum guide'.

When I got home, I discovered that soon after I left, Colin had gone into the local hospice, where he died the following Friday, and his wife Jill told me that I had kept him alive longer than would otherwise have been the case. A few days after Colin's death, I was back on the island, travelling over on the 1930s open-top ex-London fire engine that was used to transport Colin's coffin. I rode Colin's Manx as 'escort', which really meant blasting up ahead and then waiting at the roadside for the fire engine to catch up. How they got approval for this from the local authorities, I will never know. Riding a Manx in full race trim with open exhaust and no road tax or insurance is not normally tolerated, but this day was different. In fact, the route was lined by hundreds of spectators, a fitting tribute to a great and brave man. As a footnote, the undertaker who had overseen Colin's funeral subsequently purchased his ex-Trow Manx.

Mallory Park, August 2001, on Colin Pascoe's ex-Alan Trow 1955 40M Manx

Brian Hussey Mike Cross Suzette Bradnam Jill Pascoe Andrew Cross Colin Pascoe MW

As I said at the start of this chapter, I never intentionally set out to be a writer, so I found it a little surprising that Richard Rosenthal's article, 'From Racer to Writer' in August 2000's *The Classic Motor Cycle* had this intro: 'Racer, off-roader, motorcycle dealer and importer, race entrant, magazine editor, Mick Walker has been all these. But it's probably as a writer and historian that he is best known.'

I was more than flattered by what Richard went on to say, 'Mick adopted a well researched, easy to read writing style from the onset, ideal for the enthusiast, reader and researcher alike. Crammed with 'in text' data, specification panels and thoughtfully captioned pictures, it is little wonder many early out-of-print editions now change hands at far more than the cover price. My personal favourites, *German Racing Motorcycles* and *German Motorcycles* typify the Walker style. Not only are the major players covered in depth, but Mick includes snippets on Gritzner-Kayser (1903-1962), Sudbank (1949-1951), Bismarck (1904-1957) and over 100 other German marques which contribute to the tapestry of German motorcycling. Some years ago I was asked to read Mick's *Spanish Post-war Road and Racing Motorcycles* to help with a review. How could a whole book be written on the subject I wondered? Clutching the tome I laughingly announced that I would be up the pub early that night! Wrong, I was gripped by the machines, personalities and flavour of Spain and put the copy down long after closing time. With Spain in mind, I asked why pick obscure difficult to research subjects? Triumph, BSA, Mike Hailwood – surely they would be easier…'

I would like to end this phase of my life in the same way we ended our interview back then. 'I never want to write about a subject I cannot add anything new to,' I replied, 'I only have enthusiasm for topics that interest me…' Richard closed, rather flatteringly, with these words: 'A self-motivated workaholic, Mick endeavours, by meticulous research, to eliminate mistakes from his writing, believing an error in a newspaper is soon forgotten, but in a book it is there for ever'.

Maybe dogs and motorcycles are meant to go together.
It was a 'puppy' (cucciolo in Italian) that first put Ducati on wheels in 1946.

My writing companions

I have always loved animals, but they did not appear in my books until I came to dedicate my first rider biography, *John Surtees – Motorcycle Maestro*, 'to my dog Jessie, whom I found and adopted while writing this book Caithness, Scotland'. She was the first of my two Border Collies, and came into my life while I was staying with my sister Margaret and brother-in-law John at their sheep farm during the summer of 2002. This was a regular haunt where several of my books have been written, including – as the dedication suggests – *John Surtees*.

I certainly didn't go to Scotland with any idea of bringing back a dog. However, Jessie was then eight, and had begun to suffer quite badly from arthritis, making it difficult for her to continue her sheep-herding duties – so it was she who adopted me while I was writing the book, and by following me when I finally left. I remember telling Margaret and John, 'We'll probably be back within half an hour', but no, Jessie simply settled into the life of a 'writer's assistant'. When I arrived in Edinburgh, where I was due to stay for a few days at Ian and Rita Welsh's house, my plan of putting Jessie into kennels never happened; Ian said she could stay in the house. Back at Wisbech, my original idea was to find her a home, but she simply moved in with Susan, me, and our cats, and we all got along fine. Jessie would even allow the cats to have titbits out of her feeding bowl. She was the most easygoing dog you could imagine – never a disagreement with any other animal, or person for that matter. We had a wonderful 3$^{1}/_{2}$ years with Jessie before she died in November 2005.

I didn't realise how much I would miss her. Outside of motorcycling, the succession of animals that Susan and I have lived with during our 42 years of marriage has been one of my greatest sources of enjoyment. We have always had at least one cat, and on occasion, as many as five. Although I coped with losing them, losing Jessie was different. So when I visited Margaret and John again in 2006 I returned with a seven-week-old Border Collie pup. Rascal lived up to her name, but was just as loyal as Jessie. As I write, she is five. She has grown into a magnificent animal, but although she gets on perfectly with humans – and cats – the same cannot be said of some other dogs. Owning an animal is a commitment, but it's very rewarding. I have come to realise that how someone treats an animal can tell one a lot about the person. As for those who mistreat animals, well…

9 Favourite Stories

what I learnt intrigued me...

I've been actively involved in the motorcycling scene for 50 years and writing about the motorcycling scene for half of that time. Motorcycling has introduced me to many fascinating characters and given me many great stories to remember. Here, in roughly chronological order, are some of my particular favourite:

Walter Kaaden my brush with genius

Walter Kaaden was the engineering genius who created the modern two-stroke engine. I was lucky enough to meet him through Alan Shepherd, who campaigned the East German MZs that Walter had created during the 1960s. My friendship with Alan began in the early 1970s, when he used to visit the Suntester company of Kings Lynn, a few miles from my Wisbech dealership. A decade earlier, Alan was one of the world's top racing stars, having shot to prominence by winning the Junior Manx Grand Prix in 1958 on an AJS 7R. However, it was his performance – again on a 7R – in the Ulster Grand Prix in August 1960 that really put Alan in the spotlight. Race leader John Surtees (on an MV four) was pushed to the limit over the 7.4-mile road circuit by Alan and his British single. Sadly, Alan's gallant effort was to end in retirement. However, the mighty MV team was so rattled that they demanded that Alan's engine be stripped and measured. They suspected he was riding not a 7R, but a 496cc G50. However, the strip proved it to be a stock 349cc. In my opinion, it was this outstanding performance that brought Alan the opportunity to become a works rider for MV Agusta, MZ, and eventually Honda, with whom he had a serious accident which effectively ended his racing career.

Walter Kaaden (centre), Alan Shepherd (standing) and an MZ mechanic with Shepherd's TT mounts, Isle of Man TT 1964

With racing over, Alan retained an enthusiasm for motorcycling at the very highest level – and a close association with MZ. He used to organise bus trips to the East German factory for fellow enthusiasts, and was delighted when I asked him to write the foreword for my first MZ book in 1996. He concluded his piece by saying, 'During my four years as an MZ rider, I received no payment for my services as a rider from the company. But money does not buy the pleasure I have had working and riding for Walter Kaaden and MZ, and I am very proud that I still have a close association with the company and the Kaaden family.' Alan was a great admirer of Walter, and paid him this tribute, 'The ultimate demonstration of his genius was my win on the 250 MZ at Daytona (the US Grand Prix) in February 1964. Faced with unprecedented poor performance and only hours to qualify for the race, I rang Walter in East Germany for advice. During the three-minute call (the maximum allowed to an Iron Curtain country from the USA at that time) he diagnosed exactly the problem. I had been supplied with very low octane fuel – and who says there are no politics in sport? He went on to instruct me how to alter the engine specification to cope and win!'

In talking about the performance of the 125 and 250 MZ engines, Alan told me that the smaller one could easily outperform the average 350 four-stroke singles of the day such as the AJS, Norton and even the Aermacchi! 'The 250 MZ, with a maximum speed of 155mph in 1962, could easily match or exceed the best of the 500 singles,' Alan said. 'Just how Walter achieved this with such limited facilities and only pennies not pounds in the budget, never ceases to amaze me. And even though the Japanese and others blatantly copied his inventions, in over three decades everyone is still utilizing this great man's work.'

I was fortunate to meet Walter Kaaden on one of my visits to Alan's self-built home in Cumbria. Walter came across as a real gentleman; a humble man who went about his work with minimum of fuss. He was an achiever, not a self-publicist, and I instantly liked him. Walter was a true engineer, a man who could create with his brain, rather than a computer. Also, as I know, Walter could have earned vast sums of money by selling his technology to the Japanese. However, he chose to put his family and his country above riches. Certainly his attitude was in contrast to the greed culture that sadly blights much of today's high-tech society.

The third member of my 'MZ trio' was Alan's fellow rider Derek Woodman. Although I had known Alan for many years, it was not until I was compiling the 1996 MZ book with him that I met Derek. At the time, Derek owned a BMW car dealership in Blackpool – which, strangely, happened to be where my wife and I were headed on holiday after leaving Alan's home. However, when Alan telephoned, he was told that Derek was on holiday in the Lake District. However, as Alan was a close friend, Derek's secretary gave him the hotel's phone number, and the next morning my wife and I met Derek at a little restaurant just off the M6. Derek was pleased to help, sharing Alan's enthusiasm for MZ and the great engineering genius – Walter Kaaden.

The modified version of Walter Kaaden's water-cooled MZ 250cc twin that carried Mike Hailwood to his third win at the Sachsenring in the 1963 East German GP.

Leo Kuzmicki my greatest scoop

A caricature of Leo Kuzmicki during his wartime RAF service.

The gifted Polish engineer Leo Kuzmicki played a key role in the development of the Manx Norton, Vanwall racing car and Imp saloon, as well as being responsible for many lesser designs. Remarkably, nobody seemed to know much about the man himself, and, as I said in the third edition of *The Manx Norton* 'little has been written about Leo Kuzmicki – Norton's man of mystery'.

The quest to uncover the truth surrounding Kuzmicki began when one of my customers was taken seriously ill. He told me that before he died, he had a dream to find out as much as he could about the Kuzmicki story. His quest was not helped by the fact that Leo had been an extremely secretive person who was reluctant to disclose personal details – with good reason, as I discovered later. What I learnt intrigued me, so I set out to uncover the real Leo Kuzmicki for myself.

I already knew that Leo left Norton in late 1953 when he was head-hunted by former Norton director Tony Vandervell to design the Vanwall Formula 1 car engine – which was essentially four Norton top ends on a common block. After Vanwall, he joined Humber in 1956, and was promoted to Deputy Chief Engineer on the Imp project after Humber became part of the Rootes Group. Late in 1963, he became Chief Engineer responsible for design and development of the Imp range, before being put in charge of Group Engineering Co-ordination in 1965. Not long afterwards, when Rootes was absorbed by the American Chrysler Corporation, he was appointed Head of Engine and Transmission Design at the Ryton plant, Coventry.

Chrysler's operation was later taken over by the French Peugeot/Citroen combine, via which I already had some contacts at Ryton. However, the last thing anyone I spoke to could remember about Leo Kuzmicki was that he had attended an official dinner late in the 1970s. One of the people I was put in touch with was able to provide a phone number, but as this was out of date, I tried putting various numbers in front of both the code and the number itself, and hoped for the best.

I spent many telephone calls, attempting to reach the correct number, but I finally hit the jackpot. I had almost reached the point of deciding that I simply couldn't keep telephoning random numbers, when the impossible happened and I got a Mrs Kuzmicki. However, when I asked to speak to Leo, she wanted to know why. Luckily, I mentioned Norton, which acted like a password. As I was to discover, if I had said anything else it was likely that the receiver would have been put down on me.

Fortunately, after explaining that I was updating my Manx Norton story, Nancy Kuzmicki – Leo's widow, as he had died in the early 1980s – agreed to meet me, but would not give me her home address. I arrived at the place we agreed on, and sat waiting in my car until an ageing Peugeot 205 pulled up and out of it stepped a little old lady. It turned out that the owners of the Ryton car plant, where Leo had worked for over two decades, had presented Nancy with a brand new Peugeot 205 in 1984, which she was still driving (aged 83), when we met in 1993. During our lengthy meeting, which Nancy told me she enjoyed greatly, the true story of her husband gradually emerged.

Leo Kuzmicki had been born into a family of Polish nobility in October 1910. By the late 1930s, he had attended the University of Lwów (now Lviv in the Ukraine) and gained many engineering qualifications. At the outbreak of war he held a senior engineering research post, but when Germany invaded Poland at the beginning of September 1939, Leo was called up for active service with the Polish Air Force. However Poland was quickly over-run, and although he managed to escape the Germans, he found himself in a Russian ambush and was transported to Moscow. There he was incarcerated and tortured by the

KGB, before he was eventually transported to a labour camp within the Arctic Circle. When Leo realised that starvation was all that awaited him, he decided that his only option was to escape. This he did, walking overland via Tashkent, Samarkand, Krasnovodsk and through the Persian Gulf to Bombay (Mumbai). However, his trek of some 2000 miles took its toll; periods of starvation and exhaustion caused permanent damage to his circulation, which eventually led to his death in 1982. From Bombay, he travelled aboard the steamship *Empress of Russia* around the Horn of Africa, at the head of a motley group of men escaping to England. They finally arrived at Liverpool in June 1942.

In England, Leo was reunited with his brother – a professional pilot and former Squadron Leader in the Polish Air Force, who was awarded both the Croix de Guerre by General de Gaulle and the Distinguished Flying Cross (DFC) by the Royal Air Force. Sadly, Leo's brother died in a flying accident before the war ended, but Leo, too, joined the RAF in 1942, serving as a Flight Engineer until his demob in 1947 with the rank of Flight Lieutenant. His first posting was to Birmingham, where he met Nancy, whom he eventually married in 1952.

Leo's first British civilian job was with Exeter motorcycle manufacturer AJW. During his RAF service, Leo became a close friend of JO (Jackie) Ball, who acquired the AJW business after the war. Leo joined Jackie in spring 1947, and went on to design the first post-war AJW machines, including the Grey Fox and Speed Fox (both powered by JAP engines); and was even a shareholder in the company.

Next came a move to Norton Motors in Birmingham, where he was appointed as Chief Engineer with responsibility for design and development. Oddly, he had been interviewed for the job in secret by Norton MD Gilbert Smith, at a Birmingham hotel. The secrecy continued, with only a few people at Norton knowing exactly what position Leo held. This suited both parties, as Leo's boss Joe Craig was able to take all the praise while the Polish engineer simply got on with work undisturbed and with little chance of recognition or discovery, which he (and Nancy herself) feared since his experiences with the KGB.

This fear explains why the truth about Leo Kuzmicki remained hidden. Even Mick Woollett, in his otherwise excellent book *Norton* (Osprey), got things wrong: '...a lot of work was being done on engines – particularly the 500. The man behind this was a former Polish fighter pilot named Leo Kuzmicki who in pre-war days had been a lecturer on internal combustion engines at Warsaw University. After the war he had decided to stay in England and had got a job at Norton – as a sweeper-up!' In reality, while Leo was a stickler for cleanliness and was always making sure that rubbish was picked up (by himself if necessary), he was certainly not employed as a cleaner.

Certainly racing star Geoff Duke realised Leo's worth and is on record as saying just how important the Pole was to his Norton world championship success. Geoff also consulted Leo when he worked as a racing advisor to the Royal Enfield factory in the mid 1960s. However, the general public and most of the staff at the various companies where Leo subsequently worked didn't realise the truth. Nor did the press – hunt as much as you like through the motorcycle journals of the period and you will find no mention of the man. Fear of the KGB also resulted in a scarcity of photographs, and none have ever turned up showing his time with Norton or, for that matter, Vanwall.

I ended my chapter on Leo Kuzmicki by saying, 'What pleases me most is that at last motorcycle enthusiasts all over the world now have a chance of knowing something of a man who played such an important role in Norton's final Grand Prix successes of the 1950s – and how the famous cammy Norton engine featured so significantly in the Vanwall Formula 1 car's success.' One of my most treasured pieces of memorabilia is Leo's briefcase and papers, which Nancy presented to me, including a handwritten CV that Leo prepared himself.

Leo Kuzmicki at home in rural England, in the 1970s.

Share Certificate.

No. of Certificate 2 — A J W MOTOR CYCLES LTD — Number of Shares 1

AUTHORISED SHARE CAPITAL .. £ 5,000

This is to Certify that LEO KUZMICKI of Celtic House, Warren Edge Rd, Southbourne, Bournemouth, Hants is the Holder of one ordinary Shares of one pound each, numbered 1 to inclusive, in the above named Company, subject to the Memorandum and Articles of Association thereof, and that such Shares are fully paid.

Given under the Common Seal of the said Company this 1st day of July 1945

Directors.

Secretary.

Before joining Norton, Kuzmicki was chief designer for AJW, and also a shareholder in the small company.

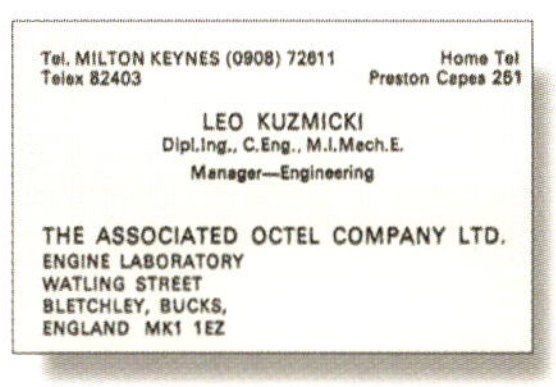

Tel. MILTON KEYNES (0908) 72611 / Telex 82403 — Home Tel Preston Capes 251

LEO KUZMICKI
Dipl.Ing., C.Eng., M.I.Mech.E.
Manager—Engineering

THE ASSOCIATED OCTEL COMPANY LTD.
ENGINE LABORATORY
WATLING STREET
BLETCHLEY, BUCKS,
ENGLAND MK1 1EZ

That episode must have given me a taste for investigative journalism. At any rate, I really enjoyed uncovering another tale for my 2010 book *Douglas The Complete Story*. It began early one morning, when Michael Gluckman phoned me in response to a news item in the London Douglas Club (LDC) magazine, requesting information for the book. Unfortunately, by the time they published my request, I had finished the manuscript. However, I felt that the story that unfolded during our telephone conversation was so interesting that publication should be delayed:

The 'lost Douglas' my 'stop-press' moment

Records of the LDC showed that only one example of the TT 600 twin was still known to exist, owned by Michael Gluckman, an arch-enthusiast who lives in China. The following is Michael's own account of how he came to own such a rare motorcycle; 'I first knew the Douglas thirty years ago when living in Port Elizabeth, in the Eastern Cape (of Southern Africa). It belonged to an elderly gentleman named Jack Cuyler, who had bought it in the early 1930s from a garage in Sydenham, Port Elizabeth. The garage owner had wanted fifteen shillings for it and Jack only had ten shillings. After some haggling he agreed a price of twelve-and-six ($62\frac{1}{2}$ pence). He then put the bike together and owned it until 2005, when I acquired it. Jack died that year aged 96.

'Jack had assembled the machine with 28 x $2\frac{1}{2}$" rims and tyres (as beaded-edge tyres were not available then) and proceeded to use it for the rest of his life, initially as a commuter machine and then seldom after he had acquired a 1929 Velocette KN. This bike I had to buy as well, in order to get the Douglas TT, and immediately passed it on to a friend who has restored it wonderfully.

The TT had been purchased new from the Douglas factory by the agent in Durban, Fritz Zurcher. Born in Beira, Mozambique of German or Swiss extraction, Zurcher used the machine competitively, especially as a scratch machine on several occasions on the Durban-Johannesburg race. This was run on appalling, un-surfaced roads for which, in theory, the Douglas was totally unsuited. It was also campaigned by the legendary South African rider Charlie Young, who worked for Zurcher. In Young's hands, the bike had broken the South African speed record, when it achieved an astonishing 107.1mph at a meeting in 1929. After Zurcher closed his business in 1930/31, Young went back to his old job in Johannesburg at Shimwells, a bicycle agent. As there were a number of important races in the Port Elizabeth area, that is perhaps how the machine ended up there in a garage, leaving a short gap in its history before Cuyler purchased it.

The ultra-rare 600cc TT twin with South African importer Fritz Zurcher and rider Charlie Young.

When Michael Gluckman acquired the Douglas in 2005 a full restoration was carried out. He told me, 'It was perhaps the first time in 70-odd years that the whole thing had been apart and the mechanicals were wonderfully rebuilt for me by Tony Lammers in Pretoria. It needed a new crankshaft, rods and bearings together with a new flywheel. The last-mentioned had numerous radial cracks and if the engine had been revved would have exploded like a hand grenade. Predictably, the magneto and carburettors also needed overhauling and the machine was rebuilt with new mudguards bought in England, new rims from America and new [beaded-edge] tyres of the original pattern and size. The springs fitted by Cuyler to secure the saddle to the frame were removed and substituted with the correct, terrifyingly uncomfortable solid rods. The ex-Zurcher 600TT differs from stock only in that there are self-aligning main bearings and larger tool panniers, presumably needed for the Durban-Johannesburg race, which was over some 375 miles.' I was delighted to have been able to tell its story.

The TT model now owned by Michael Gluckman, pictured in 2008 following its extensive restoration.

The ringless Tomos my ultimate 'oddball'

One of the most bizarre stories I came across in my writing career was the Yugoslavian Tomos 50cc GP racer, an example of which coded D7-62 (for seven-speed 1962) was featured in my *European Racing Motorcycles*. This is how I described its highly unconventional power unit: 'The heart of the newcomer was an entirely original engine unit, this sported a vertical cylinder and seven gears, with the clutch running at engine speed. But the features of most interest were hidden inside the engine itself... most unusual of all was the aluminium piston without any piston rings or even hardened stainless rubbing coils, which ran in a 38mm plated alloy cylinder bore.

Nobody really believed my story about the 'ringless piston' until one day in March 2011, when I received a telephone call from 50cc enthusiast Ernie Crust, saying he had proof that I was absolutely right. Ernie wrote to me enclosing photos of the works Tomos, of which he said, 'As you can see the flywheel assembly and con-rod with ringless piston are plainly displayed. I think great credit is due to you in uncovering this fact; and to the Tomos company for making it work.'

Strangely, the very same post brought another letter from British former three-times 50cc champion Nigel Stone, who wrote, "I have known Mick for many years purchasing many of his excellent books. There cannot be many motorcycles he has not written about... In life now and again someone comes along very special and very talented; in this case Mick Walker is that man, a genuine, honest iconic individual, it has been my pleasure to know him and class him as a friend.' Thank you Nigel!

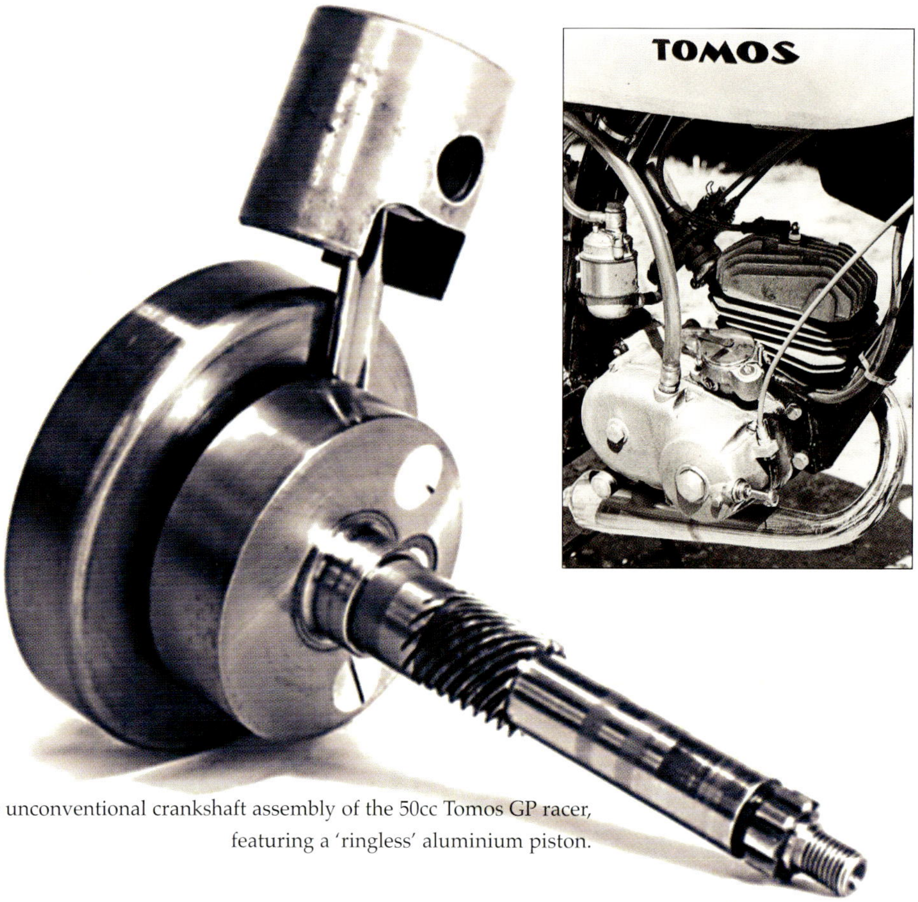

The unconventional crankshaft assembly of the 50cc Tomos GP racer, featuring a 'ringless' aluminium piston.

The 'Hitler Trophy' my brush with infamy

Over the years I have been invited to attend many functions and events, with some very pleasant trips north of the border. One of the more unusual ones came in 2006, when I and my good friend from Edinburgh Ian Welsh travelled up to the Kirkcaldy & District Motor Club's annual dinner-dance and awards night. I was delighted that Hugh and Ewen Ward (President and Social Secretary) had invited me to present the trophies won by members, but what really made this evening stand out was seeing the second of the legendary 'Hitler Trophies' that had been awarded to Norton factory star Jimmie Guthrie, about whose career I wrote in *The Manx Norton*. In 1936, when Guthrie won the European Grand Prix in Germany, he was presented with a trophy that bore the name of Adolf Hitler – who was a great supporter of motor sports, including motorcycling. The following year, Hawick's favourite son looked set to win the German Grand Prix at the Sachsenring, and was comfortably leading the last lap in front of some 250,000 spectators when he crashed and was fatally injured. The bronze trophy that was presented as a mark of respect is truly magnificent. However, while it is without doubt one of the most iconic motorsport awards, and is now in the safe keeping of the Kirkcaldy club, it is seldom seen or talked about.

Jimmie Guthrie was killed when he crashed leading the German GP in 1937. Controversially, he had been awarded the previous year's winner's trophy (which I inspected 70 years later) by the leader of the Third Reich, Adolph Hitler.

Jim Russell my boyhood hero

Although I caught the motorcycling bug at an early age, I was a teenage fan of 500cc Formula 3 car racing. The form of car racing that emerged in the immediate post-war period was a direct descendant of the earlier cyclecar racing based on machines such as the GN and Morgan three-wheelers. However, the use of motorcycle engines was the source of renewed interest in this class, in view of their high-performance, simplicity and lower cost compared to the much more expensive purpose-built multi-cylinder power units employed in the more conventional four-wheeled racing cars.

By the mid 1950s, Formula 3 car racing was at its zenith, with several well-known names competing in the class: Stirling Moss, Peter Collins and even the current F1 supremo Bernie Ecclestone. However, the true Formula 3 champion was Jim Russell. As a 13-year-old I was very impressed by the performances of this local garage owner, who was based in Downham Market, 7 miles from my home, and in 1954 I painted a montage of Formula 3 cars on a large sheet of paper, which was given to Jim Russell by an aunt of mine who lived in the town. Many years later I discovered that Jim still had the painting in the collection of memorabilia he had amassed over his racing career.

A former RAF Flight Sergeant during the war, Russell began racing in 1952 with a Cooper-JAP. In his first race, at Snetterton, on 26 June, he finished next to last. Even so, the 32 year-old Jim gained valuable experience and picked up a number of useful tips from the driver who was to become the 1952 and 1953 F3 champion, Don Parker. The following year saw Jim make the switch from JAP to Norton power. In July he travelled down to the South Norwood workshops of ace London tuner Steve Lancefield and purchased a new Manx Norton engine for £350 – the carburettor was extra. His first victory with the new power unit came the following month when he took the chequered flag at his local Snetterton circuit on August Bank Holiday Monday. Then at the end of 1953, Jim purchased a new Cooper MkVIII, into which he fitted the Lancefield dohc Manx engine.

At the beginning of 1954 a dispute broke out between Steve Lancefield and Don Parker, his top driver, over an oil contract. Jim decided to visit Lancefield to see if he could replace Don, but the tuner's answer was negative. Jim was undaunted and set about proving that he deserved serious consideration. Making his first-ever appearance at Silverstone for the *Daily Express* International Trophy meeting, he distinguished himself by finishing a notable third behind Stirling Moss and Les Leston, both in faster cars. Jim was still using his original standard Norton engine – the one he had purchased from Lancefield the previous year.

After an excellent showing at the new Aintree circuit a week after Silverstone, Steve Lancefield finally relented and agreed to provide 'some official support'. This came in time for the *Daily Telegraph* Trophy at Brands Hatch. Held on the August Bank Holiday Monday, it was the blue riband event in the F3 racing calendar. All the top stars were there, including Moss, Leston and Parker. Right from the start the 100,000-strong crowd witnessed a tremendous struggle between Moss and Russell. For lap after lap, the pair pulled further and further away from the rest of the field. It was a battle of wills between the two, with Russell leading Moss throughout to take the chequered flag, proving his right to be ranked with the very top drivers, not only in his class, but in motor racing as a whole. This was a superb performance from someone who had only started racing two years before.

From that day Jim never looked back. Among his successes in Formula 3 racing were winning the *Daily Telegraph* Trophy for four years running (1954-57). There was no actual award after 1956, as Jim had won the trophy outright

Jim Russell, *Daily Telegraph* International Trophy, Brands Hatch, August 1954

with his third victory in 1956. He also won the *Autosport* National F3 championship three times (1955-57) and numerous other victories and lap records throughout Britain and Europe, effectively making him the uncrowned king of the class. From 1955 onwards Jim Russell was an official Cooper works driver, the company providing him with various racing and sports cars. But for Formula 3, his car was always powered by a Lancefield Norton engine, and when I was compiling the original edition of *The Manx Norton*, Jim Russell told me, 'Lancefield's workshop was like going into a doctor's surgery – spotless'.

After the 1989 interview, which was conducted at his garage – a Mercedes-Benz dealership on the original Downham Market site – Jim and I became good friends. When I was updating for the second edition of the Manx book, published in spring 2001, I visited him at his mansion home between Thetford and Bury St Edmunds. He pulled out all of his memorabilia, including the painting which I had done as a schoolboy in the 1950s. Besides his racing career and car dealership, Jim Russell is perhaps best remembered for his famous racing school. This began during the 1960s at Snetterton, before expanding to include other circuits. Jim celebrated his 80th birthday in 2000 and was still very proud of his racing achievements, without, I might add, any of the egotism we see in some of today's four-wheel stars.

I also met the man who had provided Jim's race-winning engines, while working on my original Manx Norton book in 1989. SS (Steven Silvester) Lancefield was one of the truly great Norton experts during the Manx heyday, spanning the 1940s through to the mid 1960s. Born in London on 4 November 1903, Steve began his motorcycling career with a borrowed Triumph two-stroke in the 1920s, eventually transferring from the public highway to the race track – Brooklands – in 1929. However, he soon decided he was better at working on motorcycles than riding them. A trip to Donington Park with Harold Daniell in the early 1930s proved that a Lancefield-prepared Norton was superior to a Daniell one, so he joined Daniell in his Forest Hill motorcycle business, and a hobby was turned into a profession. He also married Harold's sister Claire.

During the war, Lancefield worked with Rolls-Royce, then the Bristol Aircraft Company. Lancefield and Daniell resumed their business after the cessation of hostilities and continued right up to 1949, when Lancefield was invited to join the Norton works team, which directly backed Daniell. Norton race supremo Joe Craig had noticed the Lancefield-prepared machines winning a couple of second places at Daytona the previous year. Not only that, but in 1947, for the first time ever, one rider had won three Isle of Man races in a single year. Lancefield Nortons had carried Eric Briggs to victories in the Senior Clubmans TT in June, and the Senior and Junior Manx Grand Prix that September. In 1949, Steve Lancefield replaced Craig, who went on to work with the BRM Formula 1 car project in Bourne, Lincolnshire.

For most of the 1950s, Steve spent his days preparing engines for Formula 3 (500cc) car racers, including Stirling Moss and Jim Russell. However, by the end of the decade, with the death of Formula 3, he returned to his original love, two-wheel racers. In 1960, he had the honour of preparing the first 500 single to lap the Isle of Man at over 100 mph, ridden by Derek Minter. Never one for publicity, Steve continued working on Manx engines until the late 1970s.

Although I had already met the other famous Norton tuner, Francis Beart, prior to beginning work on my Manx Norton book, I had never met Steve Lancefield. Luckily, Steve (then in his late 80s) and I shared a mutual friend, who arranged a meeting in May 1989 where I was given what can only be described as a frosty reception. This, I was later to discover, was because he hated journalists. But after 30 minutes or so the frost melted, it had become clear that I wasn't what he had expected. We were able to talk on equal terms; he was an engineer, I was an engineer; he was a motorcycle man, I was a motorcycle man. And so a kind of mutual respect grew between us.

Eventually I dragged myself away from his home, a high-ceilinged Victorian house on London's South Circular road, near Charlton Athletic football ground. Steve had filled me with interesting stories, which have since enabled me to reveal several otherwise unknown facts about the man himself, the Norton factory and its products.

Steve was totally dedicated to making the Norton single-cylinder Manx engine both fast and reliable. He himself said, 'Some people say I take racing too seriously; to me it's a religion and science and nothing is too good to ensure success. In this respect often I express my considered opinion and it is not liked.' As I said in *The Manx Norton*, 'I see this as a sensible approach. Racing at the top level is a serious business and requires 100 per cent commitment and expertise. SS Lancefield had both these attributes in abundance.'

Sadly, Steve Lancefield, Master Engineer – he told me that he never liked the word 'tuner' – died a few days before the Manx Norton book was launched at the Alexandra Palace Motorcycle Show in January 1990. The book was well received by the press, television, radio and the public alike, and has now gone on to its third edition, the last two published by my good friend Alan Wilson of Redline Books.

Master Engineer Steve Lancefield with rider Derek Minter, Brands Hatch 1960.

10 Sons of Speed

It is only natural that both my sons would have a need for speed...

I in no way encouraged my sons' interest in racing; it was just something that they themselves wanted to do. In 1983, when Steven was aged 12, he and his younger brother joined the local Anglia Roller Skating Club. At first their activities were restricted to Saturday afternoons and Sunday mornings at the Hudson Sports Centre in Wisbech. Steven remembers that in their first competitive event he came second to last, with Gary bringing up the rear. These initial efforts were on ancient quad skates, and when Susan bought new skates for the next week, things began to improve. An enjoyable part of the skating scene was the inter-club events, of which there were no less than eight categories. And with his new skates Steven went on to record his first victory at the Hudson Centre.

During the next 18 months, while Gary quit skating Steven progressed though the ranks. His first race meeting away from Wisbech was at Birmingham Wheels (an event for 13- to 15-year-olds) where, on the banked track, Steven finished second from last in his first event, the 1,500 metres race. At the time, the Birmingham venue was only one of three banked tracks available to skaters in the UK, the others being at Tatem Park, North London, and Herne Bay, Kent.

Steven became a member of the Fenland Speed Skating Club, competing regularly in local events and at various circuits throughout the country. At 16, he switched to men's events, which raised his game, competing against the top skaters in the UK. His first international race meeting was a two-day affair at Rouen in northern France. One event was the 10,000 metres, with 60 competitors on the start line. On the first day, as Steven recalls, 'It rained throughout, with truly terrible conditions'. The following day, Steven came home 17th, finishing in the main pack and telling me this was 'an excellent achievement at my first international outing'.

Steven represented Great Britain over the next few years in several countries, including France, Belgium and Germany, and also took part in the Europa Cup events. The first was at St Maxim near Marseilles in southern France, then Pamplona, Spain, in the heart of the Basque country. Steven was also drafted into the British team for two further European Championship rounds, first at Pamplona, then the Azores – technically part of Portugal despite being an island in the Atlantic Ocean.

Steven's best European Championship position was 14th; quite an accomplishment against hundreds of competitors from all over Europe. There were various categories for speed skating, ranging from the 300 metres time trial to the full marathon, which was run over a distance of 26 miles. Other disciplines included 300 to 20,000 metres on purpose-built tracks and 300 metres to full marathon on public roads.

At 15, Steven had also begun cycling to augment his skating training, and joined the local club, the Wisbech Wheelers. This club held weekly 10-mile time trials and staged a club run every Sunday. His mother Susan took up cycling with the same club and went on to win the ladies annual championship title for several years running. Even now, although Steven has long since quit skating, his interest in cycling continues.

Steven skating at Tatem Park speed oval, North London in the late 1980s.

1994, British Skating Championship in Birmingham, Steven finished 3rd in the 20,000 metres

Gary, September 1993
with the victor's laurels

52 WISBECH STANDARD — Friday, July 22, 1994 Classified (0354) 52621

Fenland Sport

Your essential guide to sport in Fenland

Walker riding in grand prix

MOTORCYCLING: Gary Walker takes the most prestigious stage in British motorcycling at the weekend.

Wisbech-based Walker lines-up in the support races of the British Grand Prix at Donington Park, Derbyshire.

On board a Honda RS 250R, the 20-year-old will become the first locally based solo rider to compete in a Grand Prix meet since Barry Sheene nearly two decades ago.

The early signs look good. He clocked a personal best of 1.43.6 minutes for a 2.5-mile lap (average speed 87mph) on Tuesday.

This followed a superb 12th place at the Masters of Mallory race the week before, an event which featured the country's top riders.

Home James

MOTORCYCLING: Wisbech's David James returns to home soil this weekend for the latest round of the Sidecar World Championship

Unlike Steven, from a young age Gary was only interested in motorcycles. His first machine was a Yamaha RD50, which he converted to 80cc. On his 17th birthday came a blue-and-white Yamaha TZR125, purchased from Denver Garage in Downham Market. His final road bike was yet another Yamaha, a 1989 TZR250 twin, but after being convicted of a speeding offence Gary decided to take to the track. So over the winter of 1991-92 he purchased a brand new Suzuki RGV250M from Carnells of Peterborough.

His racing debut on the Suzuki came at no less a meeting than the first round of the British Championships at Donington Park, Derbyshire, in May 1992. In the Superteen event, the Suzuki would only run on one cylinder. Even so, he managed to beat a similar machine that had both cylinders firing. Effectively, his '125' came out on top and avoided last place. The remainder of the 1992 season was spent learning the circuits and attempting to get the Suzuki running properly. To be competitive in Supersport 400 (for 400cc four-strokes and 250cc two-stroke production-based machines), one had to fit the race kit that Suzuki marketed – but the secret was getting it set up right. That first year we did not get anywhere near, while Gary's initial philosophy of 'win everything in sight' saw him sustain more than his share of crashes.

However, a combination of professional two-stroke tuning advice (my four-stroke expertise being of little use) from Leicester two-stroke specialist Harry Barlow during the close season of 1992-93 and a much-improved attitude from Gary himself saw things dramatically change for the 1993 season. Gary explained, 'Last season I wanted everything to happen at once, which I've now realised doesn't come about in this game. I'm much more patient now and it's paying off.'

There was a noticeable improvement in both his attitude and riding performance. In fact it was truly incredible. In 39 meetings and 108 races he was to score no less than 19 victories (his first coming at Snetterton in April 1993), 12 seconds, 17 thirds and 13 fourths. He took overall victory in the two-leg New Era Super Club Challenge, won the Bill Ivy trophy (400cc class), won the New Era P&M Trophy, came second in the Pegasus Supersport 400 Championships and fifth overall in the National Superteens Series. Gary also won the title of 'Most Improved Rider' awarded by *Motor Cycle News* that year.

After the season was finished, Gary, his girlfriend Jenny, Susan and myself were all invited to the Greenwich & District Motorcycle Club's annual dinner where Gary was awarded not only the Mark Salle Trophy, but also the legendary Greenwich Cup, which had been awarded to a long list of star riders, including Mike Hailwood.

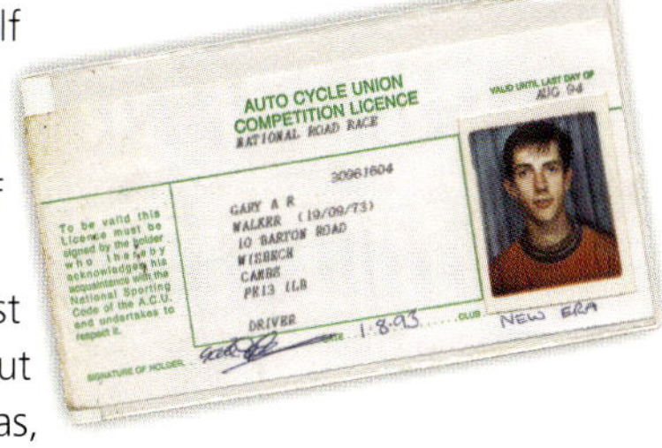

Besides the Bill Ivy meeting at Cadwell Park in June, probably the greatest day was the final round of the Superteen Series at Mallory Park. Here Gary put in a battling performance to gain a rostrum finish (third) against what was, after all, the cream of young British racing talent. Then, in the final race meeting of the year for the National Supersport 400 class Gary had a superb race at Cadwell Park, showing that he could compete against all the top adult stars.

Gary on the Suzuki RGV250 at the Snetterton Esses in the 1993 Kent Racing Combine Supersport 400 – four races, four wins.

But then came a bombshell, the ACU was axing the 400 class from the national calendar for the 1994 season. A complete rethink would have to be made. Together, Gary and I attempted to purchase what we hoped would be a competitive machine. We settled on a 1993 Honda RS250 – the first year of the single-sided-swinging-arm model. However, what we did not know at the time was that this machine was being sold because of a series of problems experienced by the previous owner. I was to discover later that although the engine had been rebuilt by a top tuner, he must have been asked to use 'time-expired' components!

We should have known we were in for trouble right from the very first run on a local byroad in February. Immediately the engine was put under load, the clutch burnt out. During the first few meetings more problems surfaced. At Snetterton, during practice for the national meeting in April, the crankshaft failed, taking with it both cylinders and pistons. To fix this blow-up cost a mind-numbing £3,500, more than a third of the bike's original cost.

At the same time I joined up with my old friend Tommy Stoner, who sadly died the following year. Tommy was a brilliant two-stroke tuner, a real 'garden shed' engineer, but one who knew what he was doing. The combination of a complete engine rebuild and Tommy's expertise at last gave us a machine that was reliable. However, even Tommy couldn't solve the machine's biggest weakness, a gearbox with all the wrong ratios. Honda should never have released the design as it was. From 1995 onwards they solved the problem with an all-new box, but that didn't help owners of the 1993 models!

Tommy, Gary, Jenny, Susan and I all got on well together. Although Tommy had a serious heart problem and was confined to a wheelchair, he was always cracking jokes. Sometimes he went too far, as I was to discover to my cost one day at Mallory Park. We were parked right next to the gate where riders went into the reception area prior to their race. Parked alongside was an ice-cream van. As the day was hot and sunny there was a constant gaggle of customers. At one stage a very attractive young lady was standing in the queue. Tommy shouted something unrepeatable to her, and the next thing 'Mr Muscles' appeared wanting revenge. As there was only Tommy and myself with our team van nearby, Mr Muscles decided it was me who had made the saucy remark to his woman. Someone in a wheelchair could not possibly have said such a thing. The next thing I knew I was being lifted off my feet by the very irate boyfriend. Luckily, Tommy owned up and apologised, which thankfully ended the matter.

With Gary, March 1993. The machine is a 1992 Suzuki RGV250 modified for Supersport 400 competition

Steven's skating championship

During the period when his brother Gary was in hospital following the Brands Hatch accident, Steven was due to take part in the British Skating Championship in Birmingham. It would have been quite understandable if he had scratched his entry but Gary would not have wanted that. Instead, Steven finished 3rd in the 20,000 metres. As he recalls, 'Somehow I managed to put in an exceptional performance that day. It seemed to work out that day, and I dedicated the result to Gary, it was as if he was with me...'

This Mallory meeting was to see Gary battle for the lead in the 250 GP class with his namesake Chris Walker, who was also racing a Honda RS250. Around the same time (July 1994) Gary competed in the British Grand Prix at Donington Park. At the point when a top-15 place in the 250 GP support race seemed in the bag, a fellow competitor who he was lapping fell off, taking Gary with him. The irony was that the end of the race was in sight. In August, Gary had a race-long duel with top British 250 star Nigel Bosworth at Pembrey in South Wales, proving that he was becoming truly competitive on his new bike.

The Cadwell Park round of the British Championship series was at the end of August. Here, at the Lincolnshire circuit, Gary was to save the life of a fellow competitor, the Portuguese rider Fernando Mendes. A fire erupted in his caravan near where we were parked, and Gary pulled him to safety. Just a week later, with Gary on the 'threshold of stardom' as one commentator described him just a few days before his 21st birthday, fate took a hand at the Brands Hatch Supercup meeting, Sunday 4 September 1994.

That Friday, I had travelled to Snetterton to meet a fellow racer who had the remainder of an RS250 for sale, having used the forks, wheels and bodywork to construct a single-cylinder racer. I bought the remaining bits, engine, electrics, carburettors, frame, exhausts and several smaller components. Gary took a quantity of the newly purchased parts – including the electrics – with him and arrived at Brands on Friday evening with Jenny, Tommy and one of Gary's fans (photographer Gary Clarke). I joined them at Brands the next morning, where another competitor – the only other rider with a Honda RS250 – approached me. Could he borrow an electrical part so that he could race? I agreed to loan the said item, little knowing what would transpire from this simple act of assistance.

Qualifying over, Gary was on the grid next to former works star Ron Haslam, who was making a return to racing that weekend. I can't remember the exact grid position, but it was somewhere around 15th out of a field of 40. Gary's race was mid-afternoon on Sunday. The race began, and after the first lap Gary came round tucked in behind Ron Haslam, somewhere midfield. But after another lap the red flag was shown, and all the riders came back to the start line.

After about five minutes the circuit was ready for action again, and I, together with others, was cleared off the grid. Then came tragedy. During the restart, Gary's machine appeared to be hit from behind. Gary and the Honda went down and the rider who had borrowed the electrics from me the day before smashed into him. We just couldn't believe it. Of course the race was stopped. It seemed ages before a helicopter arrived to transport my injured son to the Royal London Hospital in Whitechapel, East London.

The 250 race was abandoned. Susan and I were escorted and locked into an office in the main building above the start line. There we were seen by Nicola Foulston (then the Chief Executive at Brands Hatch) and the Chief Medical Officer, who informed me that Gary would be 'alright' and I would be sending him a bottle of whisky for Christmas. Nicola Foulston arranged for a taxi to take Susan, Jenny and myself to the hospital, where I asked the taxi to wait – but almost immediately we were told that we would not be going anywhere. And so the nightmare began.

As the Brands meeting was being televised live by the BBC, many people, including my brother and his wife Pat, immediately knew what had happened and were thrown into a state of shock when the news of the incident was broadcast. Also, the presenter Sue Barker subsequently gave a tribute to Gary. But we never saw it, as we were still at the hospital when it was transmitted.

We were escorted to Intensive Care where a doctor told us just how serious the situation was. Gary was not expected to survive the night. In fact he did, and we were destined to stay at the hospital for 10 long days. Halfway through this time, we were asked if we would agree to the donation of Gary's organs. Well, Susan and I decided yes we would, as we now realised there could only be one outcome, but Jenny was firmly against this. It resulted in a lot of soul-searching. Worse still, after Gary died (never regaining consciousness) we were told that because of the drugs which had been administered only his corneas could in fact have been used.

We had been accommodated in a small room next to the Intensive Care unit. It had two single beds, so I slept on the floor. There wasn't even a picture on the wall. We eventually discovered that there was a widespread theft problem. In fact, in the waiting room opposite our quarters, everything was chained down. It was here that I first met a little old lady collecting money for the Air Ambulance. I hadn't realised that this vital service was not funded by the government (shame on them!) but entirely by public donation. This lady's husband had been saved by the Air Ambulance, and even though the same had not been possible with Gary, I remain an avid supporter of the Trust.

The day after our return to Wisbech, I had to return to Kent, this time to formally identify Gary's body at Dartford. I was transported down there by my trusty brother-in-law Tony Plumridge and his wife Jean. Back home, the telephone did not stop ringing for weeks and hundreds of letters and cards arrived with messages of shared grief, support and love.

The following appeared in the *Wisbech Standard* newspaper on 16 September 1994, headed 'Gary loses fight for life'. The Sports Editor Charlie Wyatt, now one of the UK's top sports journalists, wrote, 'Fenland has lost its most promising sports star. Gary Walker was believed by many to have all the credentials to become a major force in British motorcycling. But Gary, who would have been 21 on Monday, lost his fight for life on Wednesday afternoon. He died after receiving multiple head and chest injuries following a horror crash at Brands Hatch nearly two weeks ago.' Charlie Wyatt ended with the following words, 'His family has been flooded with calls and cards from wellwishers, including some of his rivals throughout the world. Anyone who met Gary knew his complete love of motorsport. The sport is mourning the loss of a great talent who was also a superb ambassador for his town.'

Gary's funeral was attended by some 500 people. I soon gave up cursing God and asking why Gary? Instead Susan and I decided on a more positive approach. We would help other youngsters achieve their dream – we were sure this was what our son would have wished us to do.

Two negative issues did stand out, though. The first was the inquest. When this was finally held, many months after the event, not only did the rider who allegedly caused Gary's accident tell the inquest that it wasn't him, but there were several lawyers solely representing the Brands Hatch circuit. I still wonder, why were they there? I never did get any answers. The official in charge of the inquest wanted to adjourn the hearing, but I stood up and said, 'It could be Gary standing up there, if he [the rider] says he didn't do it, we have to accept that.'

The other incident was a phone call six months after the accident. The caller rang wanting to speak to Gary. When I asked where she was phoning from, the answer horrified me. She said that it was the Royal London Hospital. I told her that Gary had died there. There was an embarrassed silence and the telephone line went dead. I can only conclude that someone must have pressed the wrong computer key.

I prefer not to dwell on the negatives. Of all the hundreds of letters and cards we received, one I remember well said, 'God takes the best for himself'. This was the nearest to an answer I ever got. Rest in peace, dear son and friend.

11 Passing It On

I came up with the idea of creating a race team

With Darren North at the Springfield Show, Spalding in January 1995.

Mick Walker Racing was formed not long after Gary's tragic death. Susan and I had been invited back to Brands the following month, and before I knew what was happening I was escorted to the commentary box above the circuit's start line. While being interviewed, I came up with the idea of creating a race team to mentor young British talent. Over the next decade or so, 30 riders were to benefit. Many of my 'pupils' became well known in the road racing world, including Johnny Angel, Ollie Bridewell, Dijon Compton, Guy Etherington, Michael Gavin, Rod Hamblin, Mark Heckles, John Ingram, Dean Johnson, Robin King, Steven Neate, Darren North, Barry Rudd, James Toseland, Tom Tunstall, and Darren Wnukoski.

The first was Worksop youngster, Darren North, who I had selected after considering Chris Walker (no relation). With Chris, the set-up would have included Jack Machin, who I had known for many years. Brother of the top 1970s' racer Steve Machin, and a fellow dealer with premises in Lincoln, Jack was a skilled engineer and two-stroke tuner. Although I'm sure that the Chris Walker/Jack Machin/Mick Walker partnership would have been the more successful venture, I opted for Darren – mainly because this would be closest to the spirit of my original objective, to help youngsters. Darren was given Gary's 1993 updated RS250 Honda to race in the 1995 British 250 Championship series (at that time referred to as Supercup). I went up to Worksop to meet Darren at his parents' home, where I talked to him and Shaun Webster, his race mechanic and mentor. As it was a dark winter evening, I didn't know that Darren's dad Derek had decided to valet my car during my visit. Somebody had a nice surprise, because it wasn't my car that he cleaned!

Then came a totally unexpected tie-up with Moto Guzzi/Laverda/Cagiva importer Three Cross Motorcycles – based in Verwood, Dorset, and run by my old friend Keith Davies. Keith and I knew each other from the Coburn & Hughes days in the 1970s. Before Gary's accident I had contacted Three Cross regarding a second edition of the *Illustrated Moto Guzzi Buyers Guide*, which was to be published by Motorbooks. When I spoke to Three Cross again, the secretary asked why I had been so long in getting back to them, so I told her about Gary's death. Highly embarrassed, she put me straight through to Keith, who was as stunned to hear the news, and invited me to visit as soon as possible.

A few days later, I took up the offer and went to Dorset. After talking of old times, Keith suddenly said, 'Considering your plan to help youngsters in racing, I have a proposal for you'. Essentially, Keith's idea was for me to run a Three Cross-backed team of riders in the newly launched 125 Superteen series. This was to be held at British championship meetings during 1995, where it replaced the 250 two-stroke/400 four-stroke Superteen class of the previous few years. The new class would only be open to teenagers, riding a 125cc series-production motorcycle. At that time, two machines stood the best chance of winning the new class – the Aprilia RS125SP or the Cagiva Mito Evo SP. (SP meant Sport Production; and both machines were dominating a similar series in Italy.) I was enthusiastic for two reasons: my friendship with Keith, and because I could feel it was the right thing to do. Keith was offering me freedom to choose the riders, overall charge of the bikes, spares backup – in fact, the whole works. This arrangement worked out very nicely, for it would complement my agreement with Darren on the 250 Honda, and everyone would be racing at the same meetings.

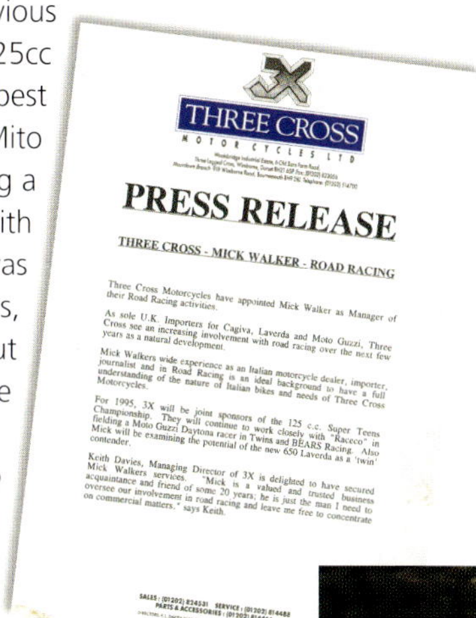
3X

THREE CROSS
MOTOR CYCLES LTD

PRESS RELEASE

THREE CROSS - MICK WALKER - ROAD RACING

Three Cross Motorcycles have appointed Mick Walker as Manager of their Road Racing activities.

As sole U.K. Importers for Cagiva, Laverda and Moto Guzzi, Three Cross see an increasing involvement with road racing over the next few years as a natural development.

Mick Walkers wide experience as an Italian motorcycle dealer, importer, journalist and in Road Racing is an ideal background to have a full understanding of the nature of Italian bikes and needs of Three Cross Motorcycles.

For 1995, 3X will be joint sponsors of the 125 c.c. Super Teens Championship. They will continue to work closely with "Raceco" in fielding a Moto Guzzi Daytona racer in Twins and BEARS Racing. Also Mick will be examining the potential of the new 650 Laverda as a 'twin' contender.

Keith Davies, Managing Director of 3X is delighted to have secured Mick Walkers services. "Mick is a valued and trusted business acquaintance and friend of some 20 years; he is just the man I need to oversee our involvement in road racing and leave me free to concentrate on commercial matters." says Keith.

SALES: (01202) 824531 SERVICE: (01202) 814488
PARTS & ACCESSORIES: (01202) 814466

The first real task for the Three Cross Cagiva effort was to select two riders. My initial choice was Dean Johnson and Rod Hamblin. Both had road-racing experience, Dean (who was from Leicestershire) in Classic racing with a Honda 350 twin, while Rod (from Lincolnshire) was competing on a Suzuki RGV 250 owned by former racer Andy Stubbs. I already knew Dean's father, Bill Johnson who ran a motorcycle dealership in Ashby De La Zouch, while Rod's uncle was well-known sidecar racer Mick Hamblin. Bill Johnson was also a friend-of-a-friend – Dave Kay – he of MV Agusta and Gilera replica fame. All the interviews and agreements were concluded before Christmas 1994, ahead of a date set for a dinner in Wisbech, where people involved with the Mick Walker Racing team could meet socially prior to the start of the racing season. This January dinner became an annual affair for the next 15 years.

Dean Johnson on a Cagiva Mito in the 1995 Snetterton Superteens.

Mick Walker Racing's Cagiva Mitos at the ACU National Awards presentation in November 1995.

The Race Team Dinners

In Gary's memory, we held a series of Mick Walker Race Team dinners, the first of which was at Mendi's, Wisbech in January 1995. From then until our final dinner at the Duke's Head, Kings Lynn in 2009, we enjoyed excellent food and comradeship as well as a huge raffle and an auction. The auction raised large amounts of money for various charities. In the early days, monies raised supported the race team's riders. Later on we were able to donate to the Air Ambulance, the Bob McIntyre Memorial Meeting and Joan Seeley Pain Relief. In January 2005, the newly crowned World Superbike Champion James Toseland (a former Mick Walker Racing teamster) brought himself and his magnificent championship-winning trophy to the dinner. We also had visitors from Europe, USA and Australia.

The dinner was always restricted to relatively small numbers. Former race secretary and official Brenda Scivyer described it as 'a lovely, family-orientated event. The great joy of the event was the tremendous atmosphere. It was never advertised, its success being spread by word of mouth. Some fantastic friendships were formed'. From 1996, the event made the 400-year-old Rose & Crown Hotel in Wisbech its home. Owned at that time by Felix Apicella and his wife Patricia, this was a wonderful venue. When Felix and Patricia sold the hotel, the new owner did not want to accommodate motorcyclists. We then moved to Knights Hill on the outskirts of Kings Lynn, where the dinner stayed until 2008. During the early years I organised the event myself, but for the last nine years the role was taken over by Paul Clarkson. Paul was also our auctioneer, responsible for the consistently high prices we achieved. In 2010, the Mick Walker Racing Dinner was cancelled because of the terrible weather; Paul and I decided it wasn't worth the risk. Little did we know at the time, this was to be the last.

James Toseland with his World Superbike championship trophy at the 2005 Team Dinner.

Darren North and his mechanic Shaun Webster had already taken delivery of the Honda RS250, but the Cagivas and the associated components were not due until just before the Superteen launch day at Snetterton in late March. This was organised by the ACU, which was running the British championship series at the time. The bikes duly arrived with no problems, and my riders looked resplendent in their brand new team leathers, manufactured by Crowtree Leathers of Louth, courtesy of Lynda and Alec Baumber.

The first round of the 1995 British Championship series for both the 250 and Superteens took place at Donington Park in April, where the Superteen race was televised by Eurosport, with Keith Heuwen as commentator. Rod Hamblin was the star of the day – even though he was to be disqualified for falling off in the race (the fact that he remounted and crossed the finishing line first did not change the official ruling). When Keith Heuwen interviewed Rod, he was too embarrassed to reply, and I had to speak on his behalf. This brought it home to me that teenagers needed coaching in media skills. There was the further problem – which ultimately turned out to have serious implications – that Rod's RGV 'sponsor' and mechanic Andy Stubbs (who I hadn't met), took part in the interview, and Rod's father Ken was also present. Rod won the Brands Hatch round on the full 2.5-mile GP circuit, but suffered a retirement at Mallory Park. It was then that he announced he wanted to concentrate on riding his 250. I tried hard to keep him in the team and his Uncle Mick and Auntie Pat tried equally hard to convince him that a team ride in a British Championship was more important than racing Andy's Suzuki at club level, but to no avail. From then on we only had one Cagiva rider pitched against the hordes of Aprilias.

However, providing Dean with two machines (his original, plus Rod's as a spare) was no bad thing, as only one rider could be champion. The night before the final race at Snetterton there was a story going around that the opposition was so rattled that they would try to bribe Dean and his dad to throw the race. Keith Davies was all for reporting this to the race officials, but I suggested that the best result would be for Dean to race, and prove his point in the only way that mattered. And this is exactly what transpired, with Dean and the Cagiva clinching the title. Happy scenes followed, with our little team of Keith Davies, Dean and Bill Johnson, mechanic Rex Caunt, plus me, celebrating a hard-fought championship win that was achieved against overwhelming odds.

The original race team in December 1994.

1995 team riders Rod Hamblin, Darren North and Dean Johnson.

Mark Heckles, August 1996, Cagiva Superteens

Obviously, this was not received with much enthusiasm by the rival camp, but we were the 1995 Superteen Champions, and I spent much of the winter of 1995/96 making plans to repeat the performance the following season. This included a test day to select a rider to replace Dean, who would not be able to defend his title because he would be 20 before the beginning of the 1996 season. He would go on (with my blessing) to join Fowlers of Bristol with a new Yamaha TZ 250 to contest the 250 British Championships.

My original plan had been to hire the Mallory Park circuit for a day in November 1995 to try out a few potential replacements for Dean. I contacted *MCN* and asked them to promote the idea via their weekly Paddock Gossip column. However, *MCN* got the story wrong, saying that it was open to all youngsters under the age of 20 – even if they had never ridden a motorcycle before!

On the day, heavy rain persisted. Over 200 keen – but inexperienced – youngsters turned up. Luckily, we had brought more than one machine, and amazingly the whole event went off without a single crash. Some of this good fortune was due to the detailed briefing session with instructions and training carried out prior to the riders actually taking to the track. The Mallory Park clubhouse/cafe did a roaring trade and David Overend, Mallory Park's Managing Director was genuinely impressed with what I was doing. At the end of the day, he generously waived all charges. Later, David and I came to an agreement where I was to organise a novice day in February, prior to the racing season getting under way. This session, with a format similar to the November 1995 test day, became an annual event at the Leicestershire circuit for several years.

Back at the test day to find Dean's replacement, among the many keen riders were Mark Heckles and James Toseland. Mark ultimately got Dean's ride, so to speak, while James (who had won the Junior Racing Association title in 1995 on an 80cc Cagiva) still joined the Cagiva ranks for the 1996 Superteen series after his stepfather Ken purchased a new Mito Evo SP for him.

Besides my Cagiva Team Manager role, my time with Three Cross also brought Laverda and Moto Guzzi racing connections. As part of my deal to run the Cagiva Superteen effort, Keith Davies had loaned me one of the newly released Laverda 650 Sport parallel twins as a road bike. Putting some 6,000 miles on the clock gave me a good feel for the machine, and I must say I was sad to hand the bike back, nine months later. The red 650 Sport was physically small, the same size as an RGV 250 Suzuki, with a near-perfect riding position for my 5ft 10in frame. My lasting impressions of the 650 Sport were that its power delivery (nothing under 5,000rpm) was almost two-stroke like, and that it had race-quality handling with brakes to match. It never broke down, or refused to start as soon as the starter button was activated. It inspired real confidence in wet conditions, which was admirably demonstrated on a 280-mile round trip from Wisbech to Darley Moor race circuit, in truly dreadful conditions, with Susan on the back. However, it seems that my experiences with the Laverda were somewhat lucky, as later batches of bikes did not feature the luxury of White Power suspension, while certain other component parts were not of the same high standard; a pity really, as it was potentially a brilliant little bike.

I was also involved with running the Three Cross 668 (essentially reconstructed from a 650 Sport) in the 1995 Snetterton 6-hour endurance race. For this event, regular rider Russell Joyner (who then worked for Three Cross) was joined by two of the Mick Walker Racing team pilots, Dean Johnson and Darren North. Unfortunately, Russell crashed out early on at Coram Curve, extensively damaging the machine. After pushing back to the pits the Laverda was repaired, and continued to circulate minus its fairing. We were all left with the what-might-have-been syndrome, because despite the mishap the team finished third in class, even after having missed two of the six hours!

James Toseland in March 1996, competing in the Superteen series.

The Moto Guzzi racing connection came after Keith and I had a meeting with Amedeo Castellani who was campaigning the Three Cross/Raceco Moto Guzzi Daytona-based racer at the time. Amedeo had been involved with Guzzis for many years, with his firm Raceco providing tuning expertise to Team Clarke Racing and their riders Peter Watson and later Ian Cobby. From the 1993 season, this turned into a highly successful joint venture with Three Cross. The Three Cross/Raceco Daytona-based racer had begun as an ex-demonstrator with 8,500 miles on the clock. In its first year, with Torquil Ross-Martin as rider, it weighed 225kg (496lbs) and produced 90bhp. By the time it was last raced in 1997 by Ian Cobby, the weight was down to 175kg (385lbs), while the power had leaped to a staggering 140bhp! Other riders to straddle the beast were Richard Defago (early 1994), Rick Lewenden (late 1994) and Aussie ex-GP star Paul Lewis (nicknamed the 'Angry Ant') in 1995. The machine won every race it competed in and more often than not, set pole in qualifying to boot.

I feel that the most important contribution I was able to make was pointing out the importance of having a top class rider on board the machine, and with the arrival of Paul Lewis my reasoning was vindicated. Paul's first-ever race on the bike was at Mallory Park. Everyone else was sure that Paul would be unable to adapt to the heavyweight Guzzi, but I was proved right. Not only did he beat Battle of the Twins expert Ian Cobby, but his performance was truly electric.

Another Three Cross engagement at the end of 1995 was an 11-day stint at the NEC Birmingham Motorcycle Show, where I displayed Dean's championship-winning Cagiva Mito Evo SP. Over the course of the show, I spoke to a vast number of race-goers and it turned out that our efforts had been followed with great enthusiasm by a lot of people, including some of the cast of television's *The Bill*. Some of our rivals also called to see me, including Nick Mead and his father, owner of the Mead Racing Superbike team.

On the brilliant Laverda 650 Sport parallel twin.

The Gary Walker Memorial meeting

On Colin Pascoe's Manx, Mallory Park 2001

The first Gary Walker Memorial Trophy meeting was held at Brands Hatch over the weekend of 7/8 October 1995, organised by the New Era Club. Riders in the 250cc open race competed for the Youngs Motors Cup, to be presented annually in Gary's memory. The winner was the same rider who had been involved in Gary's fatal accident. Somehow, this seemed to be his way of paying respect to Gary, with an outstanding performance. There was also a 'Man of the Meeting' award, the Gary Walker Memorial Trophy supplied by The Fenman Classic Bike Show and chosen by myself for the best overall performance during the day. That year saw another event in Gary's memory, the second being a Ducati single-cylinder race held at Mallory Park as part of the annual Race of the Year. Many of my old racing friends took part, including Arthur Wheeler and Stu Rogers.

The following year, Mallory became home to the memorial meeting, with all the Sunday races entitled 'Gary Walker Memorial Trophy' events. By 1997, this was an annual affair, with the magnificent Fenman Classic Bike Show main trophy, and over a dozen other sponsors contributing cups and shields. During the meeting, there was a collection on behalf of the Memorial Trust, and every rider received a specially minted medallion. Each year, Mick Walker Racing Team members took part; in 1997, it was Guy Etherington, Ian Kimberly, Tom Tunstall, Michael Gavin and Darren Wnukoski.

The 1998 event saw a new formula, described by the New Era Club president Jim Parker: 'The annual Gary Walker Memorial meeting this year is joined by Forza Italia. The two events are unique in the motorcycling calendar and it is fitting that Mick Walker, Gary's father, should be involved in both, having been connected with Italian motorcycles since 1961. With no less than 15 annual trophies at stake, this year's event promises something really special with races for not only modern racing machines, but also Formula 750 and Ducati Single Cylinder machines. There's an international flavour, with riders not only from all over Great Britain but several European countries, including Belgium, France and Germany. A special feature of the day is the various lunchtime parades – including ones for all today's competitors, Italian owners clubs, British bikes and sidecar owners. There will also be some demonstrations by Mick Walker and Roger Wilson with ex-works Gilera and MV Agusta racers!'

Channel 5 television was also in attendance, shooting a documentary on team rider Guy Etherington, about whom the programme said: 'the reigning New Era 125 GP Champion, having won the title at the age of 17 in his first year of adult racing. He first raced at the age of 14 in the Junior Racing Association's Championships, which was where he first came to the attention of Mick Walker. Over the years Mick has spotted and helped many young riders to fulfil their potential. Guy has ridden as a member of the Mick Walker Racing Team for the last four years and much of his success has been down to Mick's vast experience and knowledge of the racing scene.'

The memorial meeting was a popular feature of the British racing scene until 2007, when rising costs – particularly insurance – made me realise that sadly, enough was enough. But although there are no more memorial meetings, the many competitors there have been are a great tribute to Gary's memory.

At the time, Three Cross was one of three official UK Ducati importers (the others being Moto Cinelli and Sports Motorcycles). With Dean's Cagiva and me centre stage on the Ducati stand, I was able to help out with Ducati business when not involved in racing talk. From this, I discovered a new breed of Ducati customer, the kind who took his bike to the local dealer to have the final drive chain adjusted and lubricated. At the time, there was a huge waiting list for the 916 model. This caused a lot of ill feeling, and one member of the Sports Motorcycles staff was assaulted by an irate customer. There was also an incident involving Moto Cinelli owner Hoss Elm. One of Cinelli's customers arrived with his friends to make a complaint, as he hadn't received the part he had ordered. When Hoss Elm mentioned that he was having a similar problem with bits for his Range Rover, it turned out that the Ducati owner and his mates all worked at the local Land Rover factory, so the dispute carried on until Hoss decided to leave, not returning for several hours.

By halfway through the show, my throat was suffering and I almost lost my voice. On that very day an overseas Ducati single-cylinder enthusiast turned up saying he had waited for years for to meet me. I had to communicate by writing most of the answers on a note pad! Eleven days at the NEC show were more than long enough and I was relieved when it came to an end. Luckily it came prior to the *Motor Cycle News* day at Donington Park where Chris Walker crashed and badly damaged our number one Cagiva machine.

Much more enjoyable was the Road & Race Show at Alexandra Palace, North London, early in 1996. Again I was on duty for Three Cross, together with the race team. Alexandra Palace was a special location, entirely different to the vastness of the NEC complex. Here was a bit of history, not just because of its architectural interest, but also because back in 1935 there had been a couple of road races at the venue with many top stars of the day in attendance. In my book *British Motorcycle Racing Circuits since 1907*, I explained that the circuit was pretty dangerous due to the combination of various surfaces and widths, a steep hilly section and an equally steep incline elsewhere; there were even tramlines which were lethal in the wet. Anyone who has visited Alexandra Palace will appreciate why these races didn't continue.

Beaten in 1995, Aprilia decided to fight back by using special factory engines for selected riders during the 1996 season, although the rules clearly stated only production bikes were eligible. Although in Mark Heckles and James Toseland I probably had two of the very best riders, the standard production Cagiva Mito SP simply was not in the same league – and neither was the production Aprilia. The only circuit where we got a good result that year was Cadwell Park in August. James was runner-up and Mark third. For 1997, Aprilia went a stage further and purchased the Superteens series, making it far less interesting, as the only element of competition was the riding. The series rapidly went downhill, becoming a poorly supported number of races at club level. This was a sad end to what could have been a major stepping-stone for British youngsters. Unfortunately, as in many other sports, finance and business became more important than talent.

Even before Aprilia grabbed the Superteen class, I could see that it was a waste of time and money taking part, as the lack of a genuine choice of race bikes had effectively ruined what had previously been a very competitive form of racing. When everyone was on production power, results were governed by rider ability. But from the beginning of 1996 this changed. Now there were only a few machines capable of winning – those fitted with 'factory' Aprilia engines. Everyone else was now a second-class citizen and I told Keith not to waste his money continuing with this class.

My involvement with the Superteen series thus came to an end with the 1996 season, but my enthusiasm had died some time earlier. In part this was due to the level of gamesmanship, but also by what happened behind the scenes. In 1995 the British Championship series (including the Superteens) had been run by the sports governing body, the ACU. But from 1996 it was taken over by the MCRCB (Motor Cycle Racing Control Board), known to the racing fraternity as 'the Coal Board'. Essentially, the MCRCB was run by a couple of key ACU officials, who had been headhunted by the new set-up. To me, it seemed like a Trojan horse. By the time the ACU realised what was happening, it was all over, with the MCRCB firmly in charge of British short-circuit racing at top level, a situation that remains to the present day.

As an example of how British Championship meetings were run during this era, I recall an incident that happened some time after I had quit as the Cagiva Superteen co-ordinator. Taking in the Snetterton round as a paying customer, I arrived early on the Sunday morning, before racing had got under way, and parked my motorcycle just outside the paddock. As I took off my helmet, I heard a tannoy announcement saying, 'Would Mick Walker immediately report to race control'. I was not involved with any rider at the meeting, but I wandered over to the race office, to be confronted by a very irate-looking race director. He said, 'Right you, upstairs!' where he announced that he was giving me a lifetime ban from British Championship meetings.

To say that I was amazed would be an understatement. I asked for an explanation, but he just ranted on. Eventually it transpired that a young lad had attempted to sell two tickets at the gate that morning, and had been apprehended and brought before the race control. This young rider was wearing a Mick Walker Racing jacket, which had been given to him months earlier at my Mallory Park novice-training day in recognition of his progress on the day. I asked what the MCRCB would have done if he'd been wearing a Honda jacket and suggested that they should get their facts right before they judge someone. I walked out of the race control tower, never to hear from them again, with this incident only serving to deepen my dislike of the whole Gestapo-like circus.

Mick Walker Racing Team 1997,
left to right: Darren Wnukoski, Ian Kimberley, Tom Tunstall, Guy Etherington and Michael Gavin.

Darren Wnukoski was unbeatable on the 400 Yamaha at the beginning of 1997.

And so I switched my efforts from national to club events, which was a breath of fresh air. Instead of officious individuals, I was now dealing with genuine racing enthusiasts. I also discovered and brought on a number of promising youngsters and not-so-young riders over the next decade. One of the first was Darren Wnukoski. Darren would and could have gone much further than he did. However he was not really a team player, and found it hard to accept advice or even follow a pre-arranged policy, which was to prove to be his undoing. At the beginning of 1997 Darren was unbeatable in the Supersport 400 class at club level, but I knew sooner or later he would come up against someone his equal. It happened at Cadwell Park during a round of the ACU Clubmans 400 series, which Darren was leading quite comfortably. My pre-race instructions had been to avoid a 'dog-fight'. Instead, follow the competition, learn his moves, lines and tactics and on the final part of the last lap go through and win. But no, Darren did not take a blind bit of notice. He and the other rider, Darren Mitchell, who had raced at the highest level, and was making a come-back, proceeded to have a battle royal. They swapped places many times on each of the ten laps. Finally, almost within sight of the finish line 'my' Darren attempted a move that resulted in a high-speed crash and a broken leg. Although he did eventually return, even racing in British Superbike meetings, he was never quite the same. His riding ability had lost the potential that had been evident before his prang. This little escapade taught me a lesson, Darren was in his late twenties and, it would have been easier for me to coach a keen teenager than someone who was already set in his ways.

Another school for young riders was the JRA (Junior Racing Association), set up by Les Etherington and Adrian Pallet. Adrian ran the series after Les's son Guy became a competitor himself. The first year of the JRA national championships was 1995, and the series was won by future double-World Superbike Champion, our own James Toseland. For the 1996 season, I supported Guy Etherington, and he duly became the JRA champion, riding a Cagiva 80. We then went on to make it a hat trick with Michael Gavin in 1997.

At the final Mallory Park round of the 1997 series, Michael effectively took the title by winning the championship race before the lunch break. However, there was another, non-championship race that afternoon, for which I was invited into the commentary box. This time, the main competitor to Michael throughout the season won the race, and on this occasion the duty commentator decided – on the spur of the moment – to go down to the start line and interview him. Imagine his surprise when he discovered that the rider was not who he thought it would be, but a well-known British Championship class contender! Michael Gavin's father was absolutely furious, but nothing was done by the race officials or, for that matter, the ACU. If these antics go on at club level, heaven knows what happens at higher levels when the dealer/sponsor credibility and the financial stakes are much higher. It does not bear thinking about.

Darren Wnukoski, 400 Yamaha, Snetterton 1997

Tom Tunstall rode in the 125 championship that I organised for Mallory Park and the East Midlands Racing Association in 1996.

With the support of his parents, Les and Sally, Guy Etherington had moved up to the 125 class at club level during 1997. He was a real pleasure to work with and a quick learner. Soon he was getting up near the front of the field and collecting valuable points towards the New Era Club Championship, which he went on to win. The last round was at Brands Hatch, with the championship race postponed until after lunch, effectively a re-run. Guy's father Les was far less laid back about this than Guy, who simply took everything in his stride. This paid off and he clinched the title. But Guy was a growing lad and soon the 125 was too small for him. He progressed to larger machinery and a new entrant, Jim Blomey, for whom he rode a big Moto Guzzi and an ex-Barry Sheene Suzuki TR750. Finally he rode for Jack Lilley Motorcycles on a Triumph at British Superbike events.

Another rider with whom I was associated at around the same time was Yorkshire-based Tom Tunstall. Tom had been one of the riders of a factory-engined Aprilia in the 1996 Superteens championship. I was asked to represent Mallory Park together with the EMRA (East Midlands Racing Association) and run a championship for production 125s at their EMRA meetings during 1996. Tom had won this and so had earned the right for the Mallory Park/EMRA sponsorship (a total of some £5,000). The concept was to help a young British rider to progress into the 125 British Championship series, where Tom was to campaign an RS125 Honda. We were joined by Robin Appleyard, son of Colin, a well-known 125 rider himself as well as being a businessman. Most of the Mallory/EMRA money went to Appleyard, as did most of the publicity, and by mid-season the Tunstalls realised that once the money had been handed over, Robin Appleyard lost interest. The only bright spot was when Tom nipped past Robin on the last corner during the final round of the championship at Oulton Park. I always got on well with the Tunstall family and only ended our association due to pressure of other commitments.

Guy Etherington, 75cc Cagiva,
Mallory Park 1996 Championship winner

Barry Rudd, winner of the 1999 Honda Cup national championship series

The 1999 race team with riders Barry Rudd (left) and Robin King, plus support staff.

During 1999, I supported local rider Barry Rudd and Cambridge racer Robin King, Barry on a 600 Honda and Robin on a 400 Yamaha. As they were both contesting the New Era Super Club meetings this worked out well. Barry ultimately won his championship, but Robin suffered a major get-off mid-season, which effectively prevented him doing the same. I had also discovered Ollie Bridewell, then 12 years of age, at the Mallory Park novice day in 1999. He came to ride a recently purchased Aprilia RS125. What struck me was how keen he was and the fact that even at this young age he was a wonderful person. In some ways he was more like a little professor than a budding motorcycle racer. I was already committed to helping Barry and Robin that year, but Ollie's enthusiasm meant that he was taken on as an apprentice, and so I went to several Superteens series meetings in which he was competing that year.

For the following season, the decision was taken to race in the 125 class at New Era Club events, with Ollie soon being given the nickname 'Milky Bar Kid' by long-time race commentator/journalist Chris Carter. Ollie had two seasons on the RS125, learning the trade. Rather strangely, during this period my main problem with Ollie was his lack of belief in himself, but it was something we worked on, to a point where he was eventually awarded a 'Man of the Meeting' award; quite an achievement for one so young. The second year we also took in some other meetings, notably EMRA events at Mallory Park. Then Ollie made the move up to the new Yamaha R6 Cup, a one-model race series that was run at British Championship meetings. As I hated the whole big-time circus atmosphere of such events, I decided that Ollie and I should go our separate ways. In my case, coaching was usually spread over a specific period and by a certain point the rider would or should have progressed to a higher level, but I was also careful to ensure that I did not get too attached to any of my charges.

With an enthusiastic Ollie Bridewell and the Honda RS125, circa 2000.

So for the 2002 season I took on Steven Neate (son of ex-racer John Neate, who had competed in the 400 class at the same time as my late son, Gary). Steven was a gifted rider, who progressed while with me from a complete novice to being taken on by Red Bull in the 125 British Championship series the following year.

Ollie Bridewell at Snetterton in July 2001.

During Ollie's second year in the R6 Cup, the first couple of meetings had not gone too well for him. And so one spring evening, Ollie telephoned me to ask if I would consider coming back on board with him. I didn't want to attend any British Championship meetings, but I said I would coach him again – but this time by telephone. To be honest, the telephone idea was a long shot, but I felt that it might just work, as I knew how Ollie's mind worked. My job had always been to offer advice, transfer my experience to his on-track performances and most of all encourage his self-belief.

This was important. Ollie's self-esteem, certainly during the early competitive years, was very low. Once we went to a Bank Holiday weekend New Era meeting at Pembrey, and on the drive down the weather was marvellous: hot and not a cloud in the sky. On Saturday it was quite the reverse, cold, wet and miserable, and with this change Ollie's confidence also took a nose-dive; going from a high to a very low, just like a light switch. Ollie had the ability to do well, but the largest task was getting him to realise this.

The first meeting Ollie took in after our reunion was at Thruxton – where even if my presence was only by telephone, it immediately seemed to have made a difference, and he got a top-three finish. But better results were soon to follow. He won the prestigious British Grand Prix support race, which counted towards the R6 championship, and he ended the season as runner-up in the title chase. The Vivaldi Racing team quickly signed him up for the following season's British Superstock (1000cc). This was the major chance that Ollie had been hoping for.

One way of making the transition was being able to harness all that extra brake-horse-power, and so a cunning plan was evolved. Ollie would spend as much time as possible riding a grass-track racing machine around a local field near his Wiltshire home. This, I felt, would replicate what those great American racers of the 1970s and 1980s had achieved. They had come via the dirt and in the process were fully able to use throttle control to their advantage. It would also have the side effect of assisting and lifting Ollie's confidence levels, and it worked! Ollie was no longer overawed by the sheer power now being developed by the Kawasaki 1000cc motor. The following year, 2006, he found himself promoted to the BSB (British Superbike) series.

But Ollie still needed my advice and guidance. It was funny really, I'm sure no one at Vivaldi knew about me, and I was happy to maintain a low profile. Every year, the absolute gentleman in Ollie remained, and he would telephone me each Christmas morning to say, 'Mick will you still coach me next year?' No other rider I helped ever did this, but Ollie always made a point of saying thank you.

Steven Neate, a gifted rider who I coached as a complete novice.

The Neate family,
Snetterton, June 2002

Johnny Angel potential superstar

Johnny, Mick and Sue, Snetterton, British Superbike meeting, May 2007

Of all the young racers I coached, the one that ticked most of the boxes was the last. Johnny Angel's short, but very successful racing career revealed a great potential that was never fully realised.

Born in 1985, Johnny developed a passion for bikes from an early age. 'I would make a race track over my local car park every night and ride round it on my pedal cycle, pretending to be Carl Fogarty'. At 12, Johnny starting earning every penny he could. 'I wanted to take my car park racing to a new level, and had my sights set on a 29cc Goped sit-on scooter… after six months of saving my Goped arrived and I was scraping the belly pan off it within days and having a great time every night.'

At 17, he bought a Suzuki GSX-R400. After a few 'near misses' he quickly realised that the place to go fast was on a circuit, so made the decision to go racing. 'A lot of people told me that I would never be able to afford it, but being young and arrogant I knew what I wanted and set about achieving my dream. I sold my car, sold my bike and stopped going to clubs, to save every penny I could.' Finally, Johnny was able to afford a 1999 Yamaha R6.

Next, helped by support from his parents, came a year of track days and 'getting up to speed' to compete in the Bemsee Rookie 600 series in 2005 on an almost-new, race-prepared CBR 600RR. Johnny took in 18 races to win the Bemsee novice championship, with the final round at his local Brands Hatch circuit, 'in front of all my friends and family who had travelled all over the country to support me all year'.

In 2006, Johnny won 80 per cent of his races, securing the Bemsee club championship. 'My main memory from that year was the partnership formed between myself and my new coach Mick Walker, who coached me throughout 2006 and gave me many words of wisdom. Mick always had a calming way of putting things into perspective for me and I found this really helped keep me settled in the rush-and-go world of motorcycle racing. Mick likes to fly under the radar a little bit, like his approach to coaching, keeping his thoughts to himself most of the time, until you sit down one-to-one with him and then his years of experience shine through.'

For 2007, Johnny moved up to the 1000cc British Superstock Cup series on a Suzuki GSX-R1000K7. It took Johnny three races to get to grips with the bike, but he got onto the podium at Silverstone. All but two of the circuits used for the British Championship were new to him, but he was soon to show his potential; at the mid-season Snetterton event he totally outclassed his experienced opposition to win by over 6 seconds. Johnny was delighted. 'It was a great feeling to win at the top level, having only been a racer for two years – best of all in front of my friends and family – and also great for Mick Walker and his wife Susan to see me blossom.'

But behind the scenes things were far from perfect. Johnny Angel, potential superstar, was to make only one more British Championship outing. In July 2007, he made what he called, 'the hardest decision of my life, to hang up my leathers, but our family business, Angel Design & Print, was struggling like the rest of the economy.' Johnny did receive several offers of sponsorship, but as I explain in my final chapter, the system works on 'you pay us' – you need money to get on, talent is no longer the major factor. The last word goes to Johnny: 'In 2011, it has been over three years since I last raced a motorcycle, but it feels like yesterday. I will always look back on what I achieved with pride and will always be grateful to all the people, including Mick and Sue, who helped and supported me along the way.'

Snetterton 2007, Johnny's first win at British Championship level

Ollie Bridewell, Cadwell Park,
British Superbikes 2006

By the beginning of 2007, Ollie was becoming a major force in the BSB series, beating many of the big names, but our dialogue continued. Then came 20 July, during the unofficial Friday practice session at Mallory that usually precedes the Saturday qualifying for Sunday's BSB race. I was at my desk when Brenda Scivyer (for many years secretary of the New Era Club) phoned to tell me some dreadful news: Ollie Bridewell had suffered a fatal accident.

Strangely, Ollie had phoned me earlier that week, but unfortunately I was not at home. When I heard what had happened, I somehow felt I had come full circle. I had formed my race team to honour my son's memory, but Ollie's death and Johnny Angel's retirement both happened in the same month, and it seemed like time to close the book on this part of my life. This was my final exit from the sport I loved, and in which I had been involved since the early 1960s. In retrospect, there are many things I should have done differently. But my own experiences have helped to make the careers of others more successful than they might have been. I have also made some wonderful friends – and all the low points only make me appreciate even more the highs of what is one of the greatest sports in the world.

Ollie Bridewell, May 2007.

12 Looking Back

the machine I most regret selling is easy...

The arrival in 1969 of the all-conquering Yamaha TD2 (250) and the TR2 (350) over-the-counter production racers played a major part in the development of the classic motorcycle movement a decade later. By the early 1970s, virtually every other racing motorcycle was obsolete, even at the most humble of British club events. The 350 TR2 was not just superior to any other non-works entry in its class, but it was also faster than any single-cylinder 500! Owners of Aermacchi, AJS, Bultaco, Ducati, Greeves, Matchless and Norton racing bikes were left with mounts no longer able to achieve their main purpose – winning races. So, you either bought a Yamaha or accepted the fact that you had about as much chance of winning races as going to the moon.

In 1973, Dave Bailey, the race secretary to the local Newmarket & District Motorcycle & Light Car Club, to give it its full and official title, phoned me. He wanted to know what I thought about his club running a class for single-cylinder machines. Right from the start I was hooked, realising that the concept was suited to the support my company could provide. Dave's idea soon got off the ground. My eagerness to be involved was not only due to being a Ducati specialist, but also because I had retired from competitive riding the previous year. Ducati singles had become so hopelessly outclassed by the latest Yamahas that I had realised that it was of no use continuing, a sentiment felt by many owners who raced single-cylinder machines.

And so, one Sunday in July 1973, the very first race confined to single-cylinder machines took place at Snetterton race circuit. The huge success of this inaugural meeting exceeded everyone's hopes, including Dave Bailey's. Not only was the event grossly over-subscribed, but the array of machinery (including my Saxon-framed 350 Ducati ridden by Mick James) clearly illustrated just why spectators had become disillusioned by the sign of a grid full of screaming 'strokers' with the Yamaha logo on every fuel tank. The range of bikes in the single-cylinder class, with their diverse mixture of sounds and colour schemes, coupled with the atmosphere in the paddock, as well as the crowds, ensured that the Newmarket club made the single-cylinder event a permanent feature on their calendar. It was a historic day, and the seeds that were sown grew into what became known as the Classic Scene.

Oliver's Mount, Scarborough, mid 1990s

This instant success of the reborn singles class and its full starting grids meant that soon other clubs copied the Newmarket formula. By 1978, races were being run throughout Great Britain. However, it was left to the clubs themselves to make their own rules regarding exactly what could, or could not, take part. The Japanese by now were producing a new breed of single-cylinder street/trail bikes, such as the Yamaha XT500 and the Honda XL500, which began to appear on the starting grids. Most single-cylinder competitors tended to favour 500cc, which meant that owners of, say, a Bultaco 125 or Aermacchi 250 still didn't stand much of a chance of success.

Stephen Finch from Kenilworth, Warwickshire, a regular customer of mine, had been behind setting up the Ducati Owners' Club with me. Stephen now wanted to form an organisation to run races solely for the 'Classic' racers of the period prior to the arrival of the Yamaha TD2/TR2 models. Sadly, before Stephen could see his vision become a reality, he was involved in a fatal road accident whilst on holiday in the Isle of Man.

The event that finally moved things on to present-day Classic Racing as we know it happened in 1979. While at a Brands Hatch Vintage Motor Cycle Club (VMCC) meeting, well-known journalist Alan Cathcart offered his friend Dick Linton (the boss of FCL, the Aermacchi specialists) a ride on his Matchless G50 in a parade. It should be explained that the VMCC rules at the time outlawed G50s for vintage racing, on the grounds that they weren't old enough, but allowed them to circulate in non-competitive parades. However, even though a group of Ducati enthusiasts had been invited to take part in the parade with similar 1960s bikes, an official, Jack Walton, said that Dick Linton should not be allowed on the track with Cathcart's machine. Cathcart and Linton were so annoyed by such pettiness that they decided to form a club themselves to cater for Alan's G50 and Dick's Aermacchi, together with similar machinery of the period. All interested parties (including myself) were contacted and a meeting was organised so that the new club could become a reality.

The result of the inaugural meeting at Redgate Lodge, Donington Park in December 1979 was the formation of what today is known as the CRMC (Classic Racing Motorcycle Club), and the club's first race meeting was in 1980. The initial idea was to run races for post-war models conceived prior to the arrival of the Yamaha TD2/TR2. The point about 'conceived' was that four-strokes such as the various Ducati singles and the Honda CB350 K4 twin were eligible. However, no two-strokes after 1968 were allowed to compete, preventing history repeating itself. The recession of the early 1990s saw CRMC membership fall, resulting in a rule change, allowing separate 'post classic' races for more modern two-strokes such as the Suzuki RG500 and the ubiquitous TZ Yamahas.

The success of the CRMC formula saw other parties come into the classic racing arena; notably the Cathcart-inspired IHRO (International Historic Racing Organisation) which helped to make historic bike sport popular in countries where interest had often languished. In North America, the AHMRA (American Historic Motorcycle Racing Association) was formed, with this organisation even running classic races on the famous Daytona circuit in Florida during the same week as the legendary 200 miler.

The 1969 TR2 made virtually every other non-works bike obsolete and helped to spawn the interest in racing what were now 'classics'

Daytona Bike Week

Bob McKeever at Daytona Beach on a new Garden Gate Manx Norton in 1948.

Daytona is arguably the most important event in the US motorcycling calendar, and has been going since 1937. Over the years, the week-long festival has been the scene of many British and international racing successes – the Triumph Daytona is even named after the 500cc twins that won the premier Daytona 200 race in the 1960s. However, I had never been (or even been to America) until relatively recently.

One day in late January 2002, I received a telephone call from my friend Stu Rogers about former Daytona racer Bob McKeever. Bob, then well into his 80s, was a great motorcycle enthusiast. In his early days his marque of choice was Ariel, later followed by the Garden Gate Manx Norton on which he competed in the Daytona Beach races during the late 1940s. More recently, he had sponsored Stu over several years in the Pre-1940 Daytona Classic race, but by 2002, Stu had ceased his riding duties and was now one of two mechanics for Bob's Team Champagne Norton Racing Team, the other spannerman being none other than the legendary Nobby Clark.

It turned out that Bob was giving me an invitation to be his guest at the next year's Bike Week. The entire trip would take some six weeks, as we would start off at Bob's mansion in Brookville, some 25 miles from Washington, followed by a stay with his close friend Arvid Myhre down in Florida, some 10 miles inland from Daytona itself.

Stu and I left England in early February from Heathrow. As this was only a few months after 9/11, security was at a high level. I had packed a pile of material to enable me to work on my book *Royal Enfield The Complete Story* while I was in America, but unfortunately the airport security people associated Enfield with guns! This meant that before I had even left the UK I was strip-searched and treated like a terrorist – amazing, but entirely true. Finally I was released and able to rejoin Stu for the flight across the Atlantic, which was to be my one and only visit to the US.

After the customs formalities, we were whisked off to Bob McKeever's home, and impressive it was too. I was to share a room with Nobby, and what an experience this was to be. As we had both been around during the 1960s the stories never seemed to stop flowing. Nobby had been mechanic to many of the world's greatest riders, including Gary Hocking, Mike Hailwood and Agostini. For the next month or so, while Stu and Nobby prepared the team's bikes for the forthcoming Daytona action, I spent the days in Bob's games room writing up the Enfield manuscript. In fact, I eventually dedicated the volume to Bob and Arvid.

Eventually, the time came to move from Washington State to Florida, a 900-mile trip in the team truck. This was undertaken over two days, finally arriving at Arvid's DeLand condo where we were to spend the next couple of weeks. On that first day in the sunshine state, I managed to get sunstroke and was out of action for hours, feeling none too perky. Finally recovering, I was able to rejoin Arvid, Alex, Stu and Nobby. Prior to the Daytona Bike Week itself, there was a very well-organised and supported classic race meeting at DeLand Naval Air Force base. I decided to take myself and my camera to the far end of the runway (which was being used as the paddock) while the others went in the opposite direction towards the main action.

Little has changed from the photograph opposite, despite the intervening 50 years.

The first machines I focused on were a pair of Austrian Puch split-singles. While studying these, I heard a voice asking what my interest was in his machines. I stood up and the man noticed the tiny 'Mick Walker' emblem on my jacket. His reaction said it all – I had made a friend. But even more strangely, within a very short period in the far-off distance a tannoy requested, 'Will Mick Walker please report to the organisers' office'. Off I went – to be greeted by a large number of enthusiastic fans headed by bookseller Lee Cowie, who with his wife had a bookstall at the meeting.

Daytona Bike Week's racing programme slotted the classics into the Monday and Tuesday, while preparation for the famous '200' race was scheduled for later in the week. I spent the two days of classic action walking around the paddock, meeting friends both old and new. The enthusiasm was tremendous.

Mid-week, Stu and I accepted an invitation to visit the Tunstall family (of Ducati fame) on the other side of Florida, at St Petersburgh on the west coast. We both spent a memorable day with Syd, Iris and son Malcolm then drove back east back to Daytona.

For the Daytona 200, Stu and I had grandstand seats to watch the racing over the speedbowl and infield sections of the world-famous course. But even more memorable was the invitation to a unique event – the Daytona 200 Monument. This was a banquet celebrating the famous races since the 1930s, both on the original beach and the later, purpose-built inland circuit. Everyone attending wore a special shirt inscribed 'Daytona 200 Monument: I am a part of it', and everyone who was anyone in American racing was there; including the likes of Dick Klamfoth and Ed Kretz Junior.

After a couple of other events, it was time to head north to Washington and the flight home. My lasting impression of America was how friendly the people were and how far removed they are from what Hollywood would have us believe. I also remarked on the large number of obese people and the low cost of fuel – however, nearly a decade on and the UK has followed suit in the first, but not the second. There was a postscript to this story. While I was attending the Bob McIntyre Memorial meeting in June 2006, who should make an appearance? None other than Bob McKeever, who had flown all the way from the US to be there and purchase a signed copy of my then-new book *Bob McIntyre – The Flying Scot*, which also happened to be my 100th title.

Back in the UK, other organisers had begun to run races for classics, including the New Era, North Gloucestershire, North Western Centre ACU, Scottish Vintage, Scottish Classic Racing and the Irish Racing Championship. Finally, there was the Lansdowne Cup series that has proved to be very popular.

The Isle of Man, for so long the bastion of road racing, has seen many of yesterday's star riders take part in a parade during TT week and in the Classic Manx Grand Prix parade first staged in 1983. Australia, New Zealand, Continental Europe and even Japan have taken to the classic racing scene with great enthusiasm. A number of special meetings have emerged, notably Surtees Day at Brands Hatch, Hailwood Day at Donington Park, and the truly fabulous Centennial TT at Assen, Holland, in May 1998, which I visited with Colin Perkins.

I met Colin when I first moved to Wisbech, in 1967. Even then, he was accident-prone. Once, at Snetterton, members of the Wisbech & District Motorcycle Club were acting as marshals. At the end of the morning's racing, the marshals walked along the track to the paddock for their lunch, but Colin thought he would get in an extra lap. Unfortunately, a rope had been placed across the track to ensure that this did not take place. Colin failed to notice this, so he and his Norton twin slid down the tarmac in a shower of sparks.

When Colin approached me during the 1990s proposing that we should visit a few European circuits it sounded like a good idea. In May 1998, the Centennial TT at Assen was a truly excellent experience, even though I realised Colin had invited me because of my ability as a navigator, not to mention my ability to acquire press passes. The whole Centennial TT experience was absolutely brilliant, not just the actual racing (the best I've ever witnessed at a classic event before or since) but also the comradeship amongst enthusiasts from all over Europe. Strangely, we bumped into another Cambridgeshire man who had a Bloor Triumph with sidecar attached. And with me in the chair he did a lap of the old long Assen road circuit, which embraced public roads, rather than the modern, shorter course in use today.

Colin and I went on to visit other continental events including Montlhéry, Dijon and Spa Francorchamps. Montlhéry was wet and cold. However, I still enjoyed it; a lasting memory was of Sammy Miller being carted off in the blood wagon after crashing his Gilera 500 four replica. Amazingly Sammy, who must be made of rubber, was his old self within days, any normal person would have been out of action for weeks. At Montlhéry I discovered Colin had something of a short fuse. He had booked into a hotel, but even before we had signed in he picked an argument with the manager, and if I hadn't done my Henry Kissinger bit, we would have been out on the street.

Dijon replaced Montlhéry after this historic venue was axed (a great shame, as for me it was the French version of Brooklands, with its banked track, and wide expanse of concrete). Dijon was also a longer journey for us, but the scenic route was a particularly pleasant traffic-free drive across France. The great memory from Dijon was the George Beale Honda six replica being overtaken by a 50cc Kreidler going up a hill.

Manx Nortons ride again.
Pete Swallow heads Graham Taubman in the 2005 Manx Grand Prix Senior Classic.

The rise of the classic scene has seen the price of 'blue-chip' old motorcycles rise into the stratosphere. As a result, even their humbler stablemates, such as the Vincent Comet, can achieve five-figure sums.

It was at Spa that Colin's good luck ran out. We had hardly arrived when he disappeared, then I heard the siren of an ambulance as it screeched to a halt halfway down the pit lane. Colin had got up on the pit wall to take photos and failed to notice a big drop between two of the sections. He had fallen into the gap and had the dubious honour of being the first casualty of the weekend. The incident made him something of a minor celebrity.

The Colin/Mick partnership came to an abrupt end following a trip to the Stafford Classic Show. We arrived a minute late at the trade/press entrance and Colin was told that he could not drive in. He'd have to park in the field, no big hardship, but instead he shouted 'Haven't you heard of Mick Walker?' and drove straight at the gate attendant, almost pinning him to the car bonnet. After this embarrassing episode I politely turned down any more trips with Colin.

The first magazine to cater exclusively for classic motorcycles was *Classic Bike*, which had started out right back in 1978. Bill Haylock, who had worked for *Bike* magazine during the early 1970s, had purchased a new 450 Desmo Ducati single from Mick Walker Motorcycles, so I suppose it was no surprise that he asked me to provide information for an article in *Classic Bike*'s debut issue, and I was happy to help. Following CB's pioneering lead, many, many other classic magazines appeared during the 1980s and 1990s, including The *Classic Motor Cycle*, *Classic Bike Guide*, *Classic Racer* and *Old Bike Mart*.

It was the same in the motorcycle book world. The first publisher in this field was Osprey, with the extremely popular Collectors series, the brainchild of Tim Parker, with many others following on. One innovative book series was the *Miller's Classic Motor Cycle Price Guide*. The first edition was published in 1994, and I edited and prepared all but that first issue. *Top Gear*'s James May pointed out that Miller's was all about 'deals with real bikes that have been sold in the real world, so is much more authentic than some of the rather arbitrary price guides featured in the classic bike press'. I always enjoyed my annual visit to the Miller's editorial team at Tenterden, in Kent with my good friend Valerie Lewis at the helm. Sadly, Miller's corporate bosses at Canary Wharf in East London finally gave the motorcycle and car guides the chop in 2006, even though they still remained popular.

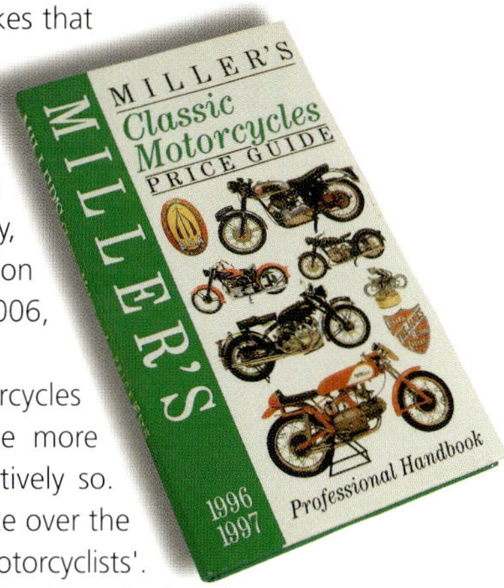

Inevitably, the rising interest has meant that old motorcycles which once could hardly be given away have become more expensive – the most desirable of them almost prohibitively so. One section of the classic scene that I have come to dislike over the years is the pure investors – I call them 'Bank-vault Motorcyclists'. Unfortunately, this breed has been largely responsible for the sharp rise in price of machinery such as Vincents and Broughs. Now, the normal motorcycle enthusiast is effectively barred from ever being able even to consider these marques. Obviously, there are genuine enthusiasts who also happen to be well off. My grudge is against those individuals who are only interested in financial gain. What this can mean was illustrated a few years ago, when Norton's Shenstone factory auction sold almost every lot for way above normal market value. Genuine Norton enthusiasts went home empty handed.

Cheffins Auctions

I have been both motorcycle consultant and a customer of Cambridge-based auctioneers Cheffins for several years. Founded in Bishops Stortford by Joshua Cheffins in 1825, Cheffins celebrated 185 years trading in 2010. Apart from the mergers and amalgamations, diversification has played a major role in creating the thriving firm of Cheffins as it is today. Driven by a need to replace lost income from changes to its core livestock market and farming activities, the company built on its long-established auctioneering traditions. The Cambridge machinery sales, now the largest in the world, were begun by Cheffins over 70 years ago when wartime restrictions limited the output of new tractors and farm machinery, creating a healthy trade in second-hand equipment.

The now thriving Vintage sales (of which motorcycles are currently an important part) were launched in a small way in 1975 selling older machinery to counter the drastic fall in income, partly due to livestock markets being closed firstly due to foot-and-mouth disease and then the gradual change in meat trading with the growth of the supermarkets and the demise of the family butcher. Car sales, added in 1999, incorporated a few motorcycles, but the bike side grew very slowly until Jerry Curzon arrived on the scene in 2004. A keen motorcyclist himself, Jerry's expertise and enthusiasm meant that this arm of the Vintage sales has seen a considerable growth ever since.

Jerry told me recently, 'The car side was outwardly very successful, but the demand of clients, costs, overheads and the like rendered that aspect unviable. Cheffins withdrew gracefully leaving me to build up the bike side including spares and memorabilia. Motorcycle sales were stand-alone events for several months, drawing an ever growing following.' July 2006 witnessed what Jerry describes as 'A genius decision to incorporate the sales into the festival that we call Vintage sales. This quadrupled the captive market at the sales as well as drawing some unlikely buyers and sellers from our clientele who would never have attended a motorcycle-only sale. Tractor and steam engine folk have an affinity with motorcyclists that car enthusiasts will never match.' When I asked Jerry why this was, his answer was pretty simple, 'All to do with being exposed to the elements, I guess.'

Bringing in motorcycle consultants, of whom I am proud to be one, Jerry says 'has introduced already well-known faces to the riding and reading public and at the same time added a much needed contact to both the sales and our networking abilities.' Besides myself, the other members of the current Cheffins two-wheel consultants are former racer and trials star Nick Jefferies (from the famous Yorkshire motorcycling dynasty) and well-respected motorcycle journalist Ian Kerr. Mike Jackson (of Andover Norton fame) has also been involved. What I always find both interesting and amazing is the sheer diversity of entries; anything from a humble moped to an exotic Vincent or Brough.

The most valuable machine I was involved with auctioning, this one-off dohc 1948 Velocette 250cc racer was built by Hunter Brothers of Melbourne, Australia. I researched these models for my book *Velocette: The Racing Story*, and when this example came up in Cheffins July 2011 sale, it excited much interest. It is now in an Australian museum.

Ducati Darmah: a great classic but not in the same league as an NCR.

Buying a classic motorcycle can be a rewarding and exciting experience, but it can also turn out to be an expensive mistake. To make sure it's the first and not the latter, a few basic rules are vital – I call them financial health warnings:

• First do your research. Never be rushed into a purchase – you will live to regret it. Knowledge is king; you simply cannot have enough of it, so research thoroughly. When I was running my Ducati spares business (up to April 2005), it amazed me how many people telephoned me after they had purchased a bike. One customer had paid £22,000 for an 'NCR Ducati', only to discover from me that – actually – the only connection with NCR was the replica tank, seat, mudguards and fairing. In truth, it was an SD Darmah, worth about 10% of the price paid. And believe me, there are plenty more horror stories that I could tell.

• Another pitfall is the potential cost of a proper restoration, which often can be more than the value of the finished article – so be warned. My advice is to carry out as much as possible of the restoration work yourself, making sure that it is for love, and not profit.

• Beware of the basket case, for not only are there likely to be vital bits missing, but an 'unfinished project' is also just as likely to have been someone else's unfinishable project.

• Finally there is the question whether you should buy your classic from a dealer, privately or at an auction. All have advantages and disadvantages. Buying from a dealer should provide the buyer with some security and peace of mind, although this depends very much on the individual dealer – remember, there are good and bad. The dealer's price will always be higher than that of a private seller to cover business costs. Buying privately should be cheaper, but has less security or 'comeback' if there is a problem. Again, a lot depends on the seller. Buying by auction is a way I have come to appreciate in recent years, both as a buyer and as a seller, and most recently as a consultant. Remember, a good auction house is like a good dealer – someone who has his reputation to consider. Established firms are the safest bet. If you are there for the long-term, you are hardly likely to take a short-term, get-rich-quick attitude. Word will get around, and bad news travels quicker than good news.

So, which are my personal favourite machines? Well, that is a difficult question, taking into consideration the thousands of motorcycles of all types and sizes that I have been lucky enough to ride. The machine I most regret selling is easy: the little Ducati 175 Formula 3 racer that I purchased from a Mr B Reynolds via the *MCN* classified advertisements of 24 February 1965 for £100 all-in, complete with leathers and the rest of the riding gear. As for the one I most regret not buying, it would have to be the immaculate Douglas 90 Plus that I was offered for £10 in 1967 – but at the time I was a hard-up racer scraping together pennies, not pounds. Setting those aside, my Top Twenty bikes are on the right (in alphabetical order, as they are impossible to rank).

These are not simply 'Dream Bikes', as my personal selection consists entirely of machines that I have owned, or I have ridden. Someone else would come up with a totally different list, but each one is there for a reason. The Yamaha Thundercat remains an ideal modern sports/tourer; the Laverda 650 Sport has brilliant handling and braking qualities; the BMW R69S is a 'Rolls-Royce' of motorcycles; and the Ducati 250 Daytona – which featured in the very first sentence of this book – was my first proper bike.

As I write, the classic scene is the most vibrant in the entire motorcycle industry. Why is this so? Partly, it is about nostalgia, and partly – in my opinion – it is because of the industry's own mistakes, as I explain in Chapter 13. I will leave you to be the judge.

The machine I most regret selling is easy: the little Ducati 175 Formula 3 racer

My Top Twenty

BMW 600 R69S (1960s)

Ducati 250 Daytona (1960s)

Honda 125 CB92 (1960s)

Kawasaki ZZR-1100 with 1340cc Wiseco big-bore kit (1990s)

Moto Guzzi 850 T3 (1970s)

Triumph 200 Formula Cub racer (1960s)

Yamaha 600 Thundercat (1990s)

BMW K75S (1980s)

Ducati 750SS (1970s)

Honda VF500 V-four (1980s)

Laverda 650 Sport (1990s)

MV Agusta 750 F4 (1990s)

Triumph 500 T100SS (1960s)

BSA 350 Gold Star (1950s)

Ducati 996 Foggy Replica – coded 916 (1990s)

Kawasaki 750 Turbo (1980s)

Moto Guzzi 850 Le Mans Mark 1 (1970s)

Southwell 650 Triton (1960s)

Velocette 350 KTT (1940s)

Zundapp 600 flat four (1930s)

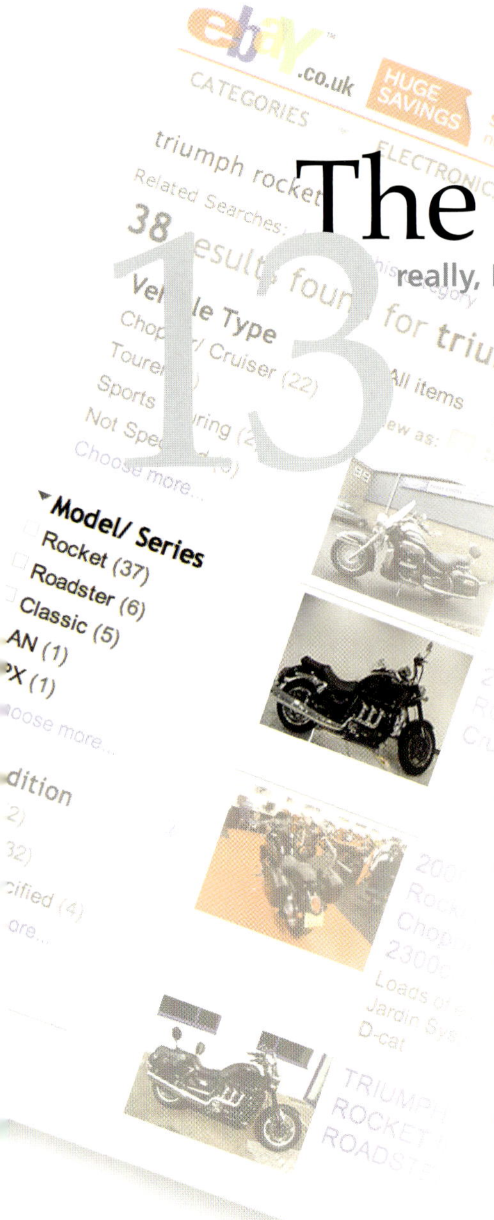

'Who really needs a 2,300cc Triumph?' Not many takers for these on eBay...

13

The Road Ahead

really, I'm optimistic about the future

The great motorcycle manufacturers of Britain, Italy, Japan and other countries were established and prospered because they offered a solution to the need for quick, efficient, economical transport. That doesn't mean that motorcycling can't, or shouldn't, be the most enjoyable activity in the world, as I discovered on my first Ducati one spring morning 50 years ago. Since then, many of my favourite road machines have been race-derived, with a keen sporting edge, but they were all designed to provide usable transport. All too often, modern motorcycling has become focused on providing expensive toys for the public highway. In recent years, instead of embracing modern technology and offering smaller, lighter, more efficient and more economical machines, the industry seems hell-bent on just the reverse. Walk into any dealer's showroom and study the machinery on offer. Who really needs a 2,300cc Triumph?

The mid-1990s saw the arrival of a breed of owners who would never consider maintaining their own bikes – not even adjusting and lubricating the final drive chain. Of course, this coincided with the introduction of electronic engine management, fuel injection, digital instruments, ABS brakes, monoshock rear suspension, inverted front forks, overhead-cam four-valve cylinder heads... and so many more complications that modern motorcyclists were frequently no longer able to understand the machinery, let alone do the maintenance work as they did in the past. Owners became reliant on dealer-based servicing, which is often more about plugging in a laptop and replacing the whole defective unit than getting out the spanners. Manufacturers and dealers were happy because this means more money, especially as few parts are interchangeable between models. The backlash against this attitude helps to explain why older (classic and vintage) bikes that can be looked after by their owners in a garden shed have become ever more popular.

The rise of the track day is another factor of modern motorcycling that encouraged the design of bikes that are sometimes little more than racing machines made legal for the road. Yes, from a track viewpoint, they are absolutely brilliant, but there is more to owning a bike than being able to turn in the best lap time, especially when it robs everyday riders of choice. A few years ago, Yamaha deleted its YZF600R Thundercat, a road-oriented sports bike, and replaced it with the YZF-R6S, an update of the pure-sports R6. The former was certainly due for replacement, but it had been an excellent all-rounder, fun to ride fast, and also supremely comfortable and capable of transporting two people. The R6 is a far more focused piece of machinery, brilliant going round the race circuit, but not the versatile machine the Thundercat was out on the public highway.

When track days first became popular, they were initially considered to be a bit dangerous by riders with racing experience, who viewed the early events as a free-for-all thrash by the sort of irresponsible riders who usually practised on the local by-pass every weekend. This attitude quite often ended up with a big spill. In order to get back home and recoup some of the repair costs, riders sometimes resorted to an insurance claim, wheeling the bike out of the circuit and claiming that it was a road accident. I know of dealers with premises near to a racetrack, who have been asked to collect a bike from a track day and take it ten miles up the road to a known accident black spot.

Worn out at under 2,000 miles. A high price to pay for high performance...

The insurance companies soon got wise to this sort of behaviour, and started checking the signing-on sheets at track day venues. Track days themselves have also become much better organized. Some of the early ones catered for all capacity classes and experience levels, all bunched together, which resulted in inevitable accidents. Thankfully, riders and their machines are now graded to ensure that there is some similarity in speeds and riding ability.

All this emphasis on performance of a very specialized kind created yet another problem for the modern motorcyclist – that of tyre choice. Most of the high-performance tyres essential for high-performance machines are made of ultra-expensive, sticky rubber with a very short life – often no more than 1,500 miles. Imagine what any car owner would say to that sort of mileage, to say nothing of the sky-high prices the motorcyclist pays for his exotic rubber.

Many modern bikes (outside of pure commuter machines designed for very short journeys) are far, far less economical than a small car of an equivalent performance. The car industry has embraced the economy issue by making fuel-efficient engines and toying with hybrid technology. Where is the same effort from the motorcycle industry? Yes, there is now an electric-bike class in the Isle of Man TT and the performance potential is already there. But the issue of battery weight and size has to have a radically new solution before a really practical two-wheeled electric machine for the public highway will be possible. Hybrid technology is a non-starter, as quite simply, a car is more suited to carrying batteries than a motorcycle.

Motorcyclists choose bikes for freedom, manoeuvrability and performance – and it has to be acknowledged that performance will probably never go hand-in-hand with economy. However, modern technology should be able to improve upon what is generally on offer today, and my own suggestions for a way forward appear on the right.

Surely it would be better for the industry to sort things out for itself, rather than wait for the inevitable harsh legislation from politicians who want to impress their electorate. The warp-speed mentality of the 'replica racers' simply cannot continue, and the whole image of motorcycling is not being helped by the increases in accident rates year after year. Considering the relatively low annual mileage achieved by the average rider, the accident rate is appalling. By acting now, the industry would reduce future problems, have a range of motorcycles more suited to the needs of future generations, create the possibility of reintroducing the motorcycle as a means of practical transport and be able to provide motorcycles at lower cost, both to the industry and its customers.

Of course, motorcycling embraces many kinds of rider. At the opposite extreme to the race-replica is the custom cruiser, which has become much more about being on show, and showering the bike with glitzy custom accessories, than it is about the bike's technology or performance. It's hard to see the impetus for change coming from there.

Racing has often been a spur to progress, but I worry, too, about the future for the sporting side of motorcycling. In the 21st century, the success, or otherwise, of any sport has become dependent upon media coverage, which is essential to attract sponsorship. Only a few years ago, rugby got limited coverage; now it receives a lot more television time and it's big business with big sponsors. In the old days, sponsorship in motorcycle sport was usually limited to companies associated with the two-wheeled game – such as tyre, oil and fuel suppliers. The

The irreducible minimum: two wheels and an engine. Everything else depends on the ingenuity of the designer.

My formula for a way forward:

1 The lightest chassis possible
- permits lighter suspension
- allows smaller brakes to be used
- fosters a rethink of tyre/wheel design
- encourages better aerodynamics

2 A lightweight, fuel-efficient engine
- less bulk permits a comparable performance with existing bikes
- lower mass assists acceleration
- improved aerodynamics reduce fuel consumption

level of sponsorship money now required means attracting corporate big businesses – the bigger the better – and at the top of the tree are the big multinationals, which often have more power than many political organisations. Attracting their money is a tough call against so many competing sports.

John Surtees wrote this very interesting postscript for my book *John Surtees – Motorcycle Maestro*: 'As I write this piece, the sad news has just come over the radio that Barry Sheene has died of cancer. It signals the end of an era, as in my opinion Barry was the last British motorcyclist to be a true household name. He revelled in the explosion of television coverage, media attention and the sponsorship that it brought in all sports. His enthusiasm and personality ensured that motorcycle sport maintained its fair share of media coverage.

'However, I have seen change in recent times with what would appear to be a dumbing down of motorcycle sport. There is no doubt that there is still an enormous amount of enthusiasm for the sport among the young and not so young, and that motorcycle racing is one of the most thrilling and exciting activities to watch. But it has become more and more isolated from the mainstream British sporting scene. When I go to the BBC Sports Personality of the Year presentations and sit there I see practically no reference to British motorcycle sport. It receives little press attention other than in specialised publications. I think that this is the result partly of self-destruction. We are fortunate in this country to have a superb selection of race circuits. But we haven't produced a world champion who could perform and communicate at the highest levels since Barry. The British scene would appear to have developed many champions of this or that – but some seem to rest on their laurels and carry on doing what they can do. Others have the talent and ambition but don't have the support. This is a familiar story. I think the ACU governing body, if they were a bit more far-sighted, would pay attention to ensuring that the structure of our racing here on the mainland allows the real talent to come through. It would give those riders a chance on the world scene. Other nations have done this with both two and four-wheeled competitors.'

I totally agree with John's views, which are just as relevant today as they were when he wrote them. His comment about racers who 'have the talent and ambition but don't have the support' touched on the difficulty for the extremely talented rider who doesn't have private funds to get him up to the level where he can attract a big-league sponsor – which I feel sure was the chief difficulty for the extremely talented Johnny Angel who I wrote about in Chapter 11. I am sure that this is a major reason for the lack of British world champions. This will only change when sponsors take a long view. In some cases, people – often ex-racers, but I won't name names – are openly selling rides to the highest bidder, regardless of their talent or ability. At its worst, skill plays so little part in the selection process that it is stifling any hope of finding true British riding talent. Of course there will always be exceptions: Mike Hailwood was a case when talent and money were there in the one person.

It would be wrong to end on a note of doom and gloom, because there is one shining star that shines through, time and again – and that is the motorcycling brotherhood. This isn't an organised club, but there are countless numbers of enthusiasts and good people who make up its ranks. To me, they are the salt of the earth, and as long as this comradeship exists, motorcycling is safe. So, really, I'm optimistic about the future.

During my half-century of involvement with motorcycling, I have been lucky to gain many true, long-lasting friends. I have travelled the world, and I have ridden an amazing array of bikes. Above all, I will always have memories that give me great pleasure.

Barry Sheene: 'the last British motorcyclist to be a true household name', September 2001

My Books

Aston Publications
Illustrated Ducati & Cagiva Buyers Guide (1987)
Manx Norton (1990)
Italian Motorcycles (1991)
Illustrated Moto Guzzi Buyers Guide (1992)

Bison Books
Classic Motorcycles (1991)

Breedon Books
John Surtees – Motorcycle Maestro (2003)
Giacomo Agostini – Champion of Champions (2004)
Mike Hailwood – The Fan's Favourite (2005)
Bob McIntyre – The Flying Scot (2006)
Geoff Duke – The Stylish Champion (2007)
Derek Minter – King of Brands (2008)
British Motorcycle Racing Circuits Since 1907 (2008)
Bill Ivy – The Will to Win (2009)
Reg Everett – Rocker to Racer – with Reg Everett (2009)

Chancellor Press
The History of Motorcycles (2002)

Crowood Press
Kawasaki Fours The Complete Story (1998)
BMW Twins The Complete Story (1998)
Moto Guzzi V-Twins The Complete Story (1998)
Café Racers of the 1960s (1998)
Laverda Twins & Triples The Complete Story (1999)
Ducati Four-Valve V Twins The Complete Story (1999)
Aprilia The Complete Story (2000)
Ducati Two-Valve V-Twins The Complete Story (2000)
MV Agusta Fours The Complete Story (2000)
Gilera The Complete Story (2000)
Ducati The Racing Story (2001)
BMW Z Series The Complete Story (2002)
Norton The Racing Story (2002)
BMW The Racing Story (2003)
Royal Enfield The Complete Story (2003)
Triumph The Racing Story (2004)
Ariel The Complete Story (2004)
Matchless The Complete Story (2004)
AJS The Complete Story (2005)
Moto Guzzi The Racing Story (2005)
Norton Dominator (2006)
BSA Pre-Unit Twins The Complete Story (2006)
Honda Production Motorcycles 1945-1980 (2007)
Suzuki Production Motorcycles 1952-1980 (2007)
Velocette Production Motorcycles (2007)
Classic Scooters 1945-1970 (2008)
Velocette The Racing Story (2009)
NSU The Complete Story (2009)
Douglas The Complete Story (2010)
Café Racers of the 1970s (2011)
Benelli The Complete Story (in preparation)

Derby Books Publishing
Sammy Miller Motorcycle Legend (2010)
Sidecar Champions Since 1923 (2011)
John Surtees (paperback) (2011)
Giacomo Agostini (paperback) (2011)
Mike Hailwood (paperback) (2011)
Bob McIntyre (paperback) (2011)
Jeff Smith (in preparation)

Grange Books
Performance Motorcycles (2001)

Hamlyn Publishing Group
Hamlyn History of Motorcycles (1997)
Hamlyn History of Motorcycles (2000)

Haynes Publishing Group
BMW K-Series Motorcycles – with Peter Dobson (1989)
Mick Walker's Italian Classic Gallery – The Road Bikes (1991)
Mick Walker's Italian Classic Gallery – The Racing Bikes (1991)

Miller's Publications
Miller's Classic Motorcycle Price Guide (1995)
Miller's Classic Motorcycle Price Guide (1996)
Miller's Classic Motorcycle Price Guide (1997)
Miller's Classic Motorcycle Price Guide (1998)
Miller's Classic Motorcycle Price Guide (1999)
Miller's Classic Motorcycle Price Guide (2000)
Miller's Classic Motorcycle Price Guide (2001)
Miller's Classic Motorcycle Price Guide (2002)
Miller's Classic Motorcycle Price Guide (2003/4)
Miller's Classic Motorcycle Price Guide (2005/6)
Miller's Collectors Cars Price Guide (2005/6)

Mitchell Beazley
Motorcycle Evolution – Design – Passion (2006)

Motorbooks
Ducati Buyer's Guide 2nd Edition (1994)
Moto Guzzi Buyer's Guide 2nd Edition (1995)
Ducati Buyers Guide 3rd Edition (2002)
Ducati Singles Restoration (2003)
Ducati Twins Restoration (2003)
BMW Twins Restoration (2004)
Moto Guzzi Twins Restoration (2004)

Osprey Publishing
Ducati Singles (1985)
Ducati Twins (1985)
Moto Guzzi Twins (1986)
Spanish Postwar Road & Racing Motorcycles (1986)
Moto Guzzi Singles (1987)
MV Agusta Production Motorcycles (1987)
Greeves – with Rob Carrick (1988)
Ducati Desmo: the Making of a Masterpiece (1989)
German Motorcycles (1989)
Classic British Racing Motorcycles (1990)
Classic Italian Racing Motorcycles (1991)
Classic Japanese Racing Motorcycles (1991)
Classic German Racing Motorcycles (1991)
Ducati Singles Restoration (1991)
BMW Twins Restoration (1992)
International Six Days Trial – with Rob Carrick (1992)
Classic European Racing Motorcycles (1992)
Classic American Racing Motorcycles (1992)
Ducati Twins Restoration (1993)
Ducati Colour series (1993)
Yamaha Colour series (1993)
Suzuki Colour series (1993)
Honda Colour series (1993)
Kawasaki Colour series (1993)
Moto Guzzi Colour series (1994)
World Endurance Racing – with Mark Wernham (1994)
Ducati Singles 2nd Edition (1997)
Ducati Twins 2nd Edition (1997)
Ducati From Clip-on Engine to 916 (1997)
Moto Guzzi Engineering from the Shores of Lake Como (1997)
Kawasaki From the Two-stroke to the ZZ-R1100 (1997)
Moto Guzzi Twins Restoration (1999)

Redline Books
Mick Walker's British Racing Motorcycles (1998)
Mick Walker's Italian Racing Motorcycles (1998)
Mick Walker's German Racing Motorcycles (1999)
Mick Walker's European Racing Motorcycles (2000)
The Manx Norton (2001)
The AJS 7R (2002)
Mick Walker's Japanese Grand Prix Racing Motorcycles (2002)
Mick Walker's Japanese Production Racing Motorcycles (2003)
The BSA Gold Star (2004)
Moto Morini Enthusiast Series (2004)
MZ Enthusiast Series (2004)
The Manx Norton New Edition (2005)
Aermacchi Harley-Davidson Motorcycles (2005)
Villiers, Everybody's Engine – with Rob Carrick (2010)

Shire Publishing
British Motorcycles of the 1940s & 1950s (2010)
British Motorcycles of the 1960s & 1970s (2011)

Silverdale
The Encyclopaedia of Motorcycles – contributor (2002)

Six-O-Five
Greeves – paperback reprint (2005)

Sutton Publishing/Motorbooks
Ducati – Taglioni and his World-Beating Motorcycles (2000)

Transport Source Books
Aermacchi (1995)
Benelli (1995)
MZ (1996)
Morini (1996)
British Performance Two-Strokes – with Rob Carrick (1998)

University of Northumbria
Ducati 2000 an Icon of the Century (2000)

Windrow & Greene
Café Racers of the 1960s (1994)
Superbike Specials of the 1970s (1995)

Index